AMERICAN
LANDLORD LAW

about

LANDLORD-TENANT LAWS

Trevor Rhodes & Nicole Février

McGraw Hill

New York   Chicago   San Francisco   Lisbon
London   Madrid   Mexico City   Milan   New Delhi
San Juan   Seoul   Singapore   Sydney   Toronto

The McGraw·Hill Companies

1 2 3 4 5 6 7 8 9 0   FGR/FGR   0 1 0 9 8

ISBN-13: P/N 978-0-07-159065-5 of set
            978-0-07-159062-4

ISBN-10: P/N 0-07-159065-X of set
            0-07-159062-5

Trademarks: EUNTK, EUNTK.com, Everything U Need to Know… and the Everything U Need to Know… horseshoe bar logo, are all trademarks of the EUNTK Corporation and may not be used without written permission. All other trademarks are the property of their respective owners.

Disclaimer: While the publisher and the author have used their best efforts in preparing this book, they make no representations or warranties with respect to the accuracy or completeness of the contents. Neither the publisher nor author shall be liable for any loss of profit or commercial damages, including but not limited to special, incidental, consequential or other damages. If legal advice or other expert assistance is required, it is strongly recommended that the services of a competent and experienced professional should be sought.

McGraw-Hill books are available at special quantity discounts to use as premiums and sales promotions, or for use in corporate training programs. To contact a representative, please visit the Contact Us pages at www.mhprofessional.com.

For information about any of the other Everything U Need to Know… products and services, visit www.EUNTK.com. If you have questions or comments, please email them to feedback@euntk.com.

McGraw-Hill Director, Business Editorial: Mary Glenn
EUNTK Managing Editor: Tomas Mureika
CD-ROM Software: TailoredApplication.com
Index: ProfessionalIndexing.com

This book is printed on acid-free paper.

Library of Congress Cataloging-in-Publication Data

Rhodes, Trevor.
   American landlord law : everything U need to know–about landlord-tenant laws / by Trevor Rhodes.
         p. cm.
   Includes bibliographical references and index.
   ISBN 0-07-159054-4 (alk. paper)
 1. Mortgage loan–United States. 2. Housing–United States–Finance. I. Title.
HG2040.5.U5R515 2008
332.7'220973–dc22

                                                    2008011675

For Bennett, Brianna, Cameron, Jacob, Leah and Tyler—

Acknowledgments

This *American Landlord Law* volume from **Everything U Need to Know...** **(EUNTK)** would not be possible without the support and assistance from the following companies and individuals: AmerUSA.net, PREMISRealty.com, Rhodes Property Management, Anthony, Linda, Janelle, Jay and Jeff Spinazzola, Christopher Rhodes, Karen Brown, Jennifer Petelle and Ed Sikora.

Table of Contents

Introduction..1

Chapter 1: Your Rent: Laying Down the Law..3
When It's Due...4
Where It's Due..4
How It's Due...5
Partial Payments...5
Increasing Rent...6
Charging Late Fees...9
Charging NSF Fees...12

Chapter 2: Security Deposits: Proper Collection and Handling...................17
How Much Can You Collect?..18
Earning and Paying Interest..21
Where to Keep the Deposit...24
Increasing the Deposit...28
Selling the Property (Transferring the Deposit).......................29

Chapter 3: Returning the Security Deposit: How to Avoid a Showdown!...................31
Move-Out Letter..32
Move-Out Inspection...35
Cleaning and Repairing...38
Time Limits..39
Normal Wear and Tear..42
Itemizing Damage and Deductions...43
Interest Earned...43
Common Disputes..46

Unpaid Rent...48

Co-tenants..49

What If a Tenant Sues Me?..49

Chapter 4: Other Deposits and Fees: What to Charge For and What Not To...........55

Application Fees...56

Cleaning Fees..56

Last Month's Rent Deposits...57

Pet Deposits...57

Chapter 5: Landlord's Duties: Maintenance and Repairs...............63

What You Must Do...64

What If You Don't Do It?..66

Chapter 6: Landlord's Entry: Getting Access to Your Property.........73

Maintenance and Repairs..74

In Case of Emergency..77

Tenants' Extended Absence...77

Showing the Property...80

Notice Required...83

Chapter 7: Landlord's Liability, Part I: Protecting Yourself and Your Tenants..........87

What Makes You Negligent...88

Condition of the Property...89

How to Protect Yourself Financially...................................90

Chapter 8: Landlord's Liability, Part II: Specific Environmental Hazards...................93

Lead in Paint and Water...94

Asbestos... 97

Mold... 98

Carbon Monoxide Gas.. 99

Radon Gas...100

Chapter 9: Modifying Lease Terms: What You Can Change and How to Do It.......103

What Can Be Changed..104

How to Cover Yourself Legally...................................... 105

Notification Requirements for Each State...........................107

Chapter 10: Occupants: Who, How and Why.................................117

Before You Find Yourself in This Situation.........................118

Defining Co-tenant, Subletting and Assignment.....................118

Co-tenant Legal Situations...119

Subletting Legal Situations..124

Assignment Legal Situations..124

How to Add a New Co-tenant, Sublet or Assign a Lease...............125

When You Should Consider Accepting Subletting or Assigning........130

Chapter 11: Retaliation: Staying on Higher Ground.....................131

What Is Retaliation..132

Time Requirements...132

How to Avoid an Accusation of Retaliation..........................141

Chapter 12: Evictions, Part I: General Information.....................143

The Steps to Eviction...144

Types of Termination: With and Without Cause......................144

Persistently Troubling Tenants....................................145

Evicting by Force or Intimidation.................................145

Chapter 13: Evictions, Part II: In Detail.............................151

Giving Notice...152

Complaint/Court Summons...159

Trial...159

Winning or Losing...160

Chapter 14: Attorneys: Friend or Foe?.....................................163

When Is It Necessary to Hire an Attorney?........................164
Finding an Attorney...165
Curbing Attorney Fees...166
Case Law Takes Precedence..167
Where to Find Laws and Statutes..167

Chapter 15: Landlord-Tenant Laws: State by State.....................169

Alabama..170
Alaska...172
Arizona...174
Arkansas..176
California...178
Colorado...180
Connecticut..182
Delaware...184
District of Columbia...186
Florida..188
Georgia...190
Hawaii...192
Idaho..194
Illinois..196
Indiana..198
Iowa...200
Kansas..202
Kentucky..204
Louisiana...206
Maine..208
Maryland...210
Massachusetts...212
Michigan..214
Minnesota..216
Mississippi...218
Missouri..220

Montana..222
Nebraska..224
Nevada...226
New Hampshire...228
New Jersey..230
New Mexico...232
New York..234
North Carolina...236
North Dakota...238
Ohio...240
Oklahoma..242
Oregon..244
Pennsylvania..246
Rhode Island..248
South Carolina..250
South Dakota..252
Tennessee...254
Texas...256
Utah..258
Vermont...260
Virginia..262
Washington...264
West Virginia..266
Wisconsin...268
Wyoming..270

Conclusion...273

Appendix A: A Radon Guide for Tenants: U.S. Environmental Protection Agency....275

Appendix B: Asbestos Standard for General Industry: U.S. Department of Labor.....287

Appendix C: Servicemembers Civil Relief Act: Title III......................................**307**

Appendix D: Protect Your Family from Lead in Your Home:
　　　　　　　U.S. Environmental Protection Agency..............................**315**

Appendix E: Carbon Monoxide Fact Sheet:
　　　　　　　U.S. Environmental Protection Agency..............................**333**

Appendix F: A Brief Guide to Mold, Moisture, and Your Home:
　　　　　　　U.S. Environmental Protection Agency..............................**337**

Appendix G: Fair Housing Poster:
　　　　　　　U.S. Department of Housing and Urban Development..........**359**

Appendix H: Fair Housing Act: Federal Housing Administration..................**363**

Appendix I: Bonus CD-ROM: The American Landlord Law Resource Center..........**393**
　　　　　　　Installation Instructions...393
　　　　　　　Terms of Use...394
　　　　　　　How to Personalize a Rental Form..394
　　　　　　　The End Result...395

Index..**397**

Introduction

There's nothing more **convoluted** and **confusing** than *the scribblings of lawmakers.* Trying to find a simple answer could takes hours or days *(you may not even find one at all)* and since most landlords and tenants don't have attorneys on retainers, there's not much help available. Sure, you can always try searching the Internet, but that will lead to you to even a more confusing world of unreliable websites maintained by people who want nothing more than to make money from advertising revenue as opposed to ensuring their content is correct.

So, you've undoubtedly started reading this introduction because you've hit a road block that's backed up by Internet traffic or maybe you've just wandered into your local bookstore looking for a reliable source of information on landlord-tenant laws so you can learn how to protect yourself.

Well, this is it – *American Landlord Law* – the most reliable source of landlord-tenant information available provided by the nation's leading tenant screening company, **AmerUSA.net.** Every states' most common landlord-tenant laws (including D.C.'s) have been referenced in a manner that can be easily read and understand, a user-friendly style inherent to every book in this **Everything U Need to Know...** series.

While this book may not always have the answer you're looking for or save you a visit to an attorney, it's sure to be your bedside companion for answers to many late night questions. And if you ever need further assistance, **check out the official website for this series** at www.EUNTK.com – for discussion groups, more laws and statutes, other subjects in the series, plus a whole lot more... *for the absolute easiest way there is to learn* **"Everything U Need to Know..."**

Chapter 1

Your Rent: Laying Down the Law

This Chapter Discusses:

★ **When It's Due**

★ **Where It's Due**

★ **How It's Due**

★ **Partial Payments**

★ **Increasing Rent**

★ **Charging Late Fees**

★ **Charging NSF Fees**

Who doesn't want to get paid, right? After all, this is why you're a landlord. Those of you that have a great deal of experience in property management have probably already learned that **if you are not careful from the get-go in defining *when, where and how* your rent should be received, then you may be in for a rude awakening** when you come across a tenant who decides to set his or her own terms **because you failed to lay down the law.** If you are a relatively new landlord or are just getting your feet wet for the very first time, **you should pay extra careful attention to the advice in this chapter** (and all others, for that matter) **to ensure you have an ironclad arrangement with your tenant for your own protection.**

When It's Due

In every state of the Union, **you have the right to specify exactly when the rent is due.** Whether it's on the first day of the month, last day of the month or any day (or days) in between, this is your call. Talk with your new tenant and see what will work out for both of you. It's not uncommon to have rent due around an odd pay schedule or a public assistance payment (this is actually required in some places such as Hawaii). **The important thing is just to make sure it's clearly spelled out in your lease agreement.** You will hear repeatedly in this *American Landlord Law* volume that **handshakes and casual agreements must be avoided.**

Failing to give an actual day could lead to serious problems and, believe it or not, **there are plenty of landlords that take a lackadaisical approach and find themselves short a month or two** (there have even been stories of more than six months – amazing, but disappointingly true). In addition, there are a number of states that will dictate for you when rental payments are due **if it is not specified in your lease**. You certainly don't want to find yourself stuck in that position.

Where It's Due

Specifying when the rent is due isn't enough; **you also need to instruct the tenant (in writing) where the rent must be paid.** Again, if you do not specify where the tenant must pay the rent, then many states will dictate that for you – often at the property itself, and it may not be convenient for you to drive all the way over there just to pick up a rent check every month.

If you have a management office onsite, great! If not, then *do not specify your home address.* This was a topic touched on in the *American Landlord* volume. It stated that you should *never lead a tenant to your home* for reasons that are too many to mention.

If you do not have a commercial location for doing business, then **set up a private mailbox** (known as a **PMB**) at any shipping center such as a UPS store – **or get an official mailbox at your local post office.** *This is an absolute necessity for any individual landlord for accepting rental payments,* as well as any official correspondence that should take place between you and your tenant (e.g., repair requests, notices and complaints).

How It's Due

Believe it or not, **you can actually dictate the manner of payment you are willing to accept.** This could be Visa, MasterCard, personal check, money order, cashier's check or even cold hard cash (however, under no circumstance should you accept cash!). Obviously, *the more difficult you make the manner of payment, the smaller the tenant litter becomes.* While this book does not necessarily advocate opening your door to credit cards (which can easily be disputed and reversed by the tenant – known as a chargeback), **it is suggested that you accept personal checks, but stipulate that if the personal check should be returned by the tenant's bank on more than two separate occasions,** *money orders and cashier's checks will only be accepted from that point on.* If you do not add in this stipulation from the beginning, in the original lease, you may find it difficult to change this later if you do have a problem with repeated bounced checks.

Partial Payments

Undoubtedly, there will come a time when a tenant cannot pay the full rent amount and offers to pay part of the rent in hopes of catching up on the rest at a later date. *Only you can decide if you are comfortable with this idea* – keeping in mind how long you have known the tenant, if the tenant has been communicating with you openly about why he or she can't make the full payment, or if the tenant recently changed his or her jobs which adjusted his or her pay dates. **If you decide to accept a partial rent payment, make sure you set a firm payment schedule and put it in writing to protect your rights to evict should the tenant never catch up.** *Do NOT allow the tenant to leave it at "I'll pay you when I can."*

A simply worded statement indicating how much he or she has paid toward that month's rent, when the remaining rent must be paid by and what late fee (if you decide to charge one or not) will be needed to be paid by what date(s), **signed by all parties** will maintain your business relationship with your tenant.

Increasing Rent

Can you charge more for your rental? *Sure, it's just a matter of when.* If you had your tenant sign a lease (and you better have in order to protect yourself!), then **that lease will dictate when you can adjust the rent.** The lease can actually give you the authority to increase the rent after giving the tenant adequate notice, but **if the lease does not give you this specific right, then you must wait until the lease has expired.**

Of course, when it's time to renew the lease, **you should give the tenant adequate notice that the new lease will include an increase of rent.** If the tenancy is less than a year, such as month-to-month, then *state laws generally dictate that you can increase the rent at any time as long as you give notice equal to the term of the tenancy.* So, for example, with a month-to-month arrangement, you would need to give 30 days' notice. Of course, **there are exceptions to this** – some states require less time for notice while others require more. **A chart outlining each state's requirement has been provided on the following pages...**

Rent Increase Notice Requirements

Alabama	No statute
Alaska	30 days
Arizona	30 days
Arkansas	No statute
California	30 days unless all increases in last 12 months total greater than 10% of the lowest amount of rent during those 12 months, then 60 days
Colorado	10 days
Connecticut	No statute
Delaware	60 days
District of Columbia	No statute
Florida	No statute
Georgia	No statute
Hawaii	45 days
Idaho	15 days
Illinois	30 days
Indiana	30 days unless lease gives different time frame
Iowa	30 days
Kansas	No statute
Kentucky	30 days
Louisiana	No statute
Maine	45 days
Maryland	1 month
Massachusetts	30 days or time frame between rental payments, whichever longer
Michigan	No statute
Minnesota	No statute
Mississippi	No statute

Missouri	No statute
Montana	15 days
Nebraska	No statute
Nevada	45 days
New Hampshire	30 days
New Jersey	1 month
New Mexico	30 days before rent due date
New York	No statute
North Carolina	No statute
North Dakota	30 days
Ohio	No statute
Oklahoma	No statute
Oregon	No statute
Pennsylvania	No statute
Rhode Island	30 days
South Carolina	No statute
South Dakota	1 month
Tennessee	No statute
Texas	No statute
Utah	No statute
Vermont	30 days
Virginia	No statute
Washington	30 days
West Virginia	No statute
Wisconsin	No statute
Wyoming	No statute

Avoid possible discrimination suits by having a consistent rent increase policy for all of your units. You don't want to give even the slightest appearance that you are singling out one particular individual or family for rent increases, leading to possible charges of discrimination. Also, **be mindful of a tenant's recent complaints.** If you increase rent within a certain period of time, which varies by state, *after a complaint is made by a tenant,* **you could be looking at a retaliation charge and find yourself in court.** Discrimination and retaliation issues are discussed in further detail in **Chapters 7 and 11** respectively.

CAUTION

The amount of any rent increase, as well as the number of times you can increase rent, is generally not regulated by the states (with the *exception* of property governed by rent control laws). Your common sense should guide you here. Obviously, **you don't want to anger your tenants and have them move out** – or go beyond what the local market is dictating and risk not having any good applicants.

Charging Late Fees

The purpose of a late fee is to give your tenants more of an incentive to pay you on time without having to always serve notice to pay or quit (more on the steps of eviction in **Chapters 12** and **13**) when someone simply forgets to send the rent on time, while still compensating you for the additional effort needed to collect the rent.

There are only 15 states that regulate late fees in some way, so chances are good that you are free to charge a late fee of what and when you like. However, *excessively high late fees can be considered usurious, and thus illegal,* in some states that don't have late fee statutes – so don't try to make a killing off of late fees. In general, to protect yourself, *a late fee should be charged when the rent is at least 3 days late and should be no more than 5% of the rent payment that is late.* **A chart covering the requirements of those 15 states that do regulate late fees specifically in statutes is listed on the next three pages.**

Late Fees

Alabama	No statute
Alaska	No statute
Arizona	Late fees must be reasonable and indicated in the lease agreement
Arkansas	No statute
California	Late fees must be close to the landlord's actual losses and indicated in the lease agreement as follows: "Because landlord and tenant agree that actual damages for late rent payments are very difficult or impossible to determine, landlord and tenant agree to the following stated late charge as liquidated damages"
Colorado	No statute
Connecticut	Late fees can be charged when rent is 9 days late
Delaware	Late fees cannot be more than 5% of the rent amount due and can be charged when the rent is more than 5 days late. If the landlord does not have an office within the rental property's county, the tenant has an additional 3 days before late fees can be charged
District of Columbia	No statute
Florida	No statute
Georgia	No statute
Hawaii	No statute
Idaho	No statute
Illinois	No statute
Indiana	No statute
Iowa	Late fees cannot be more than $10 a day with a maximum of $40 a month allowed
Kansas	No statute
Kentucky	No statute
Louisiana	No statute
Maine	Late fees cannot be more than 4% of the rent amount due for a 30-day period and must be indicated in writing to the tenant at the start of the tenancy. Late fees can be charged when rent is 15 days late
Maryland	Late fees cannot be more than 5% of the rent amount due

Massachusetts	Late fees can be charged when rent is 30 days late
Michigan	No statute
Minnesota	No statute
Mississippi	No statute
Missouri	No staute
Montana	No statute
Nebraska	No statute
Nevada	Late fees must be indicated in the lease agreement
New Hampshire	No statute
New Jersey	Late fees can be charged when rent is 5 days late
New Mexico	Late fees cannot be more than 10% of the rent amount due per rental period. Tenant must be notified of the late fee charged by the end of the next rental period
New York	No statute
North Carolina	Late fees cannot be more than 5% of the rent amount due or $15, whichever is greater, and can be charged when rent is 5 days late
North Dakota	No statute
Ohio	No statute
Oklahoma	No statute
Oregon	Late fees cannot be more than a reasonable amount charged by others in the same market if a flat fee is utilized; if a daily charge is utilized, it cannot be more than 6% of the reasonable flat fee with a maximum of 5% of the rent amount due per rental period allowed; late fees can be charged when rent is 4 days late and must be indicated in the lease agreement
Pennsylvania	No statute
Rhode Island	No statute
South Carolina	No statute
South Dakota	No statute
Tennessee	Late fees can be charged when rent is 5 days late and cannot be more than 10% of the late amount; however, if the fifth day is a weekend or holiday and the tenant pays the rent amount due on the following business day, a late fee cannot be charged

Texas	Late fees must be reasonable and close to the landlord's actual losses. Late fees must be indicated in the lease agreement and can be charged when the rent is 2 days late. Late fees can include an initial fee as well as a daily fee for each day the rent is late thereafter
Utah	No statute
Vermont	No statute
Virginia	No statute
Washington	No statute
West Virginia	No statute
Wisconsin	No statute
Wyoming	No statute

Charging NSF Fees

Like late fees, the purpose behind charging an **NSF** – **"non-sufficient funds" or bounced check fee** – is **to compensate you for the fees charged by your bank for the returned check**, as well as the additional time and resources needed to collect the rent. **The amount you can charge for a bounced check is regulated in every state, and the following chart lists each state's limit...**

Returned Check Fees

Alabama	$30 - Check writer is also responsible for all other costs of collection
Alaska	$30
Arizona	$25
Arkansas	$25
California	$25
Colorado	$20 - Check writer is also responsible for all other costs of collection
Connecticut	$20 - Check writer is also responsible for all other costs of collection
Delaware	$40
District of Columbia	$25
Florida	Checks from (1) $0.01-$50.00 = $25.00 fee, (2) $50.01-$300.00 = $30.00 fee, (3) $300.01 and over = the greater of $40.00 fee or 5% of the face amount of the check. Check writer is also responsible for all other costs of collection
Georgia	$30 or 5% of the face amount of the check, whichever is greater
Hawaii	$30 - Check writer is also responsible for all other costs of collection
Idaho	$20 - Check writer is also responsible for all other costs of collection
Illinois	$25 - Check writer is also responsible for all other costs of collection
Indiana	$20 - Check writer is also responsible for all other costs of collection
Iowa	$30
Kansas	$30
Kentucky	$25
Louisiana	$25 or 5% of the face amount of the check, whichever is greater
Maine	$25
Maryland	$35
Massachusetts	$25
Michigan	$25
Minnesota	$30 - Check writer is also responsible for all other costs of collection and civil penalties may be imposed for nonpayment

Mississippi	$40
Missouri	$25
Montana	$30
Nebraska	$35
Nevada	$25
New Hampshire	$25
New Jersey	$30
New Mexico	$30
New York	$20 - Check writer is also responsible for all other costs of collection
North Carolina	$25
North Dakota	$30
Ohio	$30 or 10% of the face amount of the check, whichever is greater
Oklahoma	$25
Oregon	$25
Pennsylvania	$30
Rhode Island	$25
South Carolina	$30
South Dakota	$40
Tennessee	$30 - Check writer is also responsible for all other costs of collection
Texas	$30 - Other costs of collection may be charged
Utah	$20 - Check writer is also responsible for all other costs of collection
Vermont	$25
Virginia	$35
Washington	$30 - This amount is assessed as a handling fee for returned checks. Check writer is also responsible for all other costs of collection
West Virginia	$25
Wisconsin	$20 - Check writer is also responsible for all other costs of collection
Wyoming	$25 - Check writer is also responsible for all other costs of collection

There are some states that allow for interest to be charged on returned checks. This may seem appealing, but *it is advisable to forget about trying to collect the couple of dollars you would be owed for one bounced check.* Sure, if things go bad and you get to the point where you are needing to collect in court during an eviction, go ahead and add the interest if you can. Otherwise, **it's not worth trying to make sure you accurately calculate** (so that you don't end up in some mathematics dispute with the tenant in front of a judge) **the interest due for a mere couple of weeks.** *Your late fee and NSF fee will be plenty compensation.*

Do not allow your bank to automatically attempt to re-deposit checks that have bounced. While this may seem convenient, chances are the check will bounce with the second attempt too – and your notification of a problem with the rent payment will only be delayed. **It's best to have the bank return the bad check to you immediately, so you can contact the tenant sooner rather than later.**

EXAMPLE

Chapter 2

Security Deposits:
Proper Collection and Handling

This Chapter Discusses:

★ **How Much Can You Collect?**

★ **Earning and Paying Interest**

★ **Where to Keep the Deposit**

★ **Increasing the Deposit**

★ **Selling the Property (Transferring the Deposit)**

This is the most commonly contested issue in the landlord-tenant relationship and, as you would expect, often a heavily regulated one - depending on the laws of your state. **This chapter will outline essential information you need to be made aware of when collecting and handling your tenant's money,** which is intended to be used to secure against property damage, pet stains, odor or even unpaid rent. As an extra measure of precaution, **you should contact your state and local housing departments to inquire about rules or regulations governing security deposits** in case they have changed or take precedence over the information contained in this chapter. For example, if you participate in a government-assisted housing program such as Section 8, it will have its own security deposit policy.

How Much Can You Collect?

The last thing you need is to be accused of violating something as simple as the maximum amount of security you are legally allowed to collect. *Each state has its own guidelines in place.* Therefore, **a chart is presented on the next two pages to show you which ones have imposed a cap on how much you can charge.** For those states that do not have any restrictions, **"No statute"** will appear instead. And so for those states, *it's reasonable to infer that you can charge as much as you want to secure your lease agreement.* However, this doesn't mean that **previous case law couldn't be used by a tenant to dispute your actions** (however remote that chance may be).

Security Deposit Limits

Alabama	1 month's rent
Alaska	2 months' rent, limit does not apply unless monthly rent exceeds $2,000
Arizona	1½ months' rent unless both parties agree to more
Arkansas	2 months' rent
California	2 months' rent if unfurnished unit, 3 months' rent if furnished unit, extra ½ month's rent if tenant has waterbed
Colorado	No statute
Connecticut	2 months' rent, 1 month's rent if tenant is 62 or older
Delaware	No limit if furnished unit or if month-to-month tenancy, 1 month's rent if year or longer lease
District of Columbia	1 month's rent
Florida	No statute
Georgia	No statute
Hawaii	1 month's rent
Idaho	No statute
Illinois	No statute
Indiana	No statute
Iowa	2 months' rent
Kansas	1 month's rent if unfurnished unit, 1½ months' rent if furnished unit
Kentucky	No statute
Louisiana	No statute
Maine	2 months' rent
Maryland	2 months' rent
Massachusetts	1 month's rent
Michigan	1½ months' rent
Minnesota	No statute
Mississippi	No statute

Missouri	2 months' rent
Montana	No statute
Nebraska	1 month's rent
Nevada	3 months' rent
New Hampshire	$100 or 1 month's rent, whichever greater, no limit if landlord and tenant share facilities
New Jersey	1½ months' rent
New Mexico	1 month's rent if less than 1-year lease, no limit if year or longer lease
New York	No limit unless covered by local rent control regulations
North Carolina	1½ months' rent if month-to-month tenancy, 2 months' rent if lease term longer than 2 months
North Dakota	1 month's rent
Ohio	No statute
Oklahoma	No statute
Oregon	No statute
Pennsylvania	2 months' rent first year of tenancy, 1 month's rent all future years
Rhode Island	1 month's rent
South Carolina	No statute
South Dakota	1 month's rent
Tennessee	No statute
Texas	No statute
Utah	No statute
Vermont	No statute
Virginia	2 months' rent
Washington	No statute
West Virginia	No statute
Wisconsin	No statute
Wyoming	No statute

Earning and Paying Interest

If you don't own a calculator or a computer, now may be the time to buy one. **There are quite a few jurisdictions around the United States that require you to pay interest on the security deposit you collect from a tenant.** After all, *it is the tenant's money you are holding onto, often for a full year* (or more), until you have good cause to claim a portion (or all) of it. If required in your jurisdiction, **landlords must pay interest on security deposits that range from at least what the average savings deposit rate is, up to 5% per year, or even whatever high rate you are able to make off of the tenant's money.** *Interest is usually required to be paid annually on the anniversary date of the lease agreement* either directly to the tenant or applied as a credit toward the next month's rent.

Due to frequent changes in the economy, **the amount of interest required to be dispersed to a tenant may vary annually for certain jurisdictions**. A guide is provided on the next three pages to summarize the **interest rate requirements** as of the date of this publication.

Security Deposit Interest Requirements

Alabama	No statute
Alaska	No statute
Arizona	No statute
Arkansas	No statute
California	No statute
Colorado	No statute
Connecticut	Pay annually and at termination, equal to average rate on savings accts at insured banks but not less than 1.5%
Delaware	No statute
District of Columbia	Pay at termination, at current passbook rate
Florida	Not required, but if made must pay annually and at termination; tenant who wrongfully terminates is not entitled to; lease agreement must give details on interest
Georgia	No statute
Hawaii	No statute
Idaho	No statute
Illinois	Required if owner has 25+ properties adjacent to each other or in same building; if security deposit held for longer than 6 months, must pay annually and at termination
Indiana	No statute
Iowa	Not required, but if paid must pay at termination; however, any interest earned during the first 5 years is landlord's
Kansas	No statute
Kentucky	No statute
Louisiana	No statute
Maine	No statute
Maryland	Must pay semi-annually, at a rate of 4% if deposit is greater than $50
Massachusetts	Must pay annually and within 30 days of termination, at a rate of 5% or the actual rate earned; no interest for last month's rent paid in advance
Michigan	No statute

Minnesota	Must pay at a rate of 1%; total interest under $1 does not need to be paid
Mississippi	No statute
Missouri	No statute
Montana	No statute
Nebraska	No statute
Nevada	No statute
New Hampshire	Only required if deposit held for a year or longer; must pay at termination; tenant can request payment every 3 years if request made within 30 days of tenancy expiration/renewal; rate must be equal to the rate paid on the bank savings account where deposited
New Jersey	Must pay annually or credit back to rent owed; landlord with less than 10 units can put deposit in any insured interest-bearing bank account; those with 10 or more must put funds in an insured money market account that matures in a year or less or in any other account that pays interest at a comparable rate to a money market account
New Mexico	Must pay annually at rate equal to passbook rate if deposit is more than 1 month's rent and there is a year lease
New York	Must pay at prevailing rate if unit is covered under rent control or stabilization requirements or if building has 6 or more units; landlord can keep 1% admin fee a year
North Carolina	No statute
North Dakota	Must pay interest if tenancy is at least 9 months; deposit must be put in an insured interest-bearing savings or checking acct
Ohio	Must pay annually and at termination, at a rate of 5% if the tenancy is 6 months or more and the deposit is greater than $50 or 1 month's rent - whichever is greater - the interest only accrues on the excess of the $50 or 1-month rent amount
Oklahoma	No statute
Oregon	No statute
Pennsylvania	Must pay if tenancy is longer than 2 years; interest accrues from start of 25th month of tenancy and must be paid annually after that point; landlord can deduct 1% fee
Rhode Island	No statute
South Carolina	No statute
South Dakota	No statute
Tennessee	No statute

Texas	No statute
Utah	No statute
Vermont	No statute
Virginia	Must pay if deposit is held for more than 13 months for continued tenancy in same unit; interest accrues from start of lease and must be paid at termination; must be at rate of 1% below FED discount rate as of Jan. 1 of each year
Washington	No statute
West Virginia	No statute
Wisconsin	No statute
Wyoming	No statute

Where to Keep the Deposit

As previously mentioned, **security deposit funds are not legally yours until you can lawfully make a claim against them.** Therefore, it's in everyone's best interest (especially yours, when worrying about complying with numerous laws and regulatory agencies) to **keep these funds separate from your business and personal accounts.** In other words, *a tenant's security deposit should be held in a separate bank account* – not in your back pocket or underneath your mattress – **in a federally insured bank**, preferably located in the same state as the property. **If you have more than one tenant, it's okay to keep all security deposits in the same account,** as long as your record keeping is accurate. *Just make sure these funds are never commingled with any of your other accounts.*

Not only will this basic practice ensure that you are compliant with the laws in all 50 states, but **it also keeps your income tax preparation nice and easy** (or at least easier), so the Internal Revenue Service can't accuse you of mishandling funds.

Now, **you don't have to follow these recommendations if your state doesn't require you to take similar steps (or precautions) when handling your tenant's money. A chart is provided on the next three pages that summarizes how security deposits should be held in accordance with each state's laws.**

Security Deposit Bank Account Requirements

Alabama	No statute
Alaska	Security deposits must be held in a separate account
Arizona	No statute
Arkansas	No statute
California	No statute
Colorado	No statute
Connecticut	Security deposits must be held in a separate account
Delaware	Security deposits must be held in a separate account; tenant must be told orally or in writing of the location of the account
District of Columbia	Security deposits must be held in a separate account
Florida	Security deposits must be held in a separate account; tenant must be told in writing within 30 days the location of the account, if the account is interest bearing or not, and the schedule and rate of any interest payments to be made; a security bond covering all security deposits may be obtained in lieu of maintaining a separate account; lease must include copy of statute § 83.49(3)
Georgia	Security deposits must be held in a separate escrow account located at a financial institution which is regulated by the state or federal government; tenant must be told of the location of the account; a security bond covering all security deposits may be obtained in lieu of maintaining a separate account
Hawaii	No statute
Idaho	No statute
Illinois	No statute
Indiana	No statute
Iowa	Security deposits must be held in a separate account
Kansas	No statute
Kentucky	Security deposits must be held in a separate account; tenant must be told orally or in writing of the location and number of the account
Louisiana	No statute
Maine	Security deposits must be held in a separate account; tenant must be told orally or in writing of the location and number of the account if the tenant requests this information

Maryland	Security deposits must be held in a separate account in a financial institution located within the state; alternatively, security deposits may be held in secured CDs or securities issued by the state or federal government
Massachusetts	Security deposits must be held in a separate account in a financial institution located within the state; tenant must be told within 30 days the location and number of the account, and the amount deposited on his or her behalf
Michigan	Security deposits must be held in a separate account located at a financial institution which is regulated by the state or federal government; tenant must be told in writing within 14 days of the location of the account and provided with the required disclosure in statute § 554.603 (3); landlord may use security deposits for any reason if a cash or surety bond covering all of the first $50,000 and 25% of all remaining funds is provided to the Secretary of State
Minnesota	No statute
Mississippi	No statute
Missouri	No statute
Montana	No statute
Nebraska	No statute
Nevada	No statute
New Hampshire	Security deposits must be held in a separate account in a financial institution located within the state; tenant must be told of the location and number of the account, the amount on deposit and the interest rate, and the tenant must be allowed to examine security deposit records if the tenant requests this information and/or to do so; tenant must be provided with a receipt for the security deposit which indicates the amount received and the name of the financial institution where it will be held if the deposit is not paid for with a personal check, certified check or check from a government or non-profit agency; a security bond covering all security deposits may be obtained in lieu of maintaining a separate account
New Jersey	Security deposits must be held in a separate interest-bearing account in a federally insured financial institution located within the state; tenant must be told within 30 days, and at the time of annual interest payments, of the location and type of the account, the amount deposited on his or her behalf and the interest rate
New Mexico	No statute
New York	Security deposits are not required to be held in a financial institution unless the property has 6 or more units, in which case the financial institution must be located in the state; if security deposits are held in a financial institution, they must be held in a separate account and the tenant must be told of the location of the account and the amount deposited on his or her behalf

North Carolina	Security deposits must be held in a separate trust account in a federally insured financial institution located within the state; tenant must be told within 30 days the location of the account; a security bond, issued from an insurance company licensed in the state, covering all security deposits may be obtained in lieu of maintaining a separate account
North Dakota	Security deposits must be held in a separate interest-bearing account in a federally insured financial institution
Ohio	No statute
Oklahoma	Security deposits must be held in a separate account
Oregon	No statute
Pennsylvania	Security deposits must be held in a separate account located at a financial institution which is regulated by the state or federal government if over $100; tenant must be told the location of the account and the amount deposited on his or her behalf; a security bond, issued from a bonding company licensed in the state, covering all security deposits may be obtained in lieu of maintaining a separate account
Rhode Island	No statute
South Carolina	No statute
South Dakota	No statute
Tennessee	Security deposits must be held in a separate account; tenant must be told orally or in writing the location of the account
Texas	No statute
Utah	No statute
Vermont	No statute
Virginia	No statute
Washington	Security deposits must be held in a separate account; tenant must be provided with a receipt for the security deposit which indicates the name and location of the financial institution where it will be held
West Virginia	No statute
Wisconsin	No statute
Wyoming	No statute

Increasing the Deposit

There are certain instances where you may need to consider increasing your security deposit to accommodate additional risks. The **most common** would be **the addition of a pet or other animal and even a new occupant.** *If the tenant wants to add an additional occupant to the lease, you have the right to charge additional security - as long as you don't go beyond allowable limits.*

The **pet deposit** is an obvious one – and **many states even allow this to be a non-refundable fee.** If that is the case, then **any funds that are non-refundable may be kept in your operating account for the rental property**, which may be your own personal bank account.

Other reasons to ask for additional security may include the tenant's request to have a waterbed, aquarium or other items that may pose a potential risk. However, *you cannot charge additional security as a means of retaliating against your tenant if that tenant complains to you or authorities about his or her living conditions* (including maintenance and repair issues). **You also cannot increase a tenant's security deposit as an act of discrimination against his or her civil rights.** *Any increase you propose must be done justly and within reason.* So, **if you increase one tenant's deposit because he or she wants to set up an aquarium,** *then* **you must increase the deposit of the next tenant who wants an aquarium.** See **Chapters 7** and **11** for more on discrimination and retaliation.

Don't expect to get a favorable response from your tenant if you decide to ask for additional security. Therefore, **you may want to consider the impact your request may have on your landlord-tenant relationship** and whether the increase is truly needed to offset a reasonable amount of risk. *Just be consistent.*

Selling the Property (Transferring the Deposit)

Your intentions may be to hold on to your investment properties for the rest of your life. But **if there comes a point in time where you decide to sell one, it's important to remember to transfer the security deposit funds along with your assignment of the lease to another landlord** – unless, upon the sale of the property, tenancy will be terminated. Then, of course, **the unit should be inspected to determine whether or not there is just cause to withhold any portion (or all) of the tenant's money.**

Chapter 3

Returning the Security Deposit: How to Avoid a Showdown!

This Chapter Discusses:

- ★ **Move-Out Letter**
- ★ **Move-Out Inspection**
- ★ **Cleaning and Repairing**
- ★ **Time Limits**
- ★ **Normal Wear and Tear**
- ★ **Itemizing Damage and Deductions**
- ★ **Interest Earned**
- ★ **Common Disputes**
- ★ **Unpaid Rent**
- ★ **Co-tenants**
- ★ **What If a Tenant Sues Me?**

You collected it and have held onto it with a clenched fist for the past year. Now finally comes the time to determine whether you are obligated by law to return the tenant's security deposit – or if you have legal grounds to retain a portion (or even the entire bankroll) and *in what time frame does all of this absolutely have to transpire?* It's far too easy for a tenant to file against you in **small claims court**, so you want to make sure you protect yourself every step of the way by following the laws of your state as outlined in this chapter.

Move-Out Letter

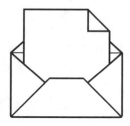

While no specific state requires a **"move-out letter"** be used, it is strongly suggested that you mail one to your tenant *approximately 30 days prior* to the lease terminating or whenever the tenant is scheduled to move.

The purpose of this letter is to keep the landlord-tenant relationship on good terms and to deter (as best as possible) any future disputes, by directly addressing the following three topics:

Three Topics to Address in a Move-Out Letter:

★ Cleaning Requirements

A reminder should be included as to what requirements were specified in the original lease agreement and/or are reasonably expected of the tenant to ensure that the tenant leave the property in the same condition it was on the day he or she moved in, except for normal wear and tear. Common issues – as well as *the definition of "normal wear and tear"* – will be discussed later in this chapter.

★ Contact Information for Inspection

You should include *how and when you are to be contacted* so that you can be called to assess the property's condition – **See the following inspection section for particular requirements by your individual state.**

★ How and When the Deposit Will Be Returned

In order to avoid dealing with impatient tenants and the amassing of unnecessary animosity, your move-out letter ought to tell the tenant *how* and *when* he or she can expect to be notified about *the returning of the security deposit*.

As with any type of correspondence between yourself and your tenant, **specific choice of language should be used to maintain a continuous state of professionalism –** *these letters should never be inflammatory, accusatory or disparaging, regardless of how the tenant chooses to behave.* You never want to appear anything less than thoroughly upstanding and respectful in the eyes of the law – thereby reducing your chances of unintentionally handing a tenant the opportunity to take legal action *against you for something you said.*

Once you have clearly addressed these three primary points, **always thank the tenant for his or her stay.** It doesn't matter what the situation is – or has been. *It is critical for you to end your letter in a cordial manner* – whatever your true feelings may be about the tenancy. **Even if the letter appears to be merely a standard form letter with the blanks filled in, a simple sentence thanking the tenant would suffice.**

An example of a standard **move-out letter** has been provided on the next page; a template has also been included **on the enclosed CD-ROM.**

Move-Out Letter

August 1, 2008

Abigail Parker
1950 Hawks Ridge
Mountain View, VA 20990

Dear Abigail,

I have received your notice to vacate 1950 Hawks Ridge on August 31, 2008. I hope your stay there has been pleasant. This letter is a reminder of move-out procedures and expectations.

The house should be left in the same good, clean order that it was in upon your arrival. Before vacating the property, please be sure to remember to clean the following:

1. Flooring – carpets should be vacuumed and, if necessary, washed; linoleums should be mopped

2. Bathroom fixtures – all showers, bathtubs, toilets, sinks, etc. should be cleaned thoroughly

3. Kitchen appliances – refrigerator, stove, oven, microwave, dishwasher should be cleaned both inside and outside

4. Countertops and cabinets – the inside of all cabinets should be cleaned as well as their exteriors and all countertops

5. Window coverings – should be dusted or laundered as appropriate

6. Walls, baseboards, shelves, doors, windows, etc. – should be dusted or cleaned as appropriate

Please remember to remove all garbage, food, plants, cleaning supplies, personal property, etc. and to be certain to have all utilities disconnected and your mail forwarded to your new address.

You may leave all keys on the kitchen counter and lock the property upon your departure. Please be sure to provide me with your forwarding address in writing. When the property is ready for an inspection, or if you have any questions, please contact me at (555) 555-5555.

In accordance with state law, your security deposit, along with an itemization of any deductions, will be returned to you within 30 days. Thank you for your tenancy.

Sincerely,

Ethan Cameron
Property Manager

Move-Out Inspection

You should inspect your rental property either the day the tenant moves out or immediately thereafter to assess the property's condition. It's recommended that you bring along the **original assessment of property condition form** you would have had the tenant complete with you at the time he or she moved in – along with any photographs that you carefully took to rely on as a reference. It's hard to argue with a printed image; memory is far more subjective…

It is customary and common courtesy to invite the tenant to be present at the time of the inspection, regardless of whether or not your state requires you give the tenant said opportunity. This way, you and the tenant can immediately address *together* any problems that may have arisen and that do not appear on the original checklist or in any of the photographs.

<u>However!</u>: In order to avoid any unhealthy altercations, you should not reveal your final decision on the fate of the security deposit while physically in the presence of the tenant. It is instead suggested that you *listen carefully* **to the tenant if he or she should choose to refute any of the problems that you decide to point out**. *Then, as diplomatically as possible, bow out of any confrontation* – do not escalate the problem by letting your innate emotions take over.

If you don't want the tenant to be present at the final inspection, you must first check to *see if your state requires that the tenant have the option of being included* or not. A guide to each state's law on this topic has been provided on the next three pages:

Inspection Notifications

Alabama	No statute
Alaska	No statute
Arizona	At move-in, the landlord must provide written notification to the tenant informing the tenant of the right to be present at the move-out inspection; the landlord must notify the tenant when the move-out inspection will occur if requested by the tenant; if the tenant is being evicted and the landlord has reasonable cause to fear violence or intimidation from the tenant, the landlord is not required to perform the move-out inspection with the tenant
Arkansas	No statute
California	Within a reasonable time after either party gives notification to the other party of the intention to terminate the lease, the landlord must notify the tenant in writing that the tenant has the right to request a preliminary move-out inspection and be present for such inspection; if the tenant requests the preliminary move-out inspection, it must take place no earlier than 2 weeks before the tenancy ends and the landlord must provide written notification of the date and time at least 48 hours in advance (this notification time frame can be waived if both parties sign a written waiver); the tenant must be provided with an itemized statement of proposed deductions from the security deposit, and this statement must include a copy of California Civil Code statute § 1950.5 paragraphs 1-4; the tenant will then have the remaining time of the tenancy to remedy any of the problems found before the final move-out inspection takes place and the landlord can proceed with any deductions from the security deposit
Colorado	No statute
Connecticut	No statute
Delaware	No statute
District of Columbia	No statute
Florida	No statute
Georgia	No statute
Hawaii	No statute
Idaho	No statute
Illinois	No statute
Indiana	No statute
Iowa	No statute

Kansas	No statute
Kentucky	No statute
Louisiana	No statute
Maine	No statute
Maryland	At the time the tenant pays the security deposit, the landlord must provide written notification to the tenant informing the tenant that he or she has the right to be present at the move-out inspection and what he or she needs to do to exercise that right; at least 15 days before the move-out date the tenant must send, via certified mail to the landlord, notification of the intent to move, the move-out date, and the tenant's forwarding address; upon receipt of this notice the landlord must send, via certified mail to the tenant, notification of the date and time the move-out inspection will occur; the move-out inspection must occur within 5 days before or after the move-out date given by the tenant; if the landlord does not comply with any of these procedures, the landlord forfeits the right to deduct from the security deposit for damages
Massachusetts	No statute
Michigan	No statute
Minnesota	No statute
Montana	No statute
Nebraska	No statute
Nevada	No statute
New Hampshire	No statute
New Jersey	No statute
New Mexico	No statute
New York	No statute
North Carolina	No statute
North Dakota	No statute
Ohio	No statute
Oklahoma	No statute
Oregon	No statute
Pennsylvania	No statute
Rhode Island	No statute

South Carolina	No statute
South Dakota	No statute
Tennessee	No statute
Texas	No statute
Utah	No statute
Vermont	No statute
Virginia	At the time the landlord requests the tenant to vacate the property, or within 5 days of the landlord's receipt of notification from the tenant of his or her intent to vacate, the landlord must make a reasonable effort to notify the tenant of the right to be present at the move-out inspection; if the tenant wishes to be at the move-out inspection, he or she must notify the landlord in writing and the landlord must then notify the tenant of the date and time of the inspection; the move-out inspection must occur within 72 hours of the landlord's repossession of the property
Washington	No statute
West Virginia	No statute
Wisconsin	No statute
Wyoming	No statute

Cleaning and Repairing

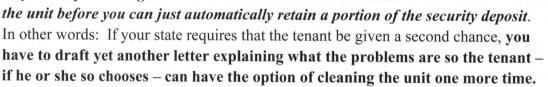

Some states require that if you plan on deducting any of the security deposit to cover a routine cleaning following the final inspection, *you must give the tenant a second chance to clean the unit before you can just automatically retain a portion of the security deposit*. In other words: If your state requires that the tenant be given a second chance, **you have to draft yet another letter explaining what the problems are so the tenant – if he or she so chooses – can have the option of cleaning the unit one more time.**

While allowing another chance at cleaning may be required by your state, **allowing a second – or even first – chance *to make repairs* is not!** Despite how much a tenant begs, *you should never (nor are you in any way obligated to) allow the tenant to* *make repairs to your property* – for the sheer and simple reason of the potential for poor performance and unlicensed work – all of which can only lead to possible increased liability on your part with regards to future tenants, not to mention the cost to the property, itself.

Use your best judgment, but **all landlords should coordinate and facilitate their own property's repairs to ensure the work is performed correctly**. You may *then* legally deduct the cost of the repairs from the tenant's security deposit.

Time Limits

As you would expect, most states have their own laws pertaining to the time period in which you must return a tenant's security deposit and/or notify the tenant of your intentions to retain some – or all – of it.

Each state has been listed on the next three pages, *along with a brief interpretation of the specific statutes, explaining the maximum amount of time that a landlord legally has in which to act*.

Deadlines for Returning Security Deposits

Alabama	35 days
Alaska	14 days if proper termination notice given, 30 days if not
Arizona	14 days
Arkansas	30 days
California	21 days
Colorado	1 month unless lease provides for longer period up to 60 days, 72 weekday non-holiday hours if emergency termination due to gas equipment hazard
Connecticut	30 days or within 15 days of receipt of forwarding address from tenant, whichever is later
Delaware	20 days
District of Columbia	45 days
Florida	15 days if no deductions, 30 days to give notice of what deductions will be made; then tenant has 15 days to dispute any deduction and remaining deposit must be returned within 30 days of initial deduction notification
Georgia	1 month
Hawaii	14 days
Idaho	21 days unless both parties agree, then up to 30 days
Illinois	45 days if no deductions, 30 days to itemize deductions
Indiana	45 days
Iowa	30 days
Kansas	30 days
Kentucky	No statute deadline for returning; if the tenant leaves owing the last month's rent and does not request the security deposit back, the landlord may apply the security deposit to the rent owed after 30 days; if the tenant leaves owing no rent and having a refund due, the landlord must send an itemization to the tenant, but if the tenant does not respond to the landlord after 60 days, the landlord may keep the deposit
Louisiana	1 month
Maine	21 days if tenancy at will, 30 days if written lease
Maryland	45 days, 10 days to itemize deductions if tenant utilizes a surety bond
Massachusetts	30 days

Michigan	30 days
Minnesota	3 weeks, 5 days if termination due to condemnation
Mississippi	45 days
Missouri	30 days
Montana	10 days if no deductions, 30 days if deductions
Nebraska	14 days
Nevada	30 days
New Hampshire	30 days; if shared facilities and deposit is more than 30 days' rent, then 20 days unless written agreement otherwise
New Jersey	30 days, 5 days if termination due to fire, flood, condemnation, evacuation; deadline does not apply if property is owner-occupied and has only 1 or 2 units if the tenant did not provide a written 30 days' notification to the landlord of the desire to invoke the law
New Mexico	30 days
New York	Reasonable time
North Carolina	30 days
North Dakota	30 days
Ohio	30 days
Oklahoma	30 days
Oregon	31 days
Pennsylvania	30 days
Rhode Island	20 days
South Carolina	30 days
South Dakota	2 weeks to return deposit and/or provide explanation for any withholding; 45 days to provide an itemized accounting of all deductions made to the security deposit if the tenant requests one
Tennessee	No statute, 10 days to itemize deductions
Texas	30 days
Utah	30 days or within 15 days of receipt of forwarding address from tenant, whichever is later
Vermont	14 days

Virginia	45 days
Washington	14 days
West Virginia	No statute
Wisconsin	21 days
Wyoming	30 days or within 15 days of receipt of forwarding address from tenant, whichever is later; 60 days if unit has damage

Normal Wear and Tear

As you've probably already surmised, most of the disputes regarding security deposits involve conflicting opinions regarding subjective definitions of what is **"normal wear and tear"** – as opposed to something that may be out of the ordinary or even rather extreme.

Unfortunately, there is no objective way of defining a line between normal, unusual – or even extreme. This topic would be much better addressed in Philosophy, Psychology or even Criminology 101. In the meantime, a basic ability to reason will prove more than adequate to help us cope with our individual differences in perception. And, as long as you've done your homework in hiring the best possible tenant (discussed in much greater detail in the *American Landlord* volume of the **"Everything U Need to Know…" series**), *you should somehow be able to come to a common agreement – especially since most sane people are really not interested in the joys of engaging in small claims court proceedings over such a relatively small sum of money*.

If your tenant turns out to be that one person who feels it was perfectly within his or her right to put a fist through your wall – then, unfortunately, **you are indeed going to have to partake in the small claims circus, should there be *any* type of dispute between landlord and tenant.**

Itemizing Damage and Deductions

If you determine that you are, in fact, going to retain *any* of the
security deposit, **most states require you to prepare a letter
that specifically addresses how much is being deducted
and for which item(s).** In addition to maintaining your
legal compliance, *an itemization is also important because
it clearly and concisely justifies this very sensitive issue
of withholding the tenant's money.*

It may go without saying for some, but we'll reiterate that any letter of such great
importance should *always* be delivered to the tenant *via certified mail or some other
type of delivery method that can have its receipt confirmed.* This way, you have
solid proof that you have acted in accordance with your state's law.

It is important to note that – even if it should be *glaringly* obvious to the tenant that
there's no way in this lifetime the tenant should expect to be getting the security
deposit back – be it on account of painfully obvious damage or because he or she owes
past due rent and is in the process of being evicted – **you must *still* send a letter to
comply with the notification requirements.**

Interest Earned

As already mentioned in **Chapter 2**, **your state may require you to
pay interest – or share any interest – that you have received from
the tenant's security deposit**, regardless of whether or not there are repairs needed.

*If required, the interest should be calculated and returned along with any other
portion of the security deposit.* **There are currently 15 states that have interest
requirements.** A summary of each state's law has been outlined again on the next
three pages. *If your state is not listed,* **then there is** *no statute at this time* **that
pertains to interest earned from security deposits.**

Security Deposit Interest Requirements

Alabama	No statute
Alaska	No statute
Arizona	No statute
Arkansas	No statute
California	No statute
Colorado	No statute
Connecticut	Pay annually and at termination, equal to average rate on savings accts at insured banks but not less than 1.5%
Delaware	No statute
District of Columbia	Pay at termination, at current passbook rate
Florida	Not required, but if made must pay annually and at termination; tenant who wrongfully terminates is not entitled to; lease agreement must give details on interest
Georgia	No statute
Hawaii	No statute
Idaho	No statute
Illinois	Required if owner has 25+ properties adjacent to each other or in same building; if security deposit held for longer than 6 months, must pay annually and at termination
Indiana	No statute
Iowa	Not required, but if paid must pay at termination; however, any interest earned during the first 5 years is landlord's
Kansas	No statute
Kentucky	No statute
Louisiana	No statute
Maine	No statute
Maryland	Must pay semi-annually, at a rate of 4% if deposit is greater than $50
Massachusetts	Must pay annually and within 30 days of termination, at a rate of 5% or the actual rate earned; no interest for last month's rent paid in advance
Michigan	No statute

Minnesota	Must pay at a rate of 1%; total interest under $1 does not need to be paid
Mississippi	No statute
Missouri	No statute
Montana	No statute
Nebraska	No statute
Nevada	No statute
New Hampshire	Only required if deposit held for a year or longer; must pay at termination; tenant can request payment every 3 years if request made within 30 days of tenancy expiration/renewal; rate must be equal to the rate paid on the bank savings account where deposited
New Jersey	Must pay annually or credit back to rent owed; landlord with less than 10 units can put deposit in any insured interest-bearing bank account; those with 10 or more must put funds in an insured money market account that matures in a year or less or in any other account that pays interest at a comparable rate to a money market account
New Mexico	Must pay annually at rate equal to passbook rate if deposit is more than 1 month's rent and there is a year lease
New York	Must pay at prevailing rate if unit is covered under rent control or stabilization requirements or if building has 6 or more units; landlord can keep 1% admin fee a year
North Carolina	No statute
North Dakota	Must pay interest if tenancy is at least 9 months; deposit must be put in an insured interest-bearing savings or checking acct
Ohio	Must pay annually and at termination, at a rate of 5% if the tenancy is 6 months or more and the deposit is greater than $50 or 1 month's rent - whichever is greater - the interest only accrues on the excess of the $50 or 1-month rent amount
Oklahoma	No statute
Oregon	No statute
Pennsylvania	Must pay if tenancy is longer than 2 years; interest accrues from start of 25th month of tenancy and must be paid annually after that point; landlord can deduct 1% fee
Rhode Island	No statute
South Carolina	No statute
South Dakota	No statute
Tennessee	No statute

Texas	No statute
Utah	No statute
Vermont	No statute
Virginia	Must pay if deposit is held for more than 13 months for continued tenancy in same unit; interest accrues from start of lease and must be paid at termination; must be at rate of 1% below FED discount rate as of Jan. 1 of each year
Washington	No statute
West Virginia	No statute
Wisconsin	No statute
Wyoming	No statute

Common Disputes

It never fails – you can usually count on *some form of a dispute or issue* to arise when performing your final inspection of your rental property. For your review and consideration, the three most common ones have been addressed below:

The Three Most Common Security Deposit Disputes:

☆ Fixtures

Anything attached to the property is typically defined as a fixture (e.g., ceiling fan, lighting, intercom, door bell, etc.). Depending on how you initially draft your lease agreement, *the tenant is commonly responsible for leaving all of the original fixtures, as well as any fixtures the tenant installed during the duration of the tenancy*.

This means that if a tenant should remove a ceiling light and replace it with a fan while living there, the tenant must then reinstall the *original* ceiling light (or a new, comparable model) upon moving out. That is, of course, unless you agree to accept the fan instead.

You can legally charge the tenant for any damage that may result from removing a fixture the tenant installed and left behind, even if you remove it *(that is – unless you gave the tenant permission to install it in the first place).*

<u>To keep matters simple</u>: *You should have the property returned to the original condition it was in before the tenant moved in, upon the tenant moving out*. Otherwise, things can easily get complicated, trying to dispute what was and what wasn't **"authorized."**

<u>Remember</u>: It takes a little more time and effort, but **having every correspondence or authorization documented in writing prevents a lot of unnecessary headaches** down the trail…

☆ Painting

State statutes don't actually specifically address who is responsible for paying for repainting – but if such an issue ever were to make it into a courtroom, judges would most likely consider *how long the tenant occupied the property*. The longer the tenancy, the more wear and tear would be expected. Therefore, **it would be less likely that the tenant would be the one responsible for paying for a fresh coat of paint**.

☆ Carpeting

The same premise for painting basically goes for carpeting, as well. However, **"normal wear and tear"** must be examined more closely here. Obviously, if the tenant spills coffee or fruit punch on the carpet (even after having lived there for several years!), it is common for **the tenant to be required to pay for at least a percentage** of the replacement. "Normal wear and tear" is commonly defined as everyday residential traffic.

> **However**: *If it was genuinely time for the carpet to be replaced anyway, the tenant should not incur* **any** *of the replacement costs*.

Unpaid Rent

Landlords are permitted to use the tenant's security deposit for any unpaid rent no matter which way you want to try to look at it! Whether it be for **additional days the tenant stays beyond the "move-out date"** or perhaps because the tenant didn't give enough notice to cover the period mutually agreed upon in the lease – **in either case, then you can prorate those extra days that notice should have been given**.

If the tenant is not on a month-to-month lease, you can also withhold the balance of the remaining lease term should the tenant leave early and you are unable to re-rent the property, after a sincere effort on your part to advertise the property's vacancy, during that time.

If you are in the process of evicting the tenant, *you should exhaust as much of the security deposit as possible toward needed cleaning and repairs before you apply it to the unpaid rent*. The **eviction process usually entitles you to a monetary judgment for the unpaid rent,** so you should be significantly more concerned with covering your other expenses first! *Unpaid rent can always be pursued using some type of collection means (such as wage garnishment) without having to go back to court as long as you have an eviction judgment recorded against the tenant*. Unfortunately, cleaning and repair fees are more difficult to collect after tenancy ends.

Co-tenants

If you have accepted a ***jointly-executed lease agreement between two or more parties***, **you are allowed to withhold the return of the security deposit until all tenants move out** – although some kinder landlords will generously refund a portion if the tenants have demonstrated exemplary behavior with cleanliness and "on time" payments…

You may also want to consider collecting the leaving tenant's share from the remaining tenant(s). Regardless of how you want to approach the final situation, you should ***definitely inspect the unit any time*** **any** *co-tenant vacates* – that way, when it comes time to return or retain a portion of the security deposit, ***all tenants should be credited or debited fairly and accordingly*** – which, ideally, should be equally. **Chapter 10** goes further into the issue of co-tenancies.

What If a Tenant Sues Me?

Well, unfortunately, it ***does*** happen. A tenant can have ***as long as 10 years in some states*** to come back at you for something ***as simple as the remaining security deposit***. Again, most of these cases are filed in a **small claims court**, which usually handles disputes of ***$5,000 or less***.

On the next four pages are two guides for every state – regarding how much time tenants have to file a case against you and the maximum amount they can collect in a small claims court.

<u>Note</u>: **Tenants always have the option of suing you in a higher court if they choose,** especially if the amount they are trying to collect ***exceeds*** the maximum amount permissible in a small claims court.

Statute of Limitations for Written Contracts (Lease Agreements)

Alabama	6 years
Alaska	6 years
Arizona	6 years
Arkansas	5 years
California	4 years
Colorado	6 years
Connecticut	6 years
Delaware	3 years
District of Columbia	3 years
Florida	5 years
Georgia	6 years
Hawaii	6 years
Idaho	5 years
Illinois	10 years
Indiana	10 years
Iowa	10 years
Kansas	5 years
Kentucky	15 years
Louisiana	10 years
Maine	6 years
Maryland	3 years
Massachusetts	6 years
Michigan	6 years
Minnesota	6 years
Mississippi	3 years
Missouri	10 years

Montana	8 years
Nebraska	5 years
Nevada	6 years
New Hampshire	3 years
New Jersey	6 years
New Mexico	6 years
New York	6 years
North Carolina	3 years
North Dakota	6 years
Ohio	15 years
Oklahoma	5 years
Oregon	6 years
Pennsylvania	6 years
Rhode Island	15 years
South Carolina	10 years
South Dakota	6 years
Tennessee	6 years
Texas	4 years
Utah	6 years
Vermont	6 years
Virginia	5 years
Washington	6 years
West Virginia	10 years
Wisconsin	6 years
Wyoming	10 years

Small Claims Court Amount Limits

Alabama	$3,000
Alaska	$10,000
Arizona	$2,500
Arkansas	$5,000
California	$7,500
Colorado	$7,500
Connecticut	$5,000; no limit if security deposit case
Delaware	$15,000
District of Columbia	$5,000
Florida	$5,000
Georgia	$15,000; no limit if eviction case
Hawaii	$3,500; no limit if security deposit case
Idaho	$5,000
Illinois	$10,000
Indiana	$6,000
Iowa	$5,000
Kansas	$4,000
Kentucky	$1,500
Louisiana	$3,000; no limit if eviction case in Justice of the Peace Courts
Maine	$4,500
Maryland	$5,000
Massachusetts	$2,000
Michigan	$3,000
Minnesota	$7,500
Mississippi	$2,500
Missouri	$3,000

Montana	$3,000
Nebraska	$2,700
Nevada	$5,000
New Hampshire	$5,000
New Jersey	$3,000; $5,000 if security deposit case; certain suits cannot be brought in small claims court
New Mexico	$10,000
New York	$5,000; $3,000 in town and village courts
North Carolina	$5,000
North Dakota	$5,000
Ohio	$3,000
Oklahoma	$6,000
Oregon	$5,000
Pennsylvania	$8,000; $10,000 in Philadelphia courts
Rhode Island	$2,500
South Carolina	$7,500
South Dakota	$8,000
Tennessee	$15,000; $25,000 if county population over 700,000; no limit if eviction case
Texas	$10,000
Utah	$7,500
Vermont	$5,000
Virginia	$5,000
Washington	$4,000
West Virginia	$5,000
Wisconsin	$5,000; no limit if eviction case
Wyoming	$7,000

Chapter 4

Other Deposits and Fees:
What to Charge For and What Not To

This Chapter Discusses:

★ **Application Fees**
★ **Cleaning Fees**
★ **Last Month's Rent Deposits**
★ **Pet Deposits**

Only 11 states specifically allow for non-refundable fees, while just a few specifically prohibit them. *This leaves the topic of non-refundable fees quite tricky to navigate.* With the exception of application fees, depending on which state you are in, **it might be best to forgo the idea of charging additional initial fees.** This chapter goes over the basics of **the most common additional fees charged to tenants,** as well as providing you with a **comprehensive chart outlining each state's requirements** – *so you can come to an informed decision* about charging your tenants anything other than a security deposit.

Application Fees

With few exceptions, non-refundable application fees are allowed in all states. ***This is one permissible fee you should take advantage of without hesitation.*** The goal is *not* to become rich by collecting a bunch of exorbitant application fees and running just a small percentage of background checks *(that, in fact, would be illegal).* The point is to **charge just enough to cover the expense of thoroughly checking out a potential tenant,** so that you actually do the background check and yet not incur any financial burden.

The most common ways states regulate application fees are either by **limiting the fee to only enough to cover your actual expenses for obtaining a credit report** or by **capping the fee at a set amount.**

One important exception to note is the state of **Wisconsin.** In this state, *you cannot charge an application fee if the prospective tenants provide you with a copy of their credit report that is less than 30 days old.*

Cleaning Fees

While it may seem like a good idea to charge in advance for what you know you are going to have to do when someone moves out – clean the unit – after careful consideration *it may not seem so wise.*

The first problem comes from the fact that **only a few states allow for a non-refundable cleaning fee, so there is a good chance your state isn't one of them.** However, if you're lucky enough to have property in a more landlord-friendly state that *does* allow such a fee, **what happens if the tenant leaves the unit in a condition that would go beyond the scope of your normal move-out cleanup, but not to the point of damaging the rental?** (Think along the lines of a carpet that has pet stains that can be removed if you hire a good, professional carpet cleaner.) *Deducting from the security deposit for cleaning when you've already charged a fee for cleaning* *could lead to a security deposit dispute in court.* **You would be better off collecting as much as you can for a security deposit** and having the freedom to use that one deposit as needed.

Last Month's Rent Deposits

Labeling a deposit – or part of a deposit – as the last month's rent invites a number of complications. First, *if you label part of the allowable security deposit as the last month's rent, then you cannot use that portion for any damage.* If the tenant then leaves the unit with lots of damage, **you might find yourself without enough of a security deposit to cover it.**

Second, **if you are expecting applicants to come up with an application fee, the first month's rent, a security deposit *and* the last month's rent just to get the keys to their new home, you may find it difficult to attract a good number of applicants.**

Third, **if you increase the rent and forget to require an increase to the last month's rent deposit, that could lead to a dispute at the end of the tenancy over whether or not the tenant owes you anything for the last month's rent** – which the tenant assumes is already pre-paid. Do you see how problematic it could quickly get? *It would be easier (not to mention reasonable) to allow the tenant to pay the last month's rent when it's due and for you to simply focus on getting as much as you can as a security deposit.*

Pet Deposits

If you allow tenants to have pets in order to broaden your applicant pool, you need to keep in mind the need to protect yourself from the possibility of additional damage that could be caused by the pets. *Some states allow for a specific pet deposit that*

is separate from – and in addition to – the security deposit. If this is the case in your state, **it is wise to take advantage of the chance to require additional funds to cover potential pet damage.**

Others require any pet deposit to be calculated with the security deposit to reach a total deposit that **cannot exceed the state's limit on security deposits.** In this case, *it's not advisable to label and restrict a portion of the deposit to pet damage only.* **If your state falls into this category, and does not allow an additional pet deposit beyond the security deposit, you can consider the option of charging more per month for rent.** *As long as the increase in rent is consistent for all applicants with pets, this is a perfectly acceptable practice.*

While pet owners, in general, are not considered a protected group when it comes to anti-discrimination laws, *it is against the law to charge an extra deposit for a pet when the pet is a trained service animal.* This shouldn't worry you, however – remember, **these animals are highly trained and are not typically left alone at home.**

On the next three pages a chart is provided to address those states which have statutes pertaining to pet deposits and any other type of additional fees that a landlord may charge and whether or not non-refundable ones are prohibited.

Pet Deposit and Additional Fee Information

Alabama	Additional deposits, beyond the security deposit limit, are allowed for pets, undoing alterations, and tenant activities that increase liability risks
Alaska	No statute
Arizona	Non-refundable fees are allowed; the purpose of any non-refundable fee must be stated in writing to the tenant; all fees are refundable unless specifically designated as non-refundable
Arkansas	No statute
California	Non-refundable fees are not allowed
Colorado	No statute
Connecticut	No statute
Delaware	Additional pet deposit of up to 1 month's rent allowed
District of Columbia	No statute
Florida	Non-refundable fees are not specifically addressed in statutes, but are customary
Georgia	Non-refundable fees are not specifically addressed in statutes, but are customary
Hawaii	Non-refundable fees are not allowed; only the first month's rent and security deposit can be collected at the start of a tenancy
Idaho	No statute
Illinois	No statute
Indiana	No statute
Iowa	No statute
Kansas	Additional pet deposit of up to ½ month's rent allowed
Kentucky	No statute
Louisiana	No statute
Maine	No statute
Maryland	No statute
Massachusetts	No statute
Michigan	No statute

Minnesota	No statute
Mississippi	No statute
Missouri	No statute
Montana	Non-refundable fees are not allowed
Nebraska	Additional pet deposit of up to ¼ month's rent allowed
Nevada	Non-refundable fees are allowed; the purpose of any non-refundable fee must be indicated in the lease agreement
New Hampshire	No statute
New Jersey	No statute
New Mexico	No statute
New York	No statute
North Carolina	Reasonable non-refundable pet deposit allowed
North Dakota	If there is a pet, the security deposit may be increased to a total of $2,500 or 2 months' rent, whichever is greater
Ohio	No statute
Oklahoma	No statute
Oregon	Non-refundable fees are allowed for reasonably anticipated landlord expenses (including those caused by a tenant not in compliance if indicated in the lease agreement) as long as the fees are not excessive
Pennsylvania	No statute
Rhode Island	No statute
South Carolina	No statute
South Dakota	A security deposit exceeding the limit is allowed if special conditions pose a danger to the maintenance of the property and all parties agree
Tennessee	No statute
Texas	No statute
Utah	Non-refundable fees are allowed; it is customary, though not specifically addressed in statutes, that the landlord must disclose in writing if any part of the security deposit is non-refundable when a written lease agreement is used
Vermont	No statute
Virginia	No statute

Washington	Non-refundable fees are allowed; any non-refundable fees must be clearly indicated in the lease agreement as non-refundable
West Virginia	No statute
Wisconsin	No statute
Wyoming	Non-refundable fees are allowed; the landlord must disclose in writing, before accepting the deposit, if any part of the security deposit is non-refundable, and the lease agreement must indicate this as well

Chapter 5

Landlord's Duties: Maintenance and Repairs

This Chapter Discusses:

★ **What You Must Do**
★ **What If You Don't Do It?**

Undoubtedly, everyone deserves a clean, well-kept, properly functioning place to live. **As a landlord, it is your responsibility to see that your tenants have such a place.** *But what does this actually mean for you?*

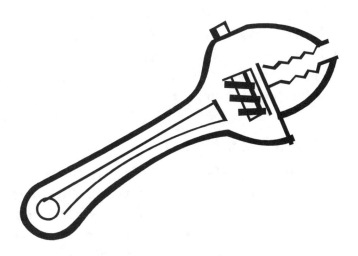

What You Must Do

Chances are most of your legal requirements for maintaining a habitable property come from not only state, but local regulations as well. This can include **local and state building codes, state housing statutes, previous judicial decisions**, and even **what is just commonly regarded as suitable.** While this can get rather confusing, there are **some basic ideas that you can grasp that will help guide you:**

Basic Ideas about a Landlord's Duties:

☆ Cleanliness and Safety

You must provide and maintain those things that will ensure clean, safe and decent housing. This includes such things as **heating and air conditioning, hot water, working locks, exterior lighting, electricity, fully operational plumbing** and **trash removal.** *You do not have to pay for the monthly electricity or gas* required for such housing basics, *but you have to ensure that these things are working properly* and able to be supplied to the tenant.

Consider what the average person or family would need to have an adequate place to live – not Thrifty Tim, who is willing to keep his winter parka on 24/7 to avoid having to install heat in his home, or Frontier Fay, who doesn't see a problem with hiking a half mile to the nearby stream for her water, so she never bothered getting plumbing installed in her home.

☆ All Properties Are Not Equal

In supplying housing basics, you need to consider where your property is located and what it specifically needs. For example, a property located in the Deep South *may not require heat* to make it habitable. Likewise, a property in the Pacific Northwest may require some *additional* protection from the elements. In fact, *the state of Oregon actually requires waterproofing by the landlord.*

Most of these unique requirements are actually fairly commonsensical. If you have lived in Florida, you know all about roaches and ants – and, if you have rental property there, you'd certainly want it and your tenants protected from them. So, it's probably no surprise that in Florida, you need to exterminate pests to be in compliance with the law. Similarly, if your rental property is located in Vermont, you'd know that most houses there do not have central air conditioning.

☆ Don't Forget about Common Areas

It is your responsibility to keep these areas maintained as well. Grass needs to be mowed, walkways need to be shoveled and de-iced in the winter, parking areas need to be lit, steps need to have secure handrails, etc. **Just because these areas are outside of the tenant's home doesn't mean they don't play a role in the safety and habitability of the property.**

☆ Maintaining Your Supplied Items

If you have supplied something, even if it is beyond a housing basic, you must maintain it and/or repair it. Items such as washing machines, microwaves, dishwashers and decorative drapes are certainly **not basic housing requirements that you must supply.** However, they undoubtedly make life more convenient and you are bound to find yourself supplying any of these amenities, or an assortment of others, to make your property more appealing to renters. **Once you do – or even promise to – you are required to supply it and keep it in safe, working condition.**

☆ Develop a Maintenance Schedule and Procedures

As explained in detail in *American Landlord,* **you need to** *have a maintenance schedule that you stick to as well as a procedure for dealing with maintenance requests.* If you can show proof that you

regularly replace air conditioning filters, respond to maintenance requests within 24 hours, provide written explanations for repair delays to tenants, etc., *you should be able to easily protect yourself if a complaint is ever filed against you.* **Just make sure everything is well documented.** *To make this easier, require all tenants to put any maintenance requests in writing.* If an emergency, such as a broken water pipe, doesn't make a written request practical, be sure you follow up with a written summary to the tenant acknowledging the problem and what you did, or are going to do, to fix the problem.

An important exception – *If your tenant causes the problem*, such as by leaving a window open during a thunderstorm, *it is still your responsibility to see that any repairs are made, but it is the tenant's responsibility to pay for those repairs.*

What If You Don't Do It?

So, **what happens if you are negligent for some reason or another?** The answer depends on what the problem is that you have failed to adequately address for your tenant, as well as where your property is located (e.g., jurisdiction).

If it is a serious matter that affects the safety or habitability of the property, then your tenants will probably have a few options to choose from. They could *file a complaint with the local housing authority,* they could *not pay their rent until you fix the problem* (commonly referred to as *"withholding"*) or they could *fix the problem themselves and deduct the cost from their rent* (commonly referred to as *"repair and deduct"*).

If the problem is a minor one, such as a leaky faucet or a storm door that is about to fall off a hinge, then *the only legal option that tenants have is to complain to the local housing authority.* **If they choose to withhold the rent or repair and deduct**

without your authorization, this is grounds for eviction. It is a *common misconception* among tenants that they can escalate a minor problem to the point of withholding rent or repairing the problem and deducting it from their rent, so *be wary of this.* A reference to each state's statute regarding **withholding** and **"repair and deduct"** options allowed to tenants is provided for you on the following four pages.

If you want to read a state's statute, just type in the statute information as it appears in this book's chart into your favorite search engine (e.g., Google, MSN, Yahoo!) and you'll find references all over. Or to make things easier, just visit the official website of this series, **www.EUNTK.com,** or its companion website, **www.AmericanLandlord.com,** for links to each state's landlord-tenant laws.

Withholding Statutes

Alabama	Ala. Code § 35-9A-405
Alaska	Alaska Stat. §§ 34.03.190 and 34.03.100(b)
Arizona	Ariz. Rev. Stat. Ann. § 33-1365
Arkansas	No statute
California	No statute
Colorado	No statute
Connecticut	Conn. Gen. Stat. Ann. §§ 47a-14a to 47a-14h
Delaware	Del. Code Ann. tit. 25, § 5308(b)(3)
District of Columbia	No statute
Florida	Fla. Stat. Ann. § 83.60
Georgia	No statute
Hawaii	Haw. Rev. Stat. § 521-78
Idaho	No statute
Illinois	765 Ill. Com. Stat. §§ 735/2 and 735/2.2
Indiana	No statute
Iowa	Iowa Code Ann. § 562A.24
Kansas	Kan. Stat. Ann. § 58-2561
Kentucky	Ky. Rev. Stat. Ann. § 383.645
Louisiana	No statute
Maine	Me. Rev. Stat. Ann. tit. 14, § 6021
Maryland	Md. Code Ann. [Real Prop.] §§ 8-211 and 8-211.1
Massachusetts	Mass. Gen. Laws Ann. ch. 239 § 8A
Michigan	Mich. Comp. Laws § 125.530
Minnesota	Minn. Stat. Ann. §§ 504B.215(3)(d) and 504B.385
Mississippi	No statute
Missouri	No statute

Montana	Mont. Code Ann. § 70-24-421
Nebraska	Neb. Rev. Stat. § 76-1428
Nevada	Nev. Rev. Stat. Ann. § 118A.490
New Hampshire	N.H. Rev. Stat. Ann. § 540:13-D
New Jersey	N.J. Stat. Ann. § 2A:42-88
New Mexico	N.M. Stat. Ann. § 47-8-27.2
New York	N.Y. Real Prop. Law § 235-B
North Carolina	No statute
North Dakota	No statute
Ohio	Ohio Rev. Code Ann. § 5321.07
Oklahoma	Okla. Stat. Ann. tit. 41 § 121
Oregon	Or. Rev. Stat. § 90.365
Pennsylvania	68 Pa. Cons. Stat. Ann. § 250.206 and 35 Pa. Cons. Stat. Ann. § 1700-1
Rhode Island	R.I. Gen. Laws § 34-18-32
South Carolina	S.C. Code Ann. § 27-40-640
South Dakota	S.D. Codified Laws Ann. § 43-32-9
Tennessee	Tenn. Code Ann. § 68-111-104
Texas	No statute
Utah	No statute
Vermont	Vt. Stat. Ann. tit. 9 § 4458
Virginia	Va. Code Ann. §§ 54-248.25 and 54-248.25.1 and 54-248.27
Washington	Wash. Rev. Code Ann. §§ 59.18.110 and 59.18.115
West Virginia	No statute
Wisconsin	Wis. Stat. Ann. § 704.07(4)
Wyoming	Wyo. Stat. § 1-21-1206

"Repair and Deduct" Statutes

Alabama	No statute
Alaska	Alaska Stat. §§ 34.03.180 and 34.03.100(b)
Arizona	Ariz. Rev. Stat. Ann. § 33-1363 and 33-1364
Arkansas	No statute
California	Cal. Civ. Code § 1942
Colorado	No statute
Connecticut	Conn. Gen. Stat. Ann. §§ 47a-13
Delaware	Del. Code Ann. tit. 25, §§ 5307 and 5308
District of Columbia	D.C. Code Ann. § 6-751.10
Florida	No statute
Georgia	No statute
Hawaii	Haw. Rev. Stat. § 521-64
Idaho	No statute
Illinois	765 Ill. Com. Stat. § 742/5
Indiana	No statute
Iowa	Iowa Code Ann. § 562A.23
Kansas	No statute
Kentucky	Ky. Rev. Stat. Ann. §§ 383.635 and 383.640
Louisiana	La. Civ. Code Ann. art. 2694
Maine	Me. Rev. Stat. Ann. tit. 14, § 6026
Maryland	No statute
Massachusetts	Mass. Gen. Laws Ann. ch. 111 § 127L
Michigan	Mich. Comp. Laws § 554.139
Minnesota	Minn. Stat. Ann. § 504B.425
Mississippi	Miss. Code Ann. § 89-8-15
Missouri	Mo. Ann. Stat. § 441.234

Montana	Mont. Code Ann. §§ 70-24-406 to 70-24-408
Nebraska	Neb. Rev. Stat. § 76-1427
Nevada	Nev. Rev. Stat. Ann. §§ 118A.360 and 118A.380
New Hampshire	No statute
New Jersey	No statute
New Mexico	No statute
New York	N.Y. Real Prop. Law § 235-A
North Carolina	No statute
North Dakota	N.D. Cent. Code § 47-16-13
Ohio	No statute
Oklahoma	Okla. Stat. Ann. tit. 41 § 121
Oregon	Or. Rev. Stat. § 90.365
Pennsylvania	No statute
Rhode Island	R.I. Gen. Laws §§ 34-18-30 and 34-18-31
South Carolina	S.C. Code Ann. § 27-40-630
South Dakota	S.D. Codified Laws Ann. § 43-32-9
Tennessee	Tenn. Code Ann. § 66-28-502
Texas	Tex. Prop. Code Ann. §§ 92.056 and 92.0561
Utah	No statute
Vermont	Vt. Stat. Ann. tit. 9 § 4459
Virginia	No statute
Washington	Wash. Rev. Code Ann. §§ 59.18.100 and 59.18.110
West Virginia	No statute
Wisconsin	No statute
Wyoming	No statute

Chapter 6

Landlord's Entry: Getting Access to Your Property

This Chapter Discusses:

- ★ Maintenance and Repairs
- ★ In Case of Emergency
- ★ Tenants' Extended Absence
- ★ Showing the Property
- ★ Notice Required

Yes, this is your property – but **you still can't just show up there any time and expect to get into it.** *Your tenants have the fundamental right to privacy.* However, that doesn't mean you're left out in the cold. *Just keep in mind that this is somebody else's home.* **A chart outlining the entry laws of each state is provided at the end of this chapter.**

Maintenance and Repairs

Since it is your duty to repair and maintain the property, **state laws allow for you to enter the property for specific reasons after providing sufficient notice to the tenant.**

When you arrange for a time to enter the rental unit, *be sure to schedule a time when the tenants will be there.* You might be tempted by the idea of setting up a time when the tenants are not there, thinking it will enable you to check a few things out like the condition of the air filter, the new refrigerator you had installed before the tenants moved in or the carpet in the bedroom where you suspect they are confining their dog during the day. But *you need to resist this temptation.* **If you – or even a contractor you hire to make a repair – enter the property when the tenants are not there, even though they gave you permission, you might open the door to a possible allegation of theft.**

Also, *even though you have agreed on a time of entry with the tenants, you cannot force your way into the property.* If the tenants change the plan when you show up and say you can't come in that day because they are unexpectedly watching their 5-month-old niece, or they just have a headache, *you can't insist upon entering.*

Entry for Maintenance and Repairs

Alabama	Yes
Alaska	Yes
Arizona	Yes
Arkansas	Yes
California	Yes
Colorado	No statute
Connecticut	Yes
Delaware	Yes
District of Columbia	No statute
Florida	Yes
Georgia	No statute
Hawaii	Yes
Idaho	No statute
Illinois	No statute
Indiana	Yes
Iowa	Yes
Kansas	Yes
Kentucky	Yes
Louisiana	Yes
Maine	Yes
Maryland	No statute
Massachusetts	Yes
Michigan	No statute
Minnesota	Yes
Mississippi	No statute
Missouri	No statute

Montana	Yes
Nebraska	Yes
Nevada	Yes
New Hampshire	Yes
New Jersey	No statute
New Mexico	Yes
New York	No statute
North Carolina	No statute
North Dakota	Yes
Ohio	Yes
Oklahoma	Yes
Oregon	Yes
Pennsylvania	No statute
Rhode Island	Yes
South Carolina	Yes
South Dakota	No statute
Tennessee	Yes
Texas	No statute
Utah	Yes
Vermont	Yes
Virginia	Yes
Washington	No
West Virginia	No statute
Wisconsin	Yes
Wyoming	No statute

In Case of Emergency

The one and only time when you can enter the property without notice – or even permission – is in the case of a *true emergency.*
So, what is actually an emergency? A basic definition to follow is *something that is a threat either to someone's life or to the property if not dealt with immediately.* Specific examples would include smoke coming out the door, water leaking into the unit below or the smell of gas from an open window. **Otherwise, if it can wait, you must give notice and get permission!**

In keeping with the mutually respected relationship you strive for with your tenants, you should leave a quick note for your tenant, indicating what happened *in the event you have entered for an emergency.*

Tenants' Extended Absence

Your lease should require that the tenants inform you in advance of any long absences they may have from the property. *Anything longer than a week should be the concern here.* **The lease should also inform them that you intend to enter the property if it becomes necessary during this time.** *Of course, you should only enter the property if it is absolutely necessary.* For example, the temperature dropped dramatically and you need to make sure the pipes haven't burst in the basement – or the gas was shut off during an emergency in the neighborhood and you need to restart the pilot light in the hot water heater, so the house doesn't fill up with gas. **Your focus should be on doing what the tenants would normally need to do to protect or maintain the safety of the property.**

A chart is provided on the following two pages showing which jurisdictions allow a landlord to enter his or her property because of an extended absence by the tenants of more than one week.

Entry During Tenants' Extended Absence

Alabama	Yes
Alaska	Yes
Arizona	No
Arkansas	No
California	No
Colorado	No statute
Connecticut	Yes
Delaware	No
District of Columbia	No statute
Florida	Yes
Georgia	No statute
Hawaii	Yes
Idaho	No statute
Illinois	No statute
Indiana	No
Iowa	Yes
Kansas	Yes
Kentucky	Yes
Louisiana	No
Maine	No
Maryland	No statute
Massachusetts	No
Michigan	No statute
Minnesota	No
Mississippi	No statute
Missouri	No statute

Montana	Yes
Nebraska	Yes
Nevada	No
New Hampshire	No
New Jersey	No statute
New Mexico	Yes
New York	No statute
North Carolina	No statute
North Dakota	No
Ohio	No
Oklahoma	No
Oregon	Yes
Pennsylvania	No statute
Rhode Island	Yes
South Carolina	Yes
South Dakota	No statute
Tennessee	Yes
Texas	No statute
Utah	No
Vermont	No
Virginia	Yes
Washington	No
West Virginia	No statute
Wisconsin	No
Wyoming	No statute

Showing the Property

While most state laws recognize your need to be able to look after your investment by showing it to the next prospective tenant or a buyer, you still must take care not to invade the **privacy of your current tenants** or anger them by parading a bunch of strangers through their home day after day. *Any showings should be limited to the last few weeks of their tenancy if possible.* If you are selling the property in the middle of their tenancy period, you should be sure to **communicate with them as openly as possible and reassure them that their lease will continue.**

There are only three states that have statutes that do not obligate the tenant to allow the landlord to show the property to prospective *tenants* or *buyers*. These are **Louisiana, Utah** and **Washington.**

You should *avoid having signs placed on the property indicating it is for sale or rent.* This would only invite strangers to show up unannounced at the property wanting to see it or know more about it from the current tenants. The same goes for **realtors' lock boxes.** *Your obligations to the tenants and their privacy must come first.*

Entry for Showing the Property

Alabama	Yes
Alaska	Yes
Arizona	Yes
Arkansas	Yes
California	Yes
Colorado	No statute
Connecticut	Yes
Delaware	Yes
District of Columbia	No statute
Florida	Yes
Georgia	No statute
Hawaii	Yes
Idaho	No statute
Illinois	No statute
Indiana	Yes
Iowa	Yes
Kansas	Yes
Kentucky	Yes
Louisiana	No
Maine	Yes
Maryland	No statute
Massachusetts	Yes
Michigan	No statute
Minnesota	Yes
Mississippi	No statute
Missouri	No statute

Montana	Yes
Nebraska	Yes
Nevada	Yes
New Hampshire	Yes
New Jersey	No statute
New Mexico	Yes
New York	No statute
North Carolina	No statute
North Dakota	Yes
Ohio	Yes
Oklahoma	Yes
Oregon	Yes
Pennsylvania	No statute
Rhode Island	Yes
South Carolina	Yes
South Dakota	No statute
Tennessee	Yes
Texas	No statute
Utah	No
Vermont	Yes
Virginia	Yes
Washington	No
West Virginia	No statute
Wisconsin	Yes
Wyoming	No statute

Notice Required

For all other entry needs, you must follow the notification requirements of your state as outlined on the next two pages. The best way to notify the tenant of anything is *in writing* – and entry requests are no exception. **If you request entry verbally, be sure to follow up with a confirmation in writing** – *document everything!* **State laws can restrict the times of day when you can enter the property,** but some states vaguely leave it at *"reasonable time."* If your state does not give specific guidelines for entry times, be sure to keep your requested time reasonable – sometime between 8:00 am and 8:00 pm on weekdays and 9:00 am and 3:00 pm on weekends should be acceptable.

Of course, **you can enter the property at any time that is convenient to both you and the tenant, so long as you both agree on the time and you don't force a late or early time on the tenant.** You can also enter the property without the notice required by state law **if the tenant gives you permission.** So, let's say you are fixing a problem for a tenant who set up an entry time in advance with you and you run across another tenant. You can ask that tenant if you can quickly check to see if he or she might be having the same problem – and, if that tenant says yes, you are well within the parameters of the law.

Notice of Entry Requirements

Alabama	2 days
Alaska	24 hours
Arizona	2 days
Arkansas	Not specified
California	24 hours, 48 hours if preliminary inspection
Colorado	No statute
Connecticut	Reasonable time
Delaware	2 days
District of Columbia	No statute
Florida	12 hours
Georgia	No statute
Hawaii	2 days
Idaho	No statute
Illinois	No statute
Indiana	Reasonable time
Iowa	24 hours
Kansas	Reasonable time
Kentucky	2 days
Louisiana	No statute
Maine	24 hours
Maryland	No statute
Massachusetts	Not specified
Michigan	No statute
Minnesota	Reasonable time
Mississippi	No statute
Missouri	No statute

Montana	24 hours
Nebraska	1 day
Nevada	24 hours
New Hampshire	Adequate notice for the circumstance
New Jersey	No statute
New Mexico	24 hours
New York	No statute
North Carolina	No statute
North Dakota	Reasonable time
Ohio	24 hours
Oklahoma	1 day
Oregon	24 hours
Pennsylvania	No statute
Rhode Island	2 days
South Carolina	24 hours
South Dakota	No statute
Tennessee	Not specified
Texas	No statute
Utah	Not specified
Vermont	24 hours
Virginia	24 hours
Washington	2 days
West Virginia	No statute
Wisconsin	Advanced notice, unless lease provides time frame
Wyoming	No statute

Chapter 7

Landlord's Liability, Part I:
Protecting Yourself and Your Tenants

This Chapter Discusses:

- ★ **What Makes You Negligent**
- ★ **Condition of the Property**
- ★ **How to Protect Yourself Financially**

Liability **refers to your legal responsibility to do something.** In this case, **to keep your property safe for those living there – or even those just visiting.** *You can be sued for potentially large amounts of money if you are negligent in your duties.* That is, if you could have reasonably done something to prevent an injury or destruction of property and you carelessly chose not to, *you are responsible.*

What Makes You Negligent

Of course, every situation is different and every jurisdiction has its own laws and unique judges interpreting them. However, in general, **negligence can be determined by considering some basic points:**

How to Determine Negligence:

⭐ ### It Must Have Been Your Responsibility

You must be responsible for the maintenance of the area or item that caused the injury or destruction of property. After all, you can't be negligent if it's not your responsibility to begin with.

⭐ ### The Problem Must Have Been Anticipated

It must be likely that the injury or destruction of property was going to happen. You can't be held responsible if a reasonable person would not anticipate a problem.

⭐ ### The Problem Must Have Had a Simple Solution

It must be relatively easy or inexpensive to fix a problem. Would some simple anti-slip tape have solved the problem or would you have to reconstruct an entire walkway to prevent a particular slip?

⭐ ### Serous Injury or Damage Occurred

Regardless of the ease or expense, **if serious injuries and/or damage can occur, then you are obligated to fix the problem.** Are you required to fix the second floor balcony that is riddled with rotten wood as soon as possible even though it will cost $5,000? Yes. Someone's life is at risk – not just the potential for a bruised arm.

★ Reasonable Action Was Not Taken

You must be able to take reasonable action to keep something from happening. If someone cuts his foot on broken glass from a mirror that fell during a tenant's move minutes after the glass shattered, you can't be expected to have been psychic and have been standing there with a broom moments before it happened and thus able to prevent the injury.

★ Your Neglect Must Lead to the Serious Injury or Damage

Your neglect must lead to the injury or property damage. Did your delay in fixing a wobbly step cause a tenant's son to slip and break his arm – or was it the slippery bubble solution the child spilled all over his shoes and the stairs while playing outside?

Condition of the Property

First and foremost, **you must make sure the property is fit to be lived in.** This includes everything from keeping the property rodent free, to having working locks on the doors, to making sure the hot water heater is functioning properly. **These are basic things any reasonable person would consider essential in a home.** See **Chapter 6** for more on *repairing and maintaining the property.*

However, **when renting a property to someone else, you must go *beyond* the basics.** When something needs repair, you must act quickly to fix it. Sure, if it were your home, you might wait a week or two until tackling a broken step on your porch – but **you simply cannot do that when it comes to rental property.** *You have a legal obligation to maintain the residence in a reasonable, albeit quick, manner.*

Certainly, there will be times when something cannot be immediately addressed. **In cases where you must wait, be sure to limit your liability risk by notifying the tenant(s) in writing what the problem is and when it will be fixed, and by warning them to be mindful of the situation.** If appropriate and feasible, be sure to place warning signs around a problem area, or even block off access entirely.

How to Protect Yourself Financially

Unequivocally, **you must have more than simply adequate insurance.** A policy that only covers the property just won't do. *You need to purchase liability insurance from your insurance provider.* **And you want the most you can afford.** Personal injury lawsuits can result in very large cash awards to the injured party – and **if you are not covered by enough insurance, you could potentially be paying off that award for the rest of your life.** Be sure to be clear with your insurance agent that the property is a rental property – as **policies differ for residential and commercial (this includes rental) use.**

Liability insurance generally covers the costs of having an attorney represent you as well as any compensatory damages. That is, *the amount you are ordered to pay to compensate the injured party for a specific loss or injury.* Depending on the state where the property is located, **your policy may also cover** *punitive damages* **– the amount you are ordered to pay beyond the value of the injured party's actual loss as an additional punishment to you to deter you and others from being negligent in a similar situation again.** To find out how your state interprets insurance policies and if punitive damages are covered by your policy, simply **ask your insurance agent.**

Not only does your insurance policy need to cover you for any potential injuries or property damage occurring at your property; **it also needs to offer some protection from claims such as discrimination and invasion of privacy.** Typically, **a policy will only cover the legal costs of such a charge because**, it is argued, **you intentionally did or said the thing that caused the damage.** But with the cost of good legal representation today, *even this limited coverage could save you tens of thousands of dollars.*

You can further protect yourself by setting up your property rental business as a limited liability company (LLC). **If you have significant personal assets and want to protect them from any potential lawsuits, this might be an option for you to consider.** Of course, there are other ways to protect assets – such as through legal trusts. **If you have significant assets, you should talk with your accountant or other tax advisor, as well as an estate or small business attorney**, for guidance with your particular situation.

Chapter 8

Landlord's Liability, Part II: Specific Environmental Hazards

This Chapter Discusses:

- ★ **Lead in Paint and Water**
- ★ **Asbestos**
- ★ **Mold**
- ★ **Carbon Monoxide Gas**
- ★ **Radon Gas**

he notion of an environmental hazard probably seems a bit farfetched to most people. It's something that maybe they hear about on the news every once in a while. Some freak, tragic accident that happens to someone else, not usually to anyone they know, or even in their part of town. So why bother worrying about it? Environmental hazards are a **serious subject with possibly grave consequences**, and something that shouldn't be taken lightly.

Lead in Paint and Water

If your rental property was built after 1988, then chances are almost certain you do not need to concern yourself with the topic of lead. Generally speaking, property built between 1978 and 1988 would only cause concern about the possibility of lead in the soldering material used to connect copper pipes together. **If your rental property was built before 1978, then you should most definitely be concerned about the possibility of lead-based paint in the unit as well – even if it may be underneath 10 layers of lead-free paint.**

If your property dates back to the 1930s and later, then, in addition to concerns over lead-based paint and solder, you must be concerned about lead pipes being in the house – unless the plumbing has been completely redone to eliminate this hazard.

So, what do you do if your property falls into any of these risky category years? Well, that all depends on what you know.

First, **if your property was built before 1978, you must have the tenant sign an Environmental Protection Agency lead-based paint disclosure form.** A sample of this **disclosure is provided on the next page** as well as on the **enclosed CD-ROM:**

Lead-Based Paint Disclosure

Disclosure of Information on Lead-Based Paint and/or Lead-Based Paint Hazards

Lead Warning Statement

Housing built before 1978 may contain lead-based paint. Lead from paint, paint chips, and dust can pose health hazards if not managed properly. Lead exposure is especially harmful to young children and pregnant women. Before renting pre-1978 housing, lessors must disclose the presence of known lead-based paint and/or lead-based paint hazards in the dwelling. Lessees must also receive a federally approved pamphlet on lead poisoning prevention.

Lessor's Disclosure

(a) Presence of lead-based paint and/or lead-based paint hazards (check (i) or (ii) below):

    (i) _____ Known lead-based paint and/or lead-based paint hazards are present in the housing (explain).

    _____

    _____

    (ii) _____ Lessor has no knowledge of lead-based paint and/or lead-based paint hazards in the housing.

(b) Records and reports available to the lessor (check (i) or (ii) below):

    (i) _____ Lessor has provided the lessee with all available records and reports pertaining to lead-based paint and/or lead-based paint hazards in the housing (list documents below).

    _____

    _____

    (ii) _____ Lessor has no reports or records pertaining to lead-based paint and/or lead-based paint hazards in the housing.

Lessee's Acknowledgment (initial)

(c) _____ Lessee has received copies of all information listed above.

(d) _____ Lessee has received the pamphlet *Protect Your Family from Lead in Your Home.*

Agent's Acknowledgment (initial)

(e) _____ Agent has informed the lessor of the lessor's obligations under 42 U.S.C. 4852d and is aware of his/her responsibility to ensure compliance.

Certification of Accuracy

The following parties have reviewed the information above and certify, to the best of their knowledge, that the information they have provided is true and accurate.

Lessor	Date	Lessor	Date
Lessee	Date	Lessee	Date
Agent	Date	Agent	Date

As you can see on the form, **you are not required to do any testing; you are simply required to disclose what you currently know about the paint in the rental.** *This is the case for any possible sources of lead.* **If you know of an actual risk, you are required to disclose it to your tenant(s).** However, if you do not know of any actual problem (i.e., you weren't told of a problem by the previous owner, or you haven't tested any part of the property for lead), then the only additional requirement you have is to **provide a copy of the Environmental Protection Agency's (EPA) booklet** *Protect Your Family from Lead in Your Home* **to all of your tenants.**

A **copy of the EPA's booklet has been provided in Appendix D and on the enclosed CD-ROM** and **additional versions in various languages may be found on the EPA's website www.EPA.gov.** You can also contact the **National Lead Information Center** at **1-800-424-LEAD (5323)** to request copies of the booklet.

If you fail to provide the lead-based paint disclosure or a copy of the booklet on lead in homes to your tenants, you can face serious penalties, including fines of over $10,000 per incident.

Asbestos

Believe it or not, **your requirement to protect your tenants from asbestos exposure stems from OSHA regulations.** The *Occupational Safety and Health Administration* **regulates your requirement to keep maintenance personnel, as well as other contractors, protected from asbestos.** So, if you ever have any work done to your property, you have to make sure there are no risks that would put those workers in harm's way. *And*, once you know about any potential asbestos risks, *you are required to notify your tenants and protect them from exposure.*

If your rental property was built before 1981, you are required to have the part of the property being worked on tested for asbestos when any maintenance or repair work is done – unless you have previously had the property thoroughly tested from top to bottom by a licensed asbestos inspector. Unlike the Environmental Protection Agency's lead regulations, *what you don't know about asbestos in the property can come back to haunt you.*

It is assumed that **there *IS* asbestos in all pre-1981 property** – *unless the entire property has been inspected.* **The risk of exposure to asbestos is complicated by the fact that it can be just about any place in a pre-1981 property** – vinyl flooring, textured wall or ceiling, attic or wall insulation, wiring, caulking, roof shingles, etc. Property built after 1981 is considered safe from asbestos.

So, what do you do if you have to have something repaired at your pre-1981 property? Your safest bet is to **hire someone to do the work and get in writing an assurance from that person that part of his or her responsibility will be to test for asbestos before starting any work.** *If asbestos is found, immediately notify your tenant(s) and reiterate the warning in writing.* **Take a moment to consider if the work really needs to be done** – *asbestos typically is not hazardous if it is not disturbed, so maybe you are better off not doing that remodeling job.* If you must do the work, be sure to notify your tenants in advance and cordon off the area if possible.

If you are aware of any asbestos in the property, be sure to put a disclosure in your lease agreement that instructs the tenants not to make any repairs or modifications to that specific area of the property (e.g., the walls, because there is asbestos in the insulation behind them), and *also* requires them to notify you immediately of any damage to an asbestos-containing item.

For additional reading pleasure, the **OSHA regulation that pertains to landlords has been provided in Appendix B and on the enclosed CD-ROM.**

Mold

No, we're not talking about your average shower mold here that can be easily sprayed and wiped away. This is all about *toxic mold* – **the serious stuff found inside and outside that can lead to hazardous health conditions.**

The regulations on mold are still in a relatively early stage of development. **There are currently no federal laws regarding mold exposure,** and only a handful of states such as California, Indiana, Maryland, Montana, New Jersey and Texas have started implementing statewide regulation. This has left some local governments such as New York City to enact their own regulations without waiting for the state to act in an attempt to protect its citizens.

So, with legal guidance lacking on the subject, **what is a landlord to do?** Your primary responsibility is to *simply maintain the property.* **If a window or pipe is leaky, you need to act quickly to repair it so that mold does not have a chance to take hold and settle into the property.** Otherwise, *if you know about the problem and fail to act, thus allowing a toxic mold to harm a tenant, you are liable.* Of course, if the mold comes about from something the tenant does (e.g., repeatedly allowing water to puddle outside of the shower leading to mold growth in the baseboard and wall), then you cannot be held liable for that.

If you can show that you are quick in addressing any problems that you are made aware of from your tenant(s) and that you are proactive in preventing problems (e.g., you provide a dehumidifier for the property's damp basement), then you should be fairly safe from liability suits. *This is where documenting everything can really come in handy!* **You can learn more about mold in Appendix F or on the EPA's website www.EPA.gov by searching for "mold."**

Carbon Monoxide Gas

If your rental property does not have any gas appliances, an oil furnace, a charcoal or gas grill or a wood or gas fireplace, then you do not have to worry about the risks associated with carbon monoxide. If *any* of these types of items are located on the property, you need to take care that you handle your responsibilities for them in a timely manner.

Your primary concerns should be to make sure all chimneys and vents are clean and functioning properly and all pilot lights are burning blue, and to prohibit such things in your lease as non-electric space heaters and using grills indoors. Of course, anything can happen – so **you should take the extra step of installing a carbon monoxide detector on every floor of the property that has a gas appliance or other item of concern.** These detectors are relatively inexpensive – around $30 for a good model that runs on electricity and also has a battery backup. *While carbon monoxide detectors are not legally required, as smoke detectors are, they should still be considered a necessity.*

To get more information on carbon monoxide and even brochures you can distribute to your tenant(s), visit the **Centers for Disease Control and Prevention's** website on carbon monoxide poisoning at **www.CDC.gov/CO** and click on **"Resources."**

Radon Gas

While you may have heard of radon gas before, chances are you probably don't know much about it. Basically, **radon is a radioactive gas that is released from natural deposits of uranium in the ground.** *It can be released in the property from a number of sources* (e.g., water from a well, natural stone fireplace, escaping from the ground itself and seeping through the foundation, etc.) and *becomes harmful when it gets trapped inside a property that is kept sealed tight.*

What can you do about it? **There are some states that may actually require you to disclose the possibility of the presence of radon in your rental property.** For example, in the state of Florida you must include the following disclosure in your lease or in a separate document acknowledged by your tenant(s): "RADON GAS: Radon is a naturally occurring radioactive gas that, when it has accumulated in a building in sufficient quantities, may present health risks to persons who are exposed to it over time. Levels of radon that exceed federal and state guidelines have been found in buildings in Florida. Additional information regarding radon and radon testing may be obtained from your county health department." **If your state does not have specific disclosure guidelines to follow, you should at the very least provide your tenants with a copy of the Environmental Protection Agency's brochure** *A Radon Guide for Tenants*, **which has been provided in Appendix A and on the enclosed CD-ROM.**

This is one of those fluid topics that will be continually changing as more is learned about radon and lawmakers come to understand the issue. **The Environmental Protection Agency estimates that 1 in 15 homes in the United States has an elevated level of radon gas.** So, regardless of your state's specific disclosure requirements, you should consider taking the extra step of testing for radon gas and remedying any high levels you find. *Again, you want to appear as accommodating and concerned for your tenants' well-being as possible if a legal situation comes up.*

Testing for radon gas is actually very inexpensive. You can find EPA-approved testing kits at your local home improvement store for less than $20, or you can even order one from the **National Safety Council** for less than $10. You can visit the NSC website at **www.NSC.org/issues/radon** for more information on radon and the testing kits offered. **And, if you actually find that your property has a high level of radon in it, repairs needed to fix the problem are generally a few hundred dollars to just a couple thousand.** Obviously, *much less than the cost of going to court over a radon health issue.* In fact, **some agencies offer assistance with the costs of making repairs to lower radon levels.**

If you find that your property has high levels of radon gas, call the National Safety Council's Radon Fit-It Program at 1-800-644-6999 and the staff can point you in the direction of state agencies that can help you, as well as certified contractors who can correctly handle radon issues. Remember, **more on the topic of radon has been provided in Appendix A and on the enclosed CD-ROM.**

Chapter 9

Modifying Lease Terms:
What You Can Change and How to Do It

This Chapter Discusses:

★ **What Can Be Changed**
★ **How to Cover Yourself Legally**
★ **Notification Requirements for Each State**

Life changes and so can leases. At some point or another, you're going to find yourself having to modify the terms of an existing lease agreement. Whether it's for *extending the terms, adding or removing a tenant or a whole list of other reasons,* **it's guaranteed to happen.** Therefore, this chapter reviews exactly what can be changed and how to go about doing it without jeopardizing your legal rights or compromising the integrity of your contract with your tenant(s).

What Can Be Changed

In theory, *anything in an existing lease can be changed as long as it does not infringe upon a tenant's legal rights.* However, practically speaking, **a tenant probably won't consent to an increase in rent.** Keep in mind that **because you have entered into a contract with your tenant, you cannot take it upon yourself to make any changes to the terms of the lease agreement.** But, *as long as all parties agree, feel free to make as many changes as you'd like.*

Some Common Reasons Why Lease Agreements Are Modified:

☆ Allowing a Tenant to Have a Pet

☆ Adding a Tenant's New Spouse

☆ Allowing a Tenant to Terminate a Lease Early

One important note of exception – If it is so provided for in the original lease, **you can implement a change without the tenant's agreement because he or she would have already consented to the change by signing the original lease.** So, for example, if your tenant's last two rent checks have bounced, you can require all future payments to be in the form of a money order *IF you reserved that right for yourself in the lease.* **You can reserve the right to do just about anything in the lease –** *just be sure your tenant(s) understand anything exceptional in the lease and you don't go overboard.* You may find it difficult to find a tenant when, for example, you reserve the right to increase the rent any time you want. *Be reasonable and clear –* "Landlord may increase rental payment by no more than 10% every 6 months if landlord provides 30-day notification of such increase to tenant."

How to Cover Yourself Legally

This can't be stressed enough – *get it in writing!* **Anything you agree on or change should be in writing.** That way, the tenants can't say later that they didn't agree to something or didn't understand it the same way you do. *Not only do you need to get the change in writing and signed off on by all parties, but you also need to be certain you follow any requirements of your state.*

A sample modification of a lease agreement form is provided on the following page, as well as on the enclosed CD-ROM. This is a generic form that can be used to change virtually anything.

Modification of Lease Agreement

Instructions:
1. Insert your IMAGE or LOGO (optional)
2. Complete AMENDMENT FIELDS
3. REPLACE ALL of this text with YOUR contact info
4. Click on 'PRINT FORM' when finished

Modification of Lease Agreement

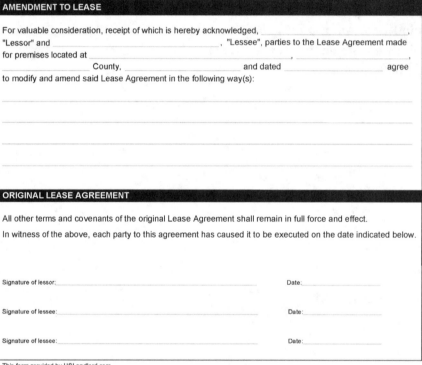

AMENDMENT TO LEASE

For valuable consideration, receipt of which is hereby acknowledged, _____,
"Lessor" and _____, "Lessee", parties to the Lease Agreement made
for premises located at _____, _____
_____ County, _____ and dated _____ agree
to modify and amend said Lease Agreement in the following way(s):

_____

_____

_____

_____

_____

ORIGINAL LEASE AGREEMENT

All other terms and covenants of the original Lease Agreement shall remain in full force and effect.

In witness of the above, each party to this agreement has caused it to be executed on the date indicated below.

Signature of lessor:_____   Date:_____

Signature of lessee:_____   Date:_____

Signature of lessee:_____   Date:_____

This form provided by USLandlord.com

Notification Requirements for Each State

There are many states that do not require a specific amount of notification time before a lease change can occur. However, *almost every state requires a certain amount of notice to terminate a tenancy.* The **following four charts lay out the requirements of each state** for their respective possible scenarios.

<u>Note:</u> You can't terminate a tenancy that still has a lease in place unless that provision was included in the lease or if there are grounds for eviction. Therefore, the first two charts only pertain to month-to-month tenancy which could be a result of either an expired annual lease term that has carried over or simply a month-to-month term from the start of tenancy.

Landlord Termination of Month-to-Month Tenancy Notice

Alabama	30 days
Alaska	30 days
Arizona	30 days
Arkansas	10 days
California	60 days
Colorado	10 days
Connecticut	3 days
Delaware	60 days
District of Columbia	30 days
Florida	15 days
Georgia	60 days
Hawaii	45 days
Idaho	1 month
Illinois	30 days
Indiana	1 month
Iowa	30 days
Kansas	30 days
Kentucky	30 days
Louisiana	10 days
Maine	30 days
Maryland	1 month; 2 months if property located in Montgomery County (except single-family residences) or in Baltimore City.
Massachusetts	30 days or time frame between rental payments, whichever longer
Michigan	Time frame between rental payments
Minnesota	3 months or time frame between rental payments, whichever shorter
Mississippi	30 days
Missouri	1 month

Montana	30 days
Nebraska	30 days
Nevada	30 days
New Hampshire	30 days; termination allowed for cause only
New Jersey	1 month; termination allowed for cause only
New Mexico	30 days
New York	1 month
North Carolina	7 days
North Dakota	30 days
Ohio	30 days
Oklahoma	30 days
Oregon	30 days
Pennsylvania	No statute
Rhode Island	30 days
South Carolina	30 days
South Dakota	1 month
Tennessee	30 days
Texas	1 month
Utah	15 days
Vermont	30 days if there is a written lease and tenant has resided at the property for 2 years or less, 60 days if longer; 60 days if there is no lease and tenant has resided at the property for 2 years or less, 90 days if longer
Virginia	30 days
Washington	20 days
West Virginia	1 month
Wisconsin	28 days
Wyoming	No statute

Tenant Termination of Month-to-Month Tenancy Notice

Alabama	30 days
Alaska	30 days
Arizona	30 days
Arkansas	No statute
California	30 days
Colorado	10 days
Connecticut	No statute
Delaware	60 days
District of Columbia	30 days
Florida	15 days
Georgia	30 days
Hawaii	28 days
Idaho	1 month
Illinois	30 days
Indiana	1 month
Iowa	30 days
Kansas	30 days
Kentucky	30 days
Louisiana	10 days
Maine	30 days
Maryland	1 month; 2 months if property located in Montgomery County (except single-family residences) or in Baltimore City.
Massachusetts	30 days or time frame between rental payments, whichever longer
Michigan	Time frame between rental payments
Minnesota	3 months or time frame between rental payments, whichever shorter
Mississippi	30 days
Missouri	1 month

Montana	30 days
Nebraska	30 days
Nevada	30 days
New Hampshire	30 days
New Jersey	1 month
New Mexico	30 days
New York	1 month
North Carolina	7 days
North Dakota	30 days; if landlord has notified tenant of a change in lease terms, then 25 days from date of notification
Ohio	30 days
Oklahoma	30 days
Oregon	30 days
Pennsylvania	No statute
Rhode Island	30 days
South Carolina	30 days
South Dakota	1 month; if landlord has notified tenant of a change in lease terms, then 15 days from date of notification
Tennessee	30 days
Texas	1 month
Utah	No statute
Vermont	1 rental period
Virginia	30 days
Washington	20 days
West Virginia	1 month
Wisconsin	28 days
Wyoming	No statute

Lease Change (Other Than Rent Amount) Notice Requirements

Alabama	No statute
Alaska	30 days
Arizona	30 days
Arkansas	No statute
California	30 days
Colorado	10 days
Connecticut	No statute
Delaware	60 days; tenant allowed to terminate tenancy within 15 days of notice
District of Columbia	No statute
Florida	No statute
Georgia	No statute
Hawaii	45 days
Idaho	15 days
Illinois	30 days
Indiana	30 days unless lease gives different time frame
Iowa	30 days
Kansas	No statute
Kentucky	30 days
Louisiana	No statute
Maine	30 days
Maryland	1 month; 2 months if property located in Montgomery County (except single-family residences) or in Baltimore City.
Massachusetts	30 days or time frame between rental payments, whichever longer
Michigan	No statute
Minnesota	No statute
Mississippi	No statute
Missouri	No statute

Montana	15 days
Nebraska	No statute
Nevada	30 days
New Hampshire	30 days
New Jersey	1 month
New Mexico	30 days
New York	No statute
North Carolina	No statute
North Dakota	30 days; tenant allowed to terminate tenancy within 25 days of notice
Ohio	No statute
Oklahoma	No statute
Oregon	No statute
Pennsylvania	No statute
Rhode Island	30 days
South Carolina	No statute
South Dakota	1 month; tenant allowed to terminate tenancy within 15 days of notice
Tennessee	No statute
Texas	No statute
Utah	No statute
Vermont	30 days
Virginia	No statute
Washington	30 days
West Virginia	No statute
Wisconsin	No statute
Wyoming	No statute

Rent Increase Notice Requirements

Alabama	No statute
Alaska	30 days
Arizona	30 days
Arkansas	No statute
California	30 days unless all increases in last 12 months total greater than 10% of the lowest amount of rent during those 12 months, then 60 days
Colorado	10 days
Connecticut	No statute
Delaware	60 days
District of Columbia	No statute
Florida	No statute
Georgia	No statute
Hawaii	45 days
Idaho	15 days
Illinois	30 days
Indiana	30 days unless lease gives different time frame
Iowa	30 days
Kansas	No statute
Kentucky	30 days
Louisiana	No statute
Maine	45 days
Maryland	1 month
Massachusetts	30 days or time frame between rental payments, whichever longer
Michigan	No statute
Minnesota	No statute
Mississippi	No statute

Missouri	No statute
Montana	15 days
Nebraska	No statute
Nevada	45 days
New Hampshire	30 days
New Jersey	1 month
New Mexico	30 days before rent due date
New York	No statute
North Carolina	No statute
North Dakota	30 days
Ohio	No statute
Oklahoma	No statute
Oregon	No statute
Pennsylvania	No statute
Rhode Island	30 days
South Carolina	No statute
South Dakota	1 month
Tennessee	No statute
Texas	No statute
Utah	No statute
Vermont	30 days
Virginia	No statute
Washington	30 days
West Virginia	No statute
Wisconsin	No statute
Wyoming	No statute

Chapter 10

Occupants:
Who, How and Why

This Chapter Discusses:

- ★ Before You Find Yourself in This Situation
- ★ Defining Co-tenant, Subletting and Assignment
- ★ Co-tenant Legal Situations
- ★ Subletting Legal Situations
- ★ Assignment Legal Situations
- ★ How to Add a New Co-tenant, Sublet or Assign a Lease
- ★ When You Should Consider Accepting Subletting or Assigning

It's bound to happen at some point or another: Your tenant wants to bring in a roommate to help pay the rent – or he or she gets a job offer in another city and wants someone to take over the remaining lease obligations, etc. What do you do? **What happens to your legal rights and your tenant's legal responsibilities?**

Before You Find Yourself in This Situation

Well before you have to consider the question of what to do if presented with any change in tenants before the end of a lease, **make sure your lease requires the tenant(s) to obtain your written authorization before any subletting or assignment agreement can be entered into.** That way, *you maintain control over your property and who lives there.* Also, keep in mind that the **best scenario for you** is to *avoid having a subtenant or assignment of the lease.* **If presented with one of these options, you should counter with the option that the replacement tenant is simply made a new tenant and the leaving tenant's tenancy is terminated.** (See **Chapter 12** for more on *terminating a tenancy*.)

This protects not only you, but the leaving tenant as well, as you'll see by how each scenario is defined. However, **if a new tenancy cannot be agreed upon, or your property is located in a state such as Florida or California where you cannot object to a subtenant unless you have a valid reason, then screen the prospective replacement tenant as thoroughly as you would any new tenant** and *read through the following sections carefully.*

Defining Co-tenant, Subletting and Assignment

Simply put: **If more than one person signs your lease as a tenant, then they are** *co-tenants* – whereas *subletting* **is when another person leases the property from your tenant.** *This subtenant would have no responsibility to you.* In contrast, an *assignment of the lease* is *when your tenant transfers his or her rights and responsibilities to another person.* That person (an *assignee*) then **leases the property from you for the remainder of the original lease – while the original tenant still has legal obligations to you as well.**

Generally speaking, a tenant who wants to sublet is looking to come back and live at the property sometime in the future, while *one looking to assign it to another does not intend to come back.*

Co-tenant Legal Situations

Regardless of how they choose to divvy up the living quarters or maintenance responsibilities among themselves, **co-tenants have an *equal* responsibility to you to pay the rent and maintain the property.** To be the most legally protected, **your lease agreement should clearly state that each tenant is jointly and severally liable for the payment of rent and all other terms of the lease agreement.** Basically, this means that *you can treat them as a group or as individuals as the situation requires.* For example, if you are renting a townhouse to 3 college students and **one does not pay his or her share of the rent, the other 2 are responsible for the missing amount.** Similarly, if one breaks a term of the lease, then you could evict them all as a group or just the offending tenant. You will have given yourself the flexibility to assess each situation individually and decide on a course of action if you made the tenants jointly and severally liable at the start of the tenancy.

If the co-tenants find themselves in the middle of a conflict over some aspect of the property – arguing over who agreed to shovel the snow on the sidewalk, or who should get the bedroom attached to the bathroom, or if a couple decides to get a divorce and both want the other to leave, etc. – *be sure to stay out of it!* **You do not want to be caught up in their battle and possibly find yourself somehow the loser.**

The best thing for you to do is to *advise them to seek out a mediator to help resolve the issue and you do not take any particular side in the matter.* Chances are you have a **local housing agency** that **offers free or low-cost mediation services for roommates. Point your tenants in the agency's direction and hopefully an amicable resolution can be made which does not affect you.** Again, *do not attempt to mediate, no matter how well intentioned* your offer to help might be.

The one time you should get involved in a dispute is when you suspect that violence has occurred or is likely to. **In this case,** *call the police immediately.* There are a number of reasons why you need to do this, from moral obligations to protecting your property to saving yourself from a legal liability suit for not protecting a tenant. **But, whatever your particular motivation,** *just do it!*

CAUTION

> ➤ *What happens when a co-tenant decides to leave?*

If a subtenant or an assignee is offered as a replacement for the leaving co-tenant, **you will need to decide if you want to accept that person's tenancy.** The *next sections of this chapter* – which deal with subletting and assigning – *will help you with making this decision.* If a subtenant or assignee is not offered as a replacement, you will simply need to deal with the security deposit and whether or not the remaining tenant(s) can afford the additional rent that was the leaving co-tenant's share.

As discussed in **Chapter 3** on **security deposits**, *you do not have to return a co-tenant's portion of the security deposit until the lease term has ended* – **even if he or she decides to move out early.** However, as you'll see, **it may not be in your best interest to hold on to it, so you should consider the other options that you have in this situation.**   Not to mention that **the person is probably going to want it back, so he or she can move into a new place with it** *and* **you want to stay on good terms with everyone involved** – *because you never know where a good referral might come from!* You basically have **three options in this situation:**

Three Options Regarding a Departing Co-tenant's Security Deposit:

★ Keep It Until the End of the Original Lease Agreement

End of story, *it's your right and it's a good solution.* At least for you – **the leaving tenant probably won't be too happy about being charged for damages done to the unit after he or she moved out.**

★ Ask the Remaining Tenants to Make Up the Difference

See if the remaining tenants can come up with the leaving tenant's portion of the security deposit. If remaining tenants are willing to come up with the extra amount, **you can return the leaving tenant's portion *AFTER* the check from the other tenants has cleared.**

However, the remaining tenants should not be held solely
responsible for any damages caused while the leaving tenant lived
there. If you are going to return the leaving tenant's portion of the
security deposit, *you should arrange (with all of the tenants) an
interim walk through inspection of the property.* Any damage found
can be noted, signed off on by all parties, and prorated by the tenant
however the situation dictates. Then, additional damage found at
the end of the lease can be deducted from the security deposit
(which would then wholly belong to the remaining tenants) without
any counter-arguments or sob stories from the remaining tenants
about how the damage was caused by the one who left early.

★ Have a Another Co-tenant Make Up the Difference

If, at any time, a new co-tenant is found for the remainder of the
lease, you can accept a portion of the security deposit from the
person and refund that portion to either the tenant who left early
or the remaining tenants, depending on the situation. Again, *you
should return the amount only after the check from the new
co-tenant has cleared your bank.* As similarly explained above,
the new co-tenant will not want to be held responsible for any
damage caused before his or her arrival, so you should arrange
an interim inspection of the property – note any damage, and have
all parties sign off on the condition of the property *at the time of the
new tenant's move-in.*

Legally speaking, the tenant who is leaving will still be responsible
for paying his or her share of the rent. *Practically speaking,* you
may not be able to find the person, let alone get him or her to
actually pay it. While the remaining tenants will be responsible for
the entire rent as previously discussed, it may not be feasible for them
to cover the additional amount every month. *If they cannot afford
the increase in rent and there is no new co-tenant, subtenant or
assignee suggested, you will need to try to work out an amicable
end to the lease.*

Perhaps they can afford the extra amount for one month while they look for a new place to live and you can simultaneously look for new tenants. Or maybe you are willing to let them stay for one more month without the one tenant's share of the rent with the expectation that the security deposit will be able to cover the rent loss because you've seen how immaculately the remaining tenants maintained the property thus far. **That way, you have at least some of your rental income still flowing while seeking a new tenant.** *Whatever you do is your decision to make, based on the situation you have at hand.* **Only** *you* **can figure out what you will be comfortable with doing considering all of the factors** such as how much time is left on the lease and what your rental market is like.

When a co-tenant leaves, unless you are going to still be receiving a portion of the rent from that person, you should *have him or her sign a lease termination agreement.* This will **allow you the option to accept another co-tenant if the remaining tenant(s) finds one in the future,** as well as **prevents the tenant who left from returning and reasserting the right to stay at the property.** A *sample lease termination agreement* is **provided on the next page** and **on the enclosed CD-ROM.**

Lease Termination Agreement

Instructions:
1. Insert your IMAGE or LOGO (optional)
2. Highlight & complete LEASE ASSIGNMENT FIELDS
3. REPLACE ALL of this text with YOUR contact info
4. Click on 'PRINT FORM' when finished

Everything U Need to Know...

Click here to insert image/logo

Residential Lease Termination

AGREEMENT TO TERMINATE

This agreement is entered into between _____, of
_____, _____ County,
_____, referred to as "Landlord," and _____, of
_____, _____ County,
_____, referred to as "Tenant."

RECITALS

Landlord and Tenant both desire to terminate and cancel the lease executed on _____.

Therefore, in consideration of the mutual covenants contained herein and other valuable consideration received, and with the intent to be legally bound, Landlord and Tenant agree as follows:

1.   Landlord and Tenant hereby mutually terminate and cancel the lease effective on _____. Tenant hereby releases to Landlord all right, title and interest in and to the premises that Tenant may have acquired by reason of the lease.

2.   Tenant will vacate the premises and surrender possession to Landlord on the effective date hereof, free of all occupants. Landlord will accept this surrender. The premises shall be delivered to Landlord in the same condition as they were at the commencement of the Lease, reasonable wear and tear excepted.

3.   Landlord and Tenant each hereby release the other from any and all claims, causes of action, demands and liabilities of whatever nature in connection with the Lease or the premises which either of them ever had, now has or hereafter may have.

This Agreement to Terminate shall be binding upon and shall inure to the benefit of Landlord and Tenant and their respective heirs, legal representatives, successors and assigns.

In witness of the above, each party to this agreement has caused it to be executed on the date indicated below.

Signature of tenant: _____   Date: _____

Signature of landlord: _____   Date: _____

This form provided by USLandlord.com

SAMPLE

Subletting Legal Situations

The most important thing to keep in mind about a sublet situation is that the **subletting tenant has *absolutely no* responsibilities to you.** *If the rent is not paid, you must go after the original tenant.* **If there is damage to the property, you can only go after the original tenant to recover payment beyond the security deposit.** However, if a situation turns bad and gets to the point of eviction, **you can evict the person who is subletting the property –** *but, at the same time, you must evict the original tenant.* On the same note, **since your original tenant is now acting as a landlord to the person who is subletting, your original tenant can have the subtenant evicted.**

Since the subletting tenant does not answer to you, and has no agreement with you, *rent payments should come directly from your original tenant.* Yes, you can take them directly from the subtenant, there is no law against it, but you want to **be sure to maintain legal boundaries – so there is no confusion later on if something goes wrong.** *But, just as the subletting tenant doesn't answer to you, you don't really answer to the subletting tenant either.* **If, for some reason, you violate the terms of the original lease, only the original tenant can sue you.** Of course, *if you do not provide a basic, habitable property, your subtenant can most likely seek intervention from the courts.*

Assignment Legal Situations

Admittedly, an assignment of a lease to a new tenant offers a landlord a lot of legal protection and is *significantly more desirable than a sublet.* **You and the assignee are directly responsible to each other for everything from rent and damages to maintenance and repairs.** Not to mention, *you can directly evict a lease assignee without getting the original tenant involved.* **It is as if the assignee is the original tenant.** However, *you would have the added bonus of having the original tenant still being responsible to you as well.* **If the assignee does not pay the rent, the original tenant must pay it!**

There are **a couple of important exceptions to consider with this type of tenancy.** First, *any part of your agreement with the original tenant that is specific and/or personal to that person does not carry over to an assignee.* For example, if your tenant is a professional landscaper, you might agree to lower the rent if the tenant maintains the landscaping at your handful of rental properties. You would not be required to give this same rent discount to the assignee. Second, *while the original tenant remains responsible to you for the rent payments should the assignee fail to pay it, the original tenant cannot be held responsible for any damage caused to your property.* **This loophole can be closed if there is a specific agreement signed by all parties that makes the original tenant responsible for the payment of damages not paid for by the assignee.** And this leads us right into **how you go about assigning a lease.**

How to Add a New Co-tenant, Sublet or Assign a Lease

Adding a new co-tenant to a lease couldn't be easier. *Everyone just needs to sign a new lease before the new person moves in.* **You can, if you feel it is necessary, change any lease terms at this point.** This includes **raising the rent** or **increasing the security deposit,** but keep in mind that *the original lease remains in effect until the new one is signed.* **If you are unreasonable with new lease terms for a roommate**, you may find yourself with **a tenant who refuses to sign the new lease** and just decides to leave at the end of the original lease – and *you lose someone who has been a good tenant.*

Basically, **for a subletting situation, you don't have to do anything.** *Remember, your original tenant becomes the landlord to the subtenant.* **Any subletting agreement has to be executed by the original tenant and the subtenant, not you.** In an effort to protect yourself and your property as best as you can, *you can offer your tenant a subletting agreement to use if you find out he or she wants to sublet.* A **sample subletting agreement** is shown on the **next two pages** and is provided **on the enclosed CD-ROM.**

Subletting Agreement

Instructions:
1. Insert your IMAGE or LOGO (optional)
2. Highlight & complete LEASE AGREEMENT FIELDS
3. REPLACE ALL of this text with YOUR contact info
4. Click on 'PRINT FORM' when finished

Residential Sublease Agreement

AGREEMENT TO SUBLEASE

This agreement is entered into between _____ , of
_____ , _____ County,
_____ , referred to as "sublessor," and _____ , of
_____ , _____ County,
_____ , referred to as "sublessee."

RECITALS

A. Sublessor is the lessee of real property that is available for subleasing.

B. Sublessee desires to sublease residential property to occupy and use as their residence.

C. Lessor of the master lease agreement described in Section VI desires to permit the sublessor the right to sublease the residential property described in Section I.

In consideration of the matters described above, and of the mutual benefits and obligations set forth in this agreement, the parties agree as follows:

SECTION I - SUBJECT OF SUBLEASE

Sublessor shall sublease to prospective sublessee the residential property leased by sublessor located at
_____ , _____ , _____ County,
_____ , for sublessee and their family to occupy and use as their residence.

SECTION II - TERM OF LEASE

The premises shall be subleased to lessee for a period of _____ starting from
_____ . Any option to renew, extend or modify this lease shall require the approval of the lessor.

SECTION III - MONTHLY RENTAL

Sublessee shall pay $ _____ per month as the monthly rental for the term of the sublease with the first payment due on or before _____ , and subsequent payments on the _____ day of each succeeding month. This rental payment shall be subject to renegotiation by the sublessee and the lessor under the master lease agreement. It is agreed that if the rental payment is not received by the _____ day of the month, then a late fee of _____ shall be assessed and due immediately. Additional terms (optional):
_____
_____

SECTION IV - SECURITY DEPOSIT

On the execution of this sublease, sublessee deposits with sublessor $ _____ , receipt of which is acknowledged by lessor, as security for the faithful performance by sublessee of the terms of this lease agreement, to be returned to sublessee, without interest (unless required by law), on the full and faithful performance by lessee of the provisions of the originial master lease agreement.

Subletting Agreement

SECTION V - NUMBER OF OCCUPANTS

Sublessee agrees that the leased apartment shall be occupied by no more _____ adults and _____ children under the age of 18 years without the prior, express, and written consent of sublessor.

SECTION VI - MASTER LEASE AGREEMENT

The sublease agreement incorporates and is subject to the master lease agreement between the sublessor and lessor, a copy of which is attached hereto, and which is hereby referred to and incorporated as if it were set out here at length. The sublessee agrees to assume all of the obligations and responsibilities of the sublessor under the master lease agreement for the duration of the sublease agreement.

SECTION VII - BINDING EFFECT

The covenants and conditions contained in this lease agreement shall apply to and bind the heirs, legal representatives, and assigns of the parties to this lease agreement, and all covenants are to be construed as conditions of this lease.

SECTION VIII - GOVERNING LAW

It is agreed that this agreement shall be governed by, construed, and enforced in accordance with the laws of the State of _____.

SECTION IX - ATTORNEY FEES

In the event that any action is filed in relation to this agreement, the unsuccessful party in the action shall pay to the successful party, in addition to all the sums that either party may be called on to pay, a reasonable sum for the successful party's attorney fees.

SECTION X - ENTIRE AGREEMENT

This agreement shall constitute the entire agreement between the parties. Any prior understanding or representation of any kind preceding the date of this agreement shall not be binding upon either party except to the extent incorporated in this agreement.

SECTION XI - MODIFICATION OF AGREEMENT

Any modification of this agreement or additional obligation assumed by either party in connection with this agreement shall be binding only if evidenced in a writing signed by each party or an authorized representative of each party.

In witness of the above, each party to this agreement has caused it to be executed on the date indicated below.

Signature of sublessor: _____   Date:_____

Signature of sublessee: _____   Date:_____

As lessor of the attached master lease agreement, I hereby give my consent to the above described provisions as set out in this sublease agreement.

Signature of lessor: _____   Date:_____

This form provided by USLandlord.com

There are **two ways you can successfully assign a lease to another person.** One way is to *indicate on the original lease that it has been assigned to the new tenant at every place where the original tenant's name appears.* **You and the original tenant should sign or initial at each of these notations – just as you would on any other contract that has changes made to it.**

Then the new tenant would need to sign the original lease as the assignee in all of the same places your original tenant signed. *All of this makes the original tenant still responsible to you only for the rent, while making the assignee responsible for the entire lease agreement.* However, as discussed earlier, **this is not the most protection you can give yourself.**

The second – and best – way you can assign a lease to a new tenant is by having all parties sign an *assignment of lease consent.* **This form lays out what is being agreed to,** *and within it you can add that the original tenant will remain responsible* **for any damage that is done to the property and not paid for by the assignee.** A sample *assignment of lease consent form* is provided on the *next page* as well as *on the enclosed CD-ROM.*

Assignment Agreement

Instructions:
1. Insert your IMAGE or LOGO (optional)
2. Highlight & complete LEASE ASSIGNMENT FIELDS
3. REPLACE ALL of this text with YOUR contact info
4. Click on 'PRINT FORM' when finished

Everything U Need to Know...

Click here to insert image/logo

Residential Lease Assignment

AGREEMENT TO ASSIGN

This agreement is entered into between _____ , of
_____ , _____ County,
_____ , referred to as "assignor," and _____ , of
_____ , _____ County,
_____ , referred to as "assignee."

RECITALS

A. Assignor has entered into a lease agreement, as lessor, with _____ ,
of _____ , _____ ,
County, _____ , referred to as "lessee." A copy of the lease agreement, containing a
description of the premises, is attached to this agreement as Exhibit A.

B. Prospective assignor desires to assign the lease agreement to prospective assignee, who will assume all
liabilities and duties as well as all rights of prospective assignor pertaining to the collection of all rents to
become due under the lease agreement after the effective date of the assignment.

In consideration of the mutual covenants contained in this agreement, the parties agree as follows:

    1.   Assignor will transfer and assign to assignee all right to the collection of all rents
required under the lease agreement provisions in the lease dated _____ on
the premises described as follows: _____ .

    2.   The assignment shall become effective on _____ , and shall apply
to all rents due thereafter until expiration of the lease agreement term.

In witness of the above, each party to this agreement has caused it to be executed on the date indicated below.

Signature of assignor: _____ Date: _____

Signature of assignee: _____ Date: _____

This form provided by USLandlord.com

When You Should Consider Accepting Subletting or Assigning

As mentioned before, *it would be much better, and simpler, if the proposed subtenant or assignee signs a new lease with you and becomes a regular tenant* – but sometimes things can't be as black and white as we'd like them to be.

Subletting is, without a doubt, **not the best situation to find yourself in.** Generally, *you are just asking for trouble if you allow a subtenant to move in.* **Assignees offer a bit more financial security for you since both parties remain responsible for the rent and damages (if you heed our advice) but this can certainly come with additional headaches if things go bad.** However, there are *some situations where it might be beneficial, or even desirable to have a subtenant or assignee.*

If your original tenant is a single mom who is a member of the National Guard and has been called up for temporary active duty, you might find yourself welcoming her mother as a subtenant or assignee who is going to take care of your tenant's child while she is away. This would be particularly true if your tenant has been a model tenant. **Again, *only you* can judge the particular situation you find yourself in.**

Chapter 11

Retaliation: Staying on Higher Ground

This Chapter Discusses:

★ **What Is Retaliation?**

★ **Time Requirements**

★ **How to Avoid an Accusation of Retaliation**

On Monday, a tenant posts a flyer in an attempt to organize some tenants who have a common complaint about the property.

On Wednesday, you send out a rent increase to that tenant because he or she has been renting from you for six months and you meant to send it out a week ago but simply forgot.

On the following Monday, **you're served with a notice that you are being sued by your tenant because of the rent increase.** *What happened?* The option for a rent increase is provided for in your lease agreement, so what did you do wrong? **One word –** *retaliation!*

What Is Retaliation?

In simple terms, *retaliation* is *punishing a tenant (through increases in rent, eviction or any other negative action) for exercising a legal right.* In the scenario above, even though your reason for the rent increase had nothing to do with the tenant's posting of the organizing flyer (because you were going to send a routine rent increase letter beforehand and simply forgot), **appearance is everything.** *Retaliation is difficult legal ground to tread.* Generally, there are **three times after which an action by a landlord can be considered retaliatory** – *when a tenant exercises some legal right, when a tenant complains to a government agency about you or the property* and *when the tenant is involved in a tenant organization or union.*

To **better understand** the notion of **retaliation and why it's important,** you should first *try to understand why such protection exists.* The **goal of retaliation laws** is **to allow tenants the opportunity to exercise their legal rights** *without fear or intimidation.* After all, what good, really, is a law that says you can seek outside help with an unsafe or unfair housing situation, if the landlord is free to then raise your rent exorbitantly or even evict you? **Such laws would be useless without retaliation laws.**

Time Requirements

While some states have no statutes regarding retaliation, some states protect tenants from retaliation in all three situations – and **some just limit the idea of an action being retaliatory if it relates to only a tenant complaining to a government agency.** There are, of course, *all sorts of levels of protection in between.*

To further complicate the matter, **you need to consider** *the time frame* **in which your state considers an action to be retaliatory.** *Some states have no statutory time frame,* while others dictate that a negative action is *considered retaliatory if it occurs within 90 days, or even up to one year, from the tenant's action.*

The **following charts will lay out for you the retaliation time frames of each state as well as which actions are deemed to be retaliatory,** so you can **have a clearer understanding of what you can and cannot do, and when.**

Retaliation Time Frames

Alabama	Not specified
Alaska	Not specified
Arizona	6 months
Arkansas	Not specified
California	180 days
Colorado	No statute
Connecticut	6 months
Delaware	90 days
District of Columbia	6 months
Florida	Not specified
Georgia	Not specified
Hawaii	Not specified
Idaho	No statute
Illinois	Not specified
Indiana	No statute
Iowa	1 year
Kansas	Not specified
Kentucky	1 year
Louisiana	No statute
Maine	6 months
Maryland	Not specified
Massachusetts	6 months
Michigan	90 days
Minnesota	90 days
Mississippi	Not specified
Missouri	No statute

Montana	6 months
Nebraska	Not specified
Nevada	Not specified
New Hampshire	6 months
New Jersey	Not specified; termination not retaliation if tenant does not renew lease within 90 days of expiration
New Mexico	6 months
New York	6 months
North Carolina	12 months
North Dakota	No statute
Ohio	Not specified
Oklahoma	No statute
Oregon	Not specified
Pennsylvania	6 months
Rhode Island	Not specified
South Carolina	Not specified
South Dakota	180 days
Tennessee	Not specified
Texas	6 months
Utah	Not specified
Vermont	Not specified
Virginia	Not specified
Washington	90 days
West Virginia	Not specified
Wisconsin	Not specified
Wyoming	No statute

Can Landlord's Action Be Considered Retaliatory After Tenant Exercises His or Her Legal Right?

Alabama	No
Alaska	Yes
Arizona	No
Arkansas	No
California	Yes
Colorado	No statute
Connecticut	Yes
Delaware	Yes
District of Columbia	Yes
Florida	No
Georgia	No statute
Hawaii	Yes
Idaho	No statute
Illinois	No
Indiana	No statute
Iowa	No
Kansas	No
Kentucky	No
Louisiana	No statute
Maine	Yes
Maryland	No
Massachusetts	Yes
Michigan	Yes
Minnesota	Yes
Mississippi	Yes
Missouri	No statute

Montana	No
Nebraska	No
Nevada	Yes
New Hampshire	Yes
New Jersey	Yes
New Mexico	Yes
New York	Yes
North Carolina	Yes
North Dakota	No statute
Ohio	No
Oklahoma	No statute
Oregon	No
Pennsylvania	Yes
Rhode Island	Yes
South Carolina	No
South Dakota	No
Tennessee	Yes
Texas	Yes
Utah	No
Vermont	No
Virginia	Yes
Washington	Yes
West Virginia	Yes
Wisconsin	Yes
Wyoming	No statute

Can Landlord's Action Be Considered Retaliatory After Tenant Complains to Landlord or Agency?

Alabama	Yes
Alaska	Yes
Arizona	Yes
Arkansas	Yes; applies to lead hazard complaints only
California	Yes
Colorado	No statute
Connecticut	Yes
Delaware	Yes
District of Columbia	Yes
Florida	Yes
Georgia	No statute
Hawaii	Yes
Idaho	No statute
Illinois	Yes
Indiana	No statute
Iowa	Yes
Kansas	Yes
Kentucky	Yes
Louisiana	No statute
Maine	Yes
Maryland	Yes
Massachusetts	Yes
Michigan	Yes
Minnesota	Yes
Mississippi	No
Missouri	No statute

Montana	Yes
Nebraska	Yes
Nevada	Yes
New Hampshire	Yes
New Jersey	Yes
New Mexico	Yes
New York	Yes
North Carolina	Yes
North Dakota	No statute
Ohio	Yes
Oklahoma	No statute
Oregon	Yes
Pennsylvania	No
Rhode Island	Yes
South Carolina	Yes
South Dakota	Yes
Tennessee	Yes
Texas	Yes
Utah	Yes
Vermont	Yes
Virginia	Yes
Washington	Yes
West Virginia	Yes
Wisconsin	Yes
Wyoming	No statute

Can Landlord's Action Be Considered Retaliatory If Tenant Is Involved in a Tenant Organization/Union?

Alabama	Yes
Alaska	Yes
Arizona	Yes
Arkansas	No
California	Yes
Colorado	No statute
Connecticut	Yes
Delaware	Yes
District of Columbia	Yes
Florida	Yes
Georgia	No statute
Hawaii	No
Idaho	No statute
Illinois	No
Indiana	No statute
Iowa	Yes
Kansas	Yes
Kentucky	Yes
Louisiana	No statute
Maine	Yes
Maryland	Yes
Massachusetts	Yes
Michigan	Yes
Minnesota	No
Mississippi	No
Missouri	No statute

Montana	Yes
Nebraska	Yes
Nevada	Yes
New Hampshire	Yes
New Jersey	Yes
New Mexico	Yes
New York	Yes
North Carolina	Yes
North Dakota	No statute
Ohio	Yes
Oklahoma	No statute
Oregon	Yes
Pennsylvania	Yes
Rhode Island	No
South Carolina	No
South Dakota	Yes
Tennessee	No
Texas	No
Utah	No
Vermont	Yes
Virginia	Yes
Washington	No
West Virginia	No
Wisconsin	No
Wyoming	No statute

How to Avoid an Accusation of Retaliation

While the legal aspects of retaliation can be rather confusing and complex, **avoiding an accusation of retaliation is actually pretty simple and straightforward** – *which is definitely good for you!* After you have **made yourself aware of your state's laws** – especially with *extra attention paid to time frame issues* – **you need to** *avoid making any negative changes* to the lease terms or housing conditions of a tenant, **who has done something that falls under the three conditions previously explained, until the time frame specified by your state has passed.** *No matter what your true intentions are...*

So, for example, in the scenario presented at the beginning of this chapter, **even though the rent increase was not in response to the tenant's invoking of his or her rights, you should wait until after 90 days have passed to mail the letter** if your property is located in Michigan. **Being patient and waiting some time before acting may be frustrating,** *but it is certainly more desirable than finding yourself in the middle of a retaliation lawsuit that you may not have a chance of winning.*

Sit and wait – *that is simple enough, right?* But **sometimes you can't wait.** Or **maybe you have a particularly difficult tenant who frequently complains.** *Avoiding, or fighting off, retaliation claims can still be fairly easy.*

As with any legal arrangement, and we've said this before, *document everything!* **Put it all in writing, keep lots of detailed notes, and have policies that you maintain.** Again, in the scenario presented at the beginning of the chapter, **if you can show through documentation that it has been your policy for years** to increase rent for *every* tenant *every* 6 months, **then the tenant's claim of retaliation won't hold up in court.** Similarly, *if you can show a string of incidences and warning letters* to a tenant you start eviction proceedings on, *you will be equally protected.*

Chapter 12

Evictions, Part I:
General Information

This Chapter Discusses:

★ **The Steps to Eviction**

★ **Types of Termination: With and Without Cause**

★ **Persistently Troubling Tenants**

★ **Evicting by Force or Intimidation**

It would be great to say that you won't need to worry about this topic and that everything will go just fine with your tenants. But, **the reality is that there is a good chance you are going to have to deal with a tenant who needs to be evicted at some point** *for any number of reasons*. These **next two chapters** will **help guide you through the process for when that unfortunate time comes…**

The Steps to Eviction

Eviction procedures are established by state law, *and can even be further modified and restricted by local-level laws.* Generally speaking, **the steps in the eviction process** include *giving notice*, a *complaint (summons to court),* the *trial, right to redemption* and, finally, *removal.*

Types of Termination: With and Without Cause

Tenancies can be terminated for a specific reason – *something the tenant has either done or not done, such as not paid the rent, damaged the property, or engaged in illegal drug dealing at the property* – **which provides you with a cause for termination.** However, **tenancies can also be terminated when there is no lease agreement, or the lease has ended** – *meaning you are terminating without the tenant directly providing you with a cause, or simply, without cause.* **This type of termination** *cannot* **occur if there is still a valid lease in place.**

Whether you are terminating a tenancy with cause or without cause, you must first serve the tenant with notice of your intention to terminate. This is *often referred to as* a *notice to quit* or a *notice to vacate.*

Notification of an intended termination with cause is usually only required a few days in advance – *commonly 3 to 5 days.* That way, **the tenant has a few (reasonable) days to remedy the situation, while not leaving you stuck for a month or more** while the situation gets worse and your potential liability increases.

Termination without cause generally requires more of an advanced notice to the tenant – usually, 1 month up to as many as 3 months, *since the tenant has not actually done something to cause it* and **it is reasonable to allow the person additional time to find a new place to live.**

Persistently Troubling Tenants

If you have previously had difficulty with specific tenants, and you have served them with termination notices in the past, only to have the tenants remedy the situation in the nick of time – for example, by catching up on their rent – **some states allow for a third option: what is commonly called an** *unconditional quit notice.*

This type of notice, *like a notice with cause,* **usually gives tenants only a few days advance notification that an eviction proceeding will be started against them.** However, the power behind this type of notification is that *the tenants cannot do anything to remedy the situation.* **They can no longer play games with you** and their rent or hide the unauthorized pet once again, etc.; **their chances are all used up.**

Because of the severity of such a termination, the states that allow it reserve it for what they deem are *the most extreme cases.*

Evicting by Force or Intimidation

Trying to evict tenants yourself through forceful methods – often referred to as a *self-help* or *do-it-yourself eviction* – **is illegal!** *Do not, under any circumstances, try to force tenants out through intimidation or other tactics – such as having the water shut off, changing the locks on the property or threatening the tenants.*

No matter how frustrated you are, or how terrible the situation has become, you must resist what can be seen as an easy way to end the reign of awful tenants. *If you give in to such a temptation, you will surely find yourself in the middle of a lawsuit that you will not win...*

Not only can a judge order you to pay damages to the tenants, as well as their attorney fees – but your state's laws may give them the right to remain in your property until the end of the lease.

Additionally, you could easily find yourself involved in a criminal case for trespass, assault or a number of other offenses depending on what you have actually done in the attempt to get the tenants to leave.

The **following pages will show you what can happen in each state if you attempt to evict a tenant through forceful or intimidating methods** – instead of *lawfully through the courts...*

Penalties for Evicting by Force or Intimidation

Alabama	Judge determines
Alaska	1½ times actual damages; tenant has the right to stay until the end of the lease; if tenant terminates, landlord must return all of the security deposit
Arizona	2 times actual damages or 2 months' rent whichever greater; tenant has the right to stay until the end of the lease; if tenant terminates, landlord must return all of the security deposit
Arkansas	No statute
California	Actual damages and $100 for each day of violation, with a minimum of $250; tenant has the right to stay until the end of the lease; tenant is entitled to receive attorney fees and court costs
Colorado	No statute
Connecticut	2 times actual damages; tenant has the right to stay until the end of the lease; tenant is entitled to receive attorney fees and court costs; landlord may be prosecuted for a misdemeanor
Delaware	3 times actual damages or 3 times daily prorated rent for the time not allowed at the property whichever greater; tenant has the right to stay until the end of the lease; tenant is entitled to receive court costs
District of Columbia	No statute
Florida	Actual damages or 3 months' rent whichever greater; tenant is entitled to receive attorney fees and court costs
Georgia	No statute
Hawaii	2 months' rent or tenant given 2 months of free occupancy if he or she was not allowed at the property for at least 1 night; tenant has the right to stay until the end of the lease; tenant is entitled to receive attorney fees and court costs
Idaho	No statute
Illinois	No statute
Indiana	No statute
Iowa	Actual damages; tenant has the right to stay until the end of the lease; tenant is entitled to receive attorney fees and court costs; if tenant terminates, landlord must return all of the security deposit
Kansas	Actual damages or 1½ months' rent whichever greater; tenant has the right to stay until the end of the lease
Kentucky	3 months' rent; tenant has the right to stay until the end of the lease; tenant is entitled to receive attorney fees and court costs

Louisiana	No statute
Maine	Actual damages or $250 whichever greater; tenant is entitled to receive attorney fees and court costs
Maryland	No statute
Massachusetts	3 times actual damages or 3 months' rent; tenant has the right to stay until the end of the lease; tenant is entitled to receive attorney fees and court costs
Michigan	3 times actual damages or $200 whichever greater; tenant has the right to stay until the end of the lease
Minnesota	Tenant has the right to stay until the end of the lease; tenant is entitled to receive attorney fees and court costs
Mississippi	No statute
Missouri	No statute
Montana	3 times actual damages or 3 months' rent whichever greater; tenant has the right to stay until the end of the lease; tenant is entitled to receive attorney fees and court costs
Nebraska	3 months' rent; tenant has the right to stay until the end of the lease; tenant is entitled to receive attorney fees and court costs
Nevada	Actual damages or $1,000 whichever greater, or tenant could be awarded both sums; tenant has the right to stay until the end of the lease; if tenant terminates, landlord must return all of the security deposit
New Hampshire	Actual damages or $1,000 whichever greater; tenant could be awarded 3 times the amount if landlord intentionally broke the law; tenant has the right to stay until the end of the lease; tenant is entitled to receive attorney fees and court costs; every day of violation is treated as a separate violation
New Jersey	No statute
New Mexico	Actual damages and 2 months' rent and prorated portion of the rent for every day of violation; tenant has the right to stay until the end of the lease; tenant is entitled to receive attorney fees and court costs
New York	3 times actual damages
North Carolina	Actual damages; tenant has the right to stay until the end of the lease
North Dakota	3 times actual damages
Ohio	Actual damages; tenant is entitled to receive attorney fees and court costs
Oklahoma	2 times actual damages or 2 times average monthly rent whichever greater; tenant has the right to stay until the end of the lease
Oregon	2 times actual damages or 2 months' rent whichever greater; tenant has the right to stay until the end of the lease

Pennsylvania	Judge determines
Rhode Island	3 times actual damages or 3 months' rent whichever greater; tenant has the right to stay until the end of the lease; tenant is entitled to receive attorney fees and court costs
South Carolina	2 times actual damages or 3 months' rent whichever greater; tenant has the right to stay until the end of the lease; tenant is entitled to receive attorney fees and court costs
South Dakota	2 months' rent; tenant has the right to stay until the end of the lease; if tenant terminates, landlord must return all of the security deposit
Tennessee	Actual damages and punitive damages; tenant has the right to stay until the end of the lease; tenant is entitled to receive attorney fees and court costs; if tenant terminates, landlord must return all of the security deposit
Texas	Actual damages and 1 month's rent and $1,000; tenant has the right to stay until the end of the lease; tenant is entitled to receive attorney fees and court costs
Utah	No statute
Vermont	Tenant has the right to stay until the end of the lease; tenant is entitled to receive attorney fees and court costs
Virginia	Actual damages; tenant has the right to stay until the end of the lease; tenant is entitled to receive attorney fees and court costs
Washington	Actual damages and $100 for each day of no utility service if service was disconnected; tenant has the right to stay until the end of the lease; tenant is entitled to receive attorney fees and court costs
West Virginia	No statute
Wisconsin	No statute
Wyoming	No statute

Even if you have done the right thing and have taken your eviction case to court and won, *you still cannot force the tenant or his or her belongings out. You can still face charges of an unlawful eviction if you do.* **This job belongs to local law enforcement,** *who will notify the tenant that he or she needs to vacate the property.* **If the tenant fails to vacate, a law enforcement officer will come on a specified day and physically remove the tenant and his or her belongings. So –** *leave it all up to your local law enforcement.*

Evictions, Part II: In Detail

This Chapter Discusses:

★ **Giving Notice**

★ **Complaint/Court Summons**

★ **Trial**

★ **Winning or Losing**

Depending on your location in relation to your rental property, the complexity of the circumstances, your general comfort level with being in a courtroom and any number of other complicating issues, **you may want to consider hiring an attorney to represent you in an eviction proceeding – or perhaps hiring just a paralegal to draft the legal documents for you.**

If you decide to handle the case on your own, this chapter will give you some insight into the basic steps involved. **Each state is different, of course, and may even use different names for the steps or procedures – but the general ideas remain the same across the country.** Your local **Clerk of the Court** will be able to **assist you with the proper documents** you need and **can tell you what steps you need to take** in your property's jurisdiction.

Giving Notice

In order for you to start the eviction process, the tenant – obviously – must have done something that violates the terms of the lease. *The process cannot officially start until you serve proper notice to the tenant that he or she has violated the lease terms and needs to correct the violation or leave the property.* If the problem is **nonpayment of rent,** this notice is commonly referred to as a **"pay or quit" notice** – and if the **problem is related to something else**, such as an unauthorized roommate, this type of notice is commonly referred to as **"cure or quit." In either case, the tenant is given a set amount of time to fix the problem before being required to vacate the property or face eviction.** This time frame is **typically a few weekdays**, but can range anywhere from three days to thirty days, depending on which state your property is in.

If your state does not have a statutory notification period, you can still give your tenant a few days to remedy the situation – *you're just not required to by law.* **Those states that do not require you to give the tenant a certain period of time to correct the problem** allow for what is often termed an **"unconditional quit."** This just means **there are no conditions that have to be met in order to avoid an eviction –** *the tenant must simply leave within the specified time frame or face eviction.* This time frame can range from immediately to thirty days.

The **charts on the following pages will lay out for you the different types of notice allowed** to be used, as well as **the time requirements of each for all of the states.** The first chart also includes *which states limit the number of times a tenant can pay you at the last minute to avoid eviction.*

Eviction Notification for Nonpayment

Alabama	7 days to pay or quit
Alaska	7 days to pay or quit
Arizona	Landlord can serve an unconditional quit notice; tenant has 10 days to move or be prosecuted for a misdemeanor and be fined
Arkansas	No statute
California	3 days to pay or quit
Colorado	3 days to pay or quit
Connecticut	Landlord can serve an unconditional quit notice once the rent is 9 days late
Delaware	5 days to pay or quit; if landlord does not have an office in the county, tenant is given 3 additional days beyond the due date before landlord can serve the 5-day pay or quit notice
District of Columbia	30 days to pay or quit
Florida	3 days to pay or quit
Georgia	Landlord can file for eviction immediately and tenant is given 7 days to pay or face eviction; if tenant has 1 previous late payment in past 12 months, an unconditional quit notice can be used immediately if landlord served notice to pay or quit every time tenant was late
Hawaii	5 days to pay or quit
Idaho	3 days to pay or quit
Illinois	5 days to pay or quit
Indiana	10 days to pay or quit
Iowa	3 days to pay or quit
Kansas	10 days to pay or quit if term of tenancy is more than 3 months, 3 days to pay or quit if term of tenancy is less than 3 months
Kentucky	7 days to pay or quit
Louisiana	Landlord can serve an unconditional quit notice immediately
Maine	7 days to pay or quit once the rent is 7 days late
Maryland	Landlord can file for eviction immediately and tenant is given 5 days to appear in court and 4 days after ruling in landlord's favor to vacate
Massachusetts	14 days to pay or quit; if tenant is a holdover, landlord can file for eviction immediately; lease may give different time frame; if tenant has 1 previous late payment in past 12 months, an unconditional quit notice can be used immediately if landlord served a notice to pay or quit every time tenant was late

Michigan	7 days to pay or quit
Minnesota	14 days to pay or quit
Mississippi	3 days to pay or quit
Missouri	Landlord can serve an unconditional quit notice
Montana	3 days to pay or quit
Nebraska	3 days to pay or quit
Nevada	5 days to pay or quit
New Hampshire	7 days to pay or quit; if tenant has 3 previous late payments in past 12 months, an unconditional quit notice can be used immediately if landlord served notice to pay or quit every time tenant was late
New Jersey	30 days to pay or quit; if tenant has been habitually late with rent payments, an unconditional quit notice can be used immediately
New Mexico	3 days to pay or quit
New York	3 days to pay or quit
North Carolina	10 days to pay or quit
North Dakota	Landlord can serve an unconditional quit notice once rent is 3 days late
Ohio	Landlord can serve an unconditional quit notice
Oklahoma	5 days to pay or quit
Oregon	72 hours to pay or quit once the rent is 8 days late, or 144 hours to pay or quit once the rent is 5 days late; landlord can choose
Pennsylvania	10 days to pay or quit
Rhode Island	5 days to pay or quit once rent is 15 days late
South Carolina	5 days to pay or quit; if lease does not conspicuously indicate that landlord may file for eviction once rent is 5 days late, landlord must give 5 days notice that eviction proceedings will be started after 5 days pay or quit notice has been given; if tenant has 1 previous late payment during his or her tenancy, an unconditional quit notice can be used immediately
South Dakota	3 days to pay or quit and landlord can serve an unconditional quit notice
Tennessee	14 days to pay or quit; then tenant is given 16 days to vacate
Texas	3 days to move; lease may give a different time frame
Utah	3 days to pay or quit
Vermont	14 days to pay or quit; if tenant has 3 previous late payments in past 12 months, an unconditional quit notice can be used immediately if landlord served notice to pay or quit every time tenant was late

Virginia	5 days to pay or quit; if tenant has 1 previous late payment in past 12 months, an unconditional quit notice can be used immediately if landlord served notice to pay or quit every time tenant was late
Washington	3 days to pay or quit
West Virginia	Landlord can file for eviction immediately
Wisconsin	5 days to pay or quit if tenancy is less than 1 year or year-to-year; 5 days to pay or quit and landlord can serve an unconditional quit notice if 14 days' notice given to tenant if tenancy is month-to-month; 30 days to pay or quit if tenancy is longer than 1 year; If tenant has 1 previous late payment in past 12 months, an unconditional quit notice can be used immediately if landlord served notice to pay or quit every time tenant was late
Wyoming	Landlord can file for eviction once rent is 3 days late and tenant is given 3 days' notice; landlord can serve an unconditional quit notice

Eviction Notification for Violation

Alabama	14 days to cure or quit
Alaska	10 days to cure or quit if health and safety issue; 3 days to cure if tenant did not pay utility and shut-off occurred and then 2 to quit
Arizona	5 days to cure or quit if health and safety issue; 10 days to cure or quit for all other violations
Arkansas	Landlord can serve an unconditional quit notice
California	3 days to cure or quit
Colorado	3 days to cure or quit; no cure time required for certain substantial violations
Connecticut	15 days to cure or quit
Delaware	7 days to cure or quit
District of Columbia	30 days to cure or quit
Florida	7 days to cure or quit; no cure time required for certain substantial violations
Georgia	Landlord can serve an unconditional quit notice
Hawaii	10 days to cure and then 20 days before landlord can file for eviction; if a nuisance issue goes beyond 24 hours, tenant has 5 days to cure and then landlord can file for eviction
Idaho	3 days to cure or quit
Illinois	Landlord can serve an unconditional quit notice
Indiana	Landlord can serve an unconditional quit notice
Iowa	7 days to cure or quit
Kansas	14 days to cure and then 16 days to vacate
Kentucky	15 days to cure or quit
Louisiana	Landlord can serve an unconditional quit notice
Maine	Landlord can serve an unconditional quit notice
Maryland	30 days to cure or quit; if clear and imminent danger, then 14 days to vacate
Massachusetts	Landlord can serve an unconditional quit notice
Michigan	30 days to cure or quit if tenancy at will or lease allows for termination if there is a violation of terms
Minnesota	Landlord can file for eviction immediately

Mississippi	30 days to cure or quit
Missouri	Landlord can serve an unconditional quit notice
Montana	14 days to cure or quit; 3 days to cure or quit if unauthorized occupant or pet
Nebraska	14 days to cure and then 16 days to vacate
Nevada	3 days to cure and then 2 days to vacate
New Hampshire	Landlord can serve an unconditional quit notice
New Jersey	3 days to cure or quit; lease must specify which violations will result in eviction
New Mexico	7 days to cure or quit
New York	No statute for property not under rent control regulations; 10 days to cure or quit if property is under rent control unless control board sets different time frame
North Carolina	Landlord can serve an unconditional quit notice if lease allows for termination for specific violation
North Dakota	Landlord can serve an unconditional quit notice if material term of lease violated
Ohio	Landlord can serve an unconditional quit notice if material term of lease violated
Oklahoma	10 days to cure and then 5 days to vacate
Oregon	14 days to cure and then 16 days to vacate; 10 days to cure or quit if unauthorized pet
Pennsylvania	Landlord can serve an unconditional quit notice
Rhode Island	20 days to cure or quit if material term of lease violated
South Carolina	14 days to cure or quit
South Dakota	Landlord can file for eviction immediately if lease allows for termination for specific violation
Tennessee	14 days to cure and then 16 days to vacate
Texas	Landlord can serve an unconditional quit notice
Utah	3 days to cure or quit
Vermont	Landlord can serve an unconditional quit notice
Virginia	21 days to cure and then 9 to vacate
Washington	10 days to cure or quit

West Virginia	Landlord can file for eviction immediately
Wisconsin	Landlord can serve an unconditional quit notice
Wyoming	Landlord can serve an unconditional quit notice

Complaint/Court Summons

The complaint is the formal document in which you ask the court to order your tenant to leave your property and pay what is owed to you. Within the complaint you need to spell out *what the tenant has done that violates the lease* – **basically the grounds on which you are seeking an eviction.** This may sound complicated, but it is actually a pretty straightforward document. **The complaint is filed with the Clerk of the Court, who will then put your case on the court's calendar.**

Once the complaint has been filed and the case has been scheduled for an appearance before a judge, **the clerk will issue a summons to your tenant.** This document tells tenants that they are being sued in an attempt to evict them, as well as when they must show up in court and what they must do if they wish to offer a defense against the charges. Not only are **the tenants required to show up in court when instructed to, but they must also provide a written answer to your complaint.** *If they do not file their answer or show up in court, you will automatically win the case.*

You are responsible for seeing that the tenant receives a copy of both the complaint and the summons. Each state has its own requirements for how this must take place and the Clerk of the Court will be able to explain your state's requirements to you. **Often, the papers must be served on (delivered to) the tenant by a law enforcement official or a process server.** You've probably seen it many times in movies – a person trying to avoid the process server, so the person is not given the summons and thus the lawsuit cannot go forward. *That is how any lawsuit must start.* But don't worry, **states allow for special handling of those who cannot be properly served after an honest effort is made to do so** – so you won't be stuck in legal limbo.

Trial

Depending on where your rental property is located, your case may be heard in what is commonly referred to as **small claims court**, or perhaps in a **special landlord-tenant court**, or it **may be heard in a formal court.** What, if anything, does it matter to you? *Basically, the difference comes down to rules.* **If you can have your case**

heard in a more relaxed setting such as a small claims court or a landlord-tenant court, you will not have to follow the very strict rules of evidence that must be followed in a formal court. *If you are representing yourself, this can save you from quite a hassle.*

Once in the courtroom, the judge and his staff will instruct everyone through the process – **you present your side of things along with any evidence you have and your tenant will do the same.** *Just be sure you bring all of your evidence with you and you lay out your case completely and accurately.* Again, **this is where your attention to detail and methodical documentation of all of your business practices will prove to be well worth the time and effort.**

Chances are, though, you will never find yourself at trial. The tenant will disappear before it gets to this point, or you will arrange for a settlement, but **something will most likely keep you out of the courtroom.** After all, who really wants to be on trial? **If you do find yourself going to trial, there is probably a good chance that you have actually done something that is questionable – or that you have provoked an action from your tenant by your doing or not doing something, such as not fixing a broken toilet, so the tenant withholds rent.** Otherwise, typically, tenants will know that they have no chance of winning an eviction suit if it's just a matter of them not paying their rent and they won't bother to fight it. So, **if you find yourself having to actually face your tenant in the courtroom, you might want to consider hiring an attorney to represent you.**

Winning or Losing

Realistically, should you win an eviction lawsuit, you may feel better, but things won't immediately be better. *While you will be able to use the tenant's security deposit to recover some of the money owed to you, it probably won't cover everything.* However, **you will now be armed with the court's judgment, which you can use to have a collection agency go after your tenant or to have part of your tenant's paychecks garnished.**

And, of course, **there is the matter of still having the tenant on the property.** As explained in **Chapter 12,** *you cannot force the tenant to leave.* **A law enforcement officer will have to deal with this for you.** You wouldn't want to find yourself having to physically remove someone anyway, so have the patience to leave this to the professionals.

But what if you lose? Then *your tenants get to stay and you may just find yourself having to pay them for any expenses related to defending themselves.* Things can be further complicated by the actual circumstances involved. **If the tenants withheld rent because they claim you failed to repair something that made the property inhabitable, the judge could require you to make the repairs.** Similarly, **if the tenants refused to pay a rent increase because they claim you discriminated against them when you increased their rent, the judge could require you to pay your tenants additional damages.**

Title III of the Servicemembers Civil Relief Act **protects** *active duty military personnel and their families from immediate eviction for failure to pay rent.* **While you can still file an eviction lawsuit against someone who is protected by this law, the case will be placed on hold for three months.** *A copy of this law can be found in* **Appendix C** and *on the enclosed CD-ROM.*

Chapter 14

Attorneys:
Friend or Foe?

This Chapter Discusses:

★ **When Is It Necessary to Hire an Attorney?**

★ **Finding an Attorney**

★ **Curbing Attorney Fees**

★ **Case Law Takes Precedence**

★ **Where to Find Laws and Statutes**

Now that you've been introduced to your rights and responsibilities as a landlord and the laws that govern them, **it's critical to understand that the issues you'll encounter with your tenants will not always be as cut and dry as this volume might unintentionally convey.** *Laws were never meant to be easy to interpret and enforce.* **If they were, then such a complex judicial system and the attorneys who make their living navigating it wouldn't be necessary.** It's almost as if laws were written to perpetuate the need for attorneys. After all, many of the lawmakers who wrote the laws were attorneys.

When Is It Necessary to Hire an Attorney?

First of all, **it is true that most of your landlord-tenant disputes can be effectively handled on your own without professional legal representation.** However, it's the more complex and riskier issues that may require an attorney to ensure your rights are fully protected under the law.

The following is a brief list to illustrate the types of issues that may require an attorney. *NOTE: Any time any legal action is brought against you that is above and beyond the realm of small claims court, seek the advice of an attorney.*

Common Types of Issues That Require an Attorney:

☆ Discrimination

Being accused of **discriminating against a tenant is a serious issue that can lead to a tarnished reputation and significant monetary awards.** Right from the start, *you should consider consulting an attorney even if you haven't been served with a lawsuit.* **Friendly, professional advice may prevent future litigation and trials.**

☆ Death or Injury of a Tenant

If a *tenant dies or is injured on the premises, you should consult an attorney as soon as you feel the cause may be partially attributed to you* – or anything of yours contained within the entire perimeter of the rental property, from surveyor stake to surveyor stake.

☆ Eviction

Granted, **you can usually handle an eviction by yourself without the assistance of an attorney as long as you follow the procedures carefully.** However, **if the tenant decides to put up a defense or is causing serious problems to the unit, it couldn't hurt to hand over the matter to a professional.**

★ Abandonment

You would actually think this doesn't happen, but **if a tenant appears to have abandoned the property, you should consult an attorney regarding what steps to take.** It's a particularly complex issue, especially if there is personal property still visible in the unit or even outside, such as automobiles. *Taking the wrong action may result in substantial penalties.* For example, the state of Florida allows for up to three times the amount of the rent or the total amount of damage caused by the landlord when handling the tenant's personal property (whichever is greater). This is why **it's worth a few hundred dollars to consult an attorney if you encounter such a problem.**

★ Serious Damage

As you know (and as mentioned in this book), **it's very difficult to collect on a judgment awarded to you in the case of a lawsuit against a tenant.** However, *if there is serious damage that is outrageously expensive to repair* (beyond the limits of your local small claims court), *you may want to take serious legal action against the tenant* – especially if the tenant either is a government employee or has had a well-established job for many years. This way, you can always collect on your judgment by garnishing the tenant's wages (as permitted in the state of California and others). And, fortunately, **most jurisdictions throughout the United States will even allow you to collect your attorney's fees from the tenant.**

Finding an Attorney

After you decide it's in your best interest to hire an attorney, **you need to find a good one who has experience in real estate law (specifically, landlord-tenant law).** Now, this doesn't necessarily mean an expensive one. *Good attorneys are known by their reputation, not by their fees.* Therefore, instead of looking at bus bench ads,

billboards and the Yellow Pages, **look to your friends, family and colleagues for a referral to a trusted legal professional.** Better yet, *if you've developed a good relationship with a real estate agent or loan officer, he or she may be the ideal source for a friendly referral.*

If you are unable to solicit a referral from your personal Rolodex, **contact your state's bar association** (not the beverage bureau, but the legal organization that licenses and governs attorneys in your state) **and ask how to locate such an attorney for your needs.** Upon receiving the attorney's contact information, **contact the attorney for an initial consultation and ask about his or her experience and qualifications.** *You must only hire an attorney who has experience in handling legal matters that are relative to your own.*

Curbing Attorney Fees

Attorneys usually charge a flat fee for filing and handling an eviction while retaining the right to charge additional fees should the tenant put up a defense and drag matters out in court. These types of flat fee arrangements are usually reasonable (a few hundred dollars). *It's the hourly fees that can get you* (especially when it comes to complicated legal matters). **As you discuss fees with your attorney, don't hesitate to ask for a reduction in the hourly rate on the pretense of establishing a long-term relationship concerning your real estate ventures and the ongoing need you'll have for him or her.**

The main focus of this section, however, is not to barter with your attorney. Instead, it's about *being prepared.* **The more legwork you can do for your attorney, the better! When *you* do the work instead of having the attorney research or assemble documents you should already possess (or can easily obtain from public records), the less time you can be billed for at the attorney's hourly rate.** Not to mention, *this is a learning process* which you should take advantage of every step of the way, for your own benefit. **While attorneys are quite capable of handling everything on their own, it's hard to pass up an opportunity to educate yourself, especially when your asset is on the line.**

Case Law Takes Precedence

This section of this chapter is to serve as a reminder that **not all matters are black and white in the eyes of the law.** While this book relies heavily on current state laws and statutes, **it's nearly impossible to take into account the ever-changing *"case law"* (also known as *"civil law"*).** *Case law* **is when a court sets a precedent by interpreting an existing law (or lack thereof) in a slightly different way that has never been done before.**

Therefore, **it's important to note that while you may think your legal rights are protected with the steps you take,** *today's attorneys or judges can rely on any prior court's decision as a basis for arguing or ruling on a case with similar circumstances to interpret the current law in a different manner.* Confusing, isn't it? But don't worry, **most of the time the state laws and statutes are adhered to closely.** It's *usually only those matters left open to interpretation* (those that you are unsure about) *that can lead you into uncharted territory* – such as the issue of abandonment mentioned earlier.

By the way, don't bother wasting your time researching case law. If you get yourself into a legal bind that gets you wondering, it's best to seek the assistance of an attorney. **Researching, reading and interpreting case law is very labor intensive and is best left up to the attorneys and their staff.**

Where to Find Laws and Statutes

Laws and statutes (unlike case law) are much easier to read (although just as dry) **and much easier to find.** While this book provides summaries of most of the laws you'll need, **you may want to read the entire statutes that address the very topic you're interested in.** But be warned, *laws and statutes can be several pages long and incredibly difficult to navigate.* If you would like to see what is currently listed for your state, visit either the website for this book series at **www.EUNTK.com** or **www.AmericanLandlord.com** for **links to each state's laws and statutes.**

Chapter 15

Landlord-Tenant Laws:
State by State

This Chapter Discusses:

★ **All 50 States - plus D.C. (in alphabetical order)**

In case you haven't read **Chapters 1 through 13, you should take the time to review them to understand basic principles and situations before jumping ahead to the summary of your state's landlord-tenant laws and procedures**. With that being said, this chapter is in fact *a collection of individual state summaries from every chart referenced in the earlier chapters*.

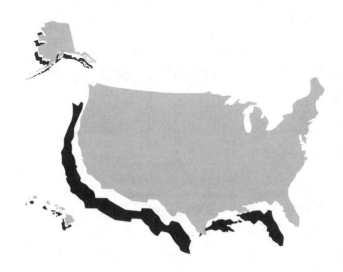

Alabama

Rent Increase Notice	No statute
Late Fees	No statute
Returned Check Fees	$30 - Check writer is also responsible for all other costs of collection
Security Deposit Limits	1 month's rent
Security Deposit Interest	No statute
Security Deposit Bank Account	No statute
Inspection Notification	No statute
Deadline for Returning Security Deposit	35 days
Statute of Limitations for Written Contracts	6 years
Small Claims Court Limits	$3,000
Pet Deposits and Additional Fees	Additional deposits, beyond the security deposit limit, are allowed for pets, undoing alterations, and tenant activities that increase liability risks
Entry for Maintenance and Repairs	Yes
Entry During Tenant's Extended Absence	Yes
Entry for Showing the Property	Yes
Notice of Entry	2 days
Landlord Termination of Month-to-Month	30 days
Tenant Termination of Month-to-Month	30 days
Lease Change (Other Than Rent Amt) Notice	No statute
Retaliation Time Frame	Not specified
Tenant Exercises Legal Right	No
Tenant Complains to Landlord or Agency	Yes
Tenant Is Involved in Tenant Org or Union	Yes
Penalty for Evicting by Force or Intimidation	Judge determines
Eviction Notice for Nonpayment	7 days to pay or quit

Alaska

Rent Increase Notice	30 days
Late Fees	No statute
Returned Check Fees	$30
Security Deposit Limits	2 months' rent, limit does not apply unless monthly rent exceeds $2,000
Security Deposit Interest	No statute
Security Deposit Bank Account	Security deposits must be held in separate account
Inspection Notification	No statute
Deadline for Returning Security Deposit	14 days if proper termination notice given, 30 days if not
Statute of Limitations for Written Contracts	6 years
Small Claims Court Limits	$10,000
Pet Deposits and Additional Fees	No statute
Entry for Maintenance and Repairs	Yes
Entry During Tenant's Extended Absence	Yes
Entry for Showing the Property	Yes
Notice of Entry	24 hours
Landlord Termination of Month-to-Month	30 days
Tenant Termination of Month-to-Month	30 days
Lease Change (Other Than Rent Amt) Notice	30 days
Retaliation Time Frame	Not specified
Tenant Exercises Legal Right	Yes
Tenant Complains to Landlord or Agency	Yes
Tenant Is Involved in Tenant Org or Union	Yes
Penalty for Evicting by Force or Intimidation	1½ times actual damages; tenant has the right to stay until the end of the lease; if tenant terminates, landlord must return all of the security deposit

Eviction Notice for Nonpayment	7 days to pay or quit
Eviction Notice for Violation	10 days to cure or quit if health and safety issue; 3 days to cure if tenant did not pay utility and shut-off occurred and then 2 to quit

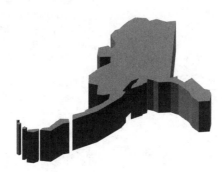

Arizona

Rent Increase Notice	30 days
Late Fees	Late fees must be reasonable and indicated in the lease agreement
Returned Check Fees	$25
Security Deposit Limits	1½ months' rent unless both parties agree to more
Security Deposit Interest	No statute
Security Deposit Bank Account	No statute
Inspection Notification	At move-in, the landlord must provide written notification to the tenant informing the tenant of the right to be present at the move-out inspection; the landlord must notify the tenant when the move-out inspection will occur if requested by the tenant; if the tenant is being evicted and the landlord has reasonable cause to fear violence or intimidation from the tenant, the landlord is not required to perform the move-out inspection with the tenant
Deadline for Returning Security Deposit	14 days
Statute of Limitations for Written Contracts	6 years
Small Claims Court Limits	$2,500
Pet Deposits and Additional Fees	Non-refundable fees are allowed; the purpose of any non-refundable fee must be stated in writing to the tenant; all fees are refundable unless specifically designated as non-refundable
Entry for Maintenance and Repairs	Yes
Entry During Tenant's Extended Absence	No
Entry for Showing the Property	Yes
Notice of Entry	2 days
Landlord Termination of Month-to-Month	30 days
Tenant Termination of Month-to-Month	30 days
Lease Change (Other Than Rent Amt) Notice	30 days
Retaliation Time Frame	6 months

Tenant Exercises Legal Right	No
Tenant Complains to Landlord or Agency	Yes
Tenant Is Involved in Tenant Org or Union	Yes
Penalty for Evicting by Force or Intimidation	2 times actual damages or 2 months' rent whichever greater; tenant has the right to stay until the end of the lease; if tenant terminates, landlord must return all of the security deposit
Eviction Notice for Nonpayment	Landlord can serve an unconditional quit notice; tenant has 10 days to move or be prosecuted for a misdemeanor and be fined
Eviction Notice for Violation	5 days to cure or quit if health and safety issue; 10 days to cure or quit for all other violations

Arkansas

Rent Increase Notice	No statute
Late Fees	No statute
Returned Check Fees	$25
Security Deposit Limits	2 months' rent
Security Deposit Interest	No statute
Security Deposit Bank Account	No statute
Inspection Notification	No statute
Deadline for Returning Security Deposit	30 days
Statute of Limitations for Written Contracts	5 years
Small Claims Court Limits	$5,000
Pet Deposits and Additional Fees	No statute
Entry for Maintenance and Repairs	Yes
Entry During Tenant's Extended Absence	No
Entry for Showing the Property	Yes
Notice of Entry	Not specified
Landlord Termination of Month-to-Month	10 days
Tenant Termination of Month-to-Month	No statute
Lease Change (Other Than Rent Amt) Notice	No statute
Retaliation Time Frame	Not specified
Tenant Exercises Legal Right	No
Tenant Complains to Landlord or Agency	Yes; applies to lead hazard complaints only
Tenant Is Involved in Tenant Org or Union	No
Penalty for Evicting by Force or Intimidation	No statute
Eviction Notice for Nonpayment	No statute
Eviction Notice for Violation	Landlord can serve an unconditional quit notice

California

Rent Increase Notice	30 days unless all increases in last 12 months total greater than 10% of the lowest amount of rent during those 12 months, then 60 days
Late Fees	Late fees must be close to the landlord's actual losses and indicated in the lease agreement as follows: "Because landlord and tenant agree that actual damages for late rent payments are very difficult or impossible to determine, landlord and tenant agree to the following stated late charge as liquidated damages"
Returned Check Fees	$25
Security Deposit Limits	2 months' rent if unfurnished unit, 3 months' rent if furnished unit, extra ½ month's rent if tenant has waterbed
Security Deposit Interest	No statute
Security Deposit Bank Account	No statute
Inspection Notification	Within a reasonable time after either party gives notification to the other party of the intention to terminate the lease, the landlord must notify the tenant in writing that the tenant has the right to request a preliminary move-out inspection and be present for such inspection; if the tenant requests the preliminary move-out inspection, it must take place no earlier than 2 weeks before the tenancy ends and the landlord must provide written notification of the date and time at least 48 hours in advance (this notification time frame can be waived if both parties sign a written waiver); the tenant must be provided with an itemized statement of proposed deductions from the security deposit, and this statement must include a copy of California Civil Code statute §1950.5 paragraphs 1-4; the tenant will then have the remaining time of the tenancy to remedy any of the problems found before the final move-out inspection takes place and the landlord can proceed with any deductions from the security deposit
Deadline for Returning Security Deposit	21 days
Statute of Limitations for Written Contracts	4 years
Small Claims Court Limits	$7,500

Pet Deposits and Additional Fees	Non-refundable fees are not allowed
Entry for Maintenance and Repairs	Yes
Entry During Tenant's Extended Absence	No
Entry for Showing the Property	Yes
Notice of Entry	24 hours, 48 hours if preliminary inspection
Landlord Termination of Month-to-Month	60 days
Tenant Termination of Month-to-Month	30 days
Lease Change (Other Than Rent Amt) Notice	30 days
Retaliation Time Frame	180 days
Tenant Exercises Legal Right	Yes
Tenant Complains to Landlord or Agency	Yes
Tenant Is Involved in Tenant Org or Union	Yes
Penalty for Evicting by Force or Intimidation	Actual damages and $100 for each day of violation, with a minimum of $250; tenant has the right to stay until the end of the lease; tenant is entitled to receive attorney fees and court costs
Eviction Notice for Nonpayment	3 days to pay or quit
Eviction Notice for Violation	3 days to cure or quit

Colorado

Rent Increase Notice	10 days
Late Fees	No statute
Returned Check Fees	$20 - Check writer is also responsible for all other costs of collection
Security Deposit Limits	No statute
Security Deposit Interest	No statute
Security Deposit Bank Account	No statute
Inspection Notification	No statute
Deadline for Returning Security Deposit	1 month unless lease provides for longer period up to 60 days, 72 weekday non-holiday hours if emergency termination due to gas equipment hazard
Statute of Limitations for Written Contracts	6 years
Small Claims Court Limits	$7,500
Pet Deposits and Additional Fees	No statute
Entry for Maintenance and Repairs	No statute
Entry During Tenant's Extended Absence	No statute
Entry for Showing the Property	No statute
Notice of Entry	No statute
Landlord Termination of Month-to-Month	10 days
Tenant Termination of Month-to-Month	10 days
Lease Change (Other Than Rent Amt) Notice	10 days
Retaliation Time Frame	No statute
Tenant Exercises Legal Right	No statute
Tenant Complains to Landlord or Agency	No statute
Tenant Is Involved in Tenant Org or Union	No statute
Penalty for Evicting by Force or Intimidation	No statute
Eviction Notice for Nonpayment	3 days to pay or quit

| Eviction Notice for Violation | 3 days to cure or quit; no cure time required for certain substantial violations |

Connecticut

Rent Increase Notice	No statute
Late Fees	Late fees can be charged when rent is 9 days late
Returned Check Fees	$20 - Check writer is also responsible for all other costs of collection
Security Deposit Limits	2 months' rent, 1 month's rent if tenant is 62 or older
Security Deposit Interest	Pay annually and at termination, equal to average rate on savings accts at insured banks but not less than 1.5%
Security Deposit Bank Account	Security deposits must be held in a separate account
Inspection Notification	No statute
Deadline for Returning Security Deposit	30 days or within 15 days of receipt of forwarding address from tenant, whichever is later
Statute of Limitations for Written Contracts	6 years
Small Claims Court Limits	$5,000; no limit if security deposit case
Pet Deposits and Additional Fees	No statute
Entry for Maintenance and Repairs	Yes
Entry During Tenant's Extended Absence	Yes
Entry for Showing the Property	Yes
Notice of Entry	Reasonable time
Landlord Termination of Month-to-Month	3 days
Tenant Termination of Month-to-Month	No statute
Lease Change (Other Than Rent Amt) Notice	No statute
Retaliation Time Frame	6 months
Tenant Exercises Legal Right	Yes
Tenant Complains to Landlord or Agency	Yes
Tenant Is Involved in Tenant Org or Union	Yes

Penalty for Evicting by Force or Intimidation	2 times actual damages; tenant has the right to stay until the end of the lease; tenant is entitled to receive attorney fees and court costs; landlord may be prosecuted for a misdemeanor
Eviction Notice for Nonpayment	Landlord can serve an unconditional quit notice once the rent is 9 days late
Eviction Notice for Violation	15 days to cure or quit

Delaware

Rent Increase Notice	No statute
Late Fees	Late fees cannot be more than 5% of the rent amount due and can be charged when the rent is more than 5 days late. If the landlord does not have an office within the rental property's county, the tenant has an additional 3 days before late fees can be charged
Returned Check Fees	$20 - Check writer is also responsible for all other costs of collection
Security Deposit Limits	2 months' rent, 1 month's rent if tenant is 62 or older
Security Deposit Interest	Pay annually and at termination, equal to average rate on savings accts at insured banks but not less than 1.5%
Security Deposit Bank Account	Security deposits must be held in a separate account
Inspection Notification	No statute
Deadline for Returning Security Deposit	30 days or within 15 days of receipt of forwarding address from tenant, whichever is later
Statute of Limitations for Written Contracts	6 years
Small Claims Court Limits	$5,000; no limit if security deposit case
Pet Deposits and Additional Fees	No statute
Entry for Maintenance and Repairs	Yes
Entry During Tenant's Extended Absence	Yes
Entry for Showing the Property	Yes
Notice of Entry	Reasonable time
Landlord Termination of Month-to-Month	3 days
Tenant Termination of Month-to-Month	No statute
Lease Change (Other Than Rent Amt) Notice	No statute
Retaliation Time Frame	6 months
Tenant Exercises Legal Right	Yes

Tenant Complains to Landlord or Agency	Yes
Tenant Is Involved in Tenant Org or Union	Yes
Penalty for Evicting by Force or Intimidation	3 times actual damages or 3 times daily prorated rent for the time not allowed at the property whichever greater; tenant has the right to stay until the end of the lease; tenant is entitled to receive court costs
Eviction Notice for Nonpayment	5 days to pay or quit; if landlord does not have an office in the county, tenant is given 3 additional days beyond the due date before landlord can serve the 5-day pay or quit notice
Eviction Notice for Violation	7 days to cure or quit

District of Columbia

Rent Increase Notice	No statute
Late Fees	No statute
Returned Check Fees	$25
Security Deposit Limits	1 month's rent
Security Deposit Interest	Pay at termination, equal to average rate on savings accts at insured banks but not less than 1.5%
Security Deposit Bank Account	Security deposits must be held in a separate account
Inspection Notification	No statute
Deadline for Returning Security Deposit	45 days
Statute of Limitations for Written Contracts	3 years
Small Claims Court Limits	$5,000
Pet Deposits and Additional Fees	No statute
Entry for Maintenance and Repairs	No statute
Entry During Tenant's Extended Absence	No statute
Entry for Showing the Property	No statute
Notice of Entry	No statute
Landlord Termination of Month-to-Month	30 days
Tenant Termination of Month-to-Month	30 days
Lease Change (Other Than Rent Amt) Notice	No statute
Retaliation Time Frame	6 months
Tenant Exercises Legal Right	Yes
Tenant Complains to Landlord or Agency	Yes
Tenant Is Involved in Tenant Org or Union	Yes

Penalty for Evicting by Force or Intimidation	No statute
Eviction Notice for Nonpayment	30 days to pay or quit
Eviction Notice for Violation	30 days to cure or quit

Florida

Rent Increase Notice	No statute
Late Fees	No statute
Returned Check Fees	Checks from (1) $0.01-$50.00 = $25.00 fee, (2) $50.01-$300.00 = $30.00 fee, (3) $300.01 and over = the greater of $40.00 fee or 5% of the face amount of the check. Check writer is also responsible for all other costs of collection
Security Deposit Limits	No statute
Security Deposit Interest	Not required; but if made, must pay annually and at termination; tenant who wrongfully terminates is not entitled to; lease agreement must give details on interest
Security Deposit Bank Account	Security deposits must be held in a separate account; tenant must be told in writing within 30 days the location of the account, if the account is interest bearing or not and the schedule and rate of any interest payments to be made; a security bond covering all security deposits may be obtained in lieu of maintaining a separate account; lease must include copy of statute §83.49(3)
Inspection Notification	No statute
Deadline for Returning Security Deposit	15 days if no deductions, 30 days to give notice of what deductions will be made; then tenant has 15 days to dispute any deduction and remaining deposit must be returned within 30 days of initial deduction notification
Statute of Limitations for Written Contracts	5 years
Small Claims Court Limits	$5,000
Pet Deposits and Additional Fees	Non-refundable fees are not specifically addressed in statutes, but are customary
Entry for Maintenance and Repairs	Yes
Entry During Tenant's Extended Absence	Yes
Entry for Showing the Property	Yes
Notice of Entry	12 hours
Landlord Termination of Month-to-Month	15 days

Tenant Termination of Month-to-Month	15 days
Lease Change (Other Than Rent Amt) Notice	No statute
Retaliation Time Frame	Not specified
Tenant Exercises Legal Right	No
Tenant Complains to Landlord or Agency	Yes
Tenant Is Involved in Tenant Org or Union	Yes
Penalty for Evicting by Force or Intimidation	Actual damages or 3 months' rent whichever greater; tenant is entitled to receive attorney fees and court costs
Eviction Notice for Nonpayment	3 days to pay or quit
Eviction Notice for Violation	7 days to cure or quit; no cure time required for certain substantial violations

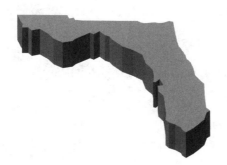

Georgia

Rent Increase Notice	No statute
Late Fees	No statute
Returned Check Fees	$30 or 5% of the face amount of the check, whichever is greater
Security Deposit Limits	No statute
Security Deposit Interest	No statute
Security Deposit Bank Account	Security deposits must be held in a separate escrow account located at a financial institution which is regulated by the state or federal government; tenant must be told of the location of the account; a security bond covering all security deposits may be obtained in lieu of maintaining a separate account
Inspection Notification	No statute
Deadline for Returning Security Deposit	1 month
Statute of Limitations for Written Contracts	6 years
Small Claims Court Limits	$15,000; no limit if eviction case
Pet Deposits and Additional Fees	Non-refundable fees are not specifically addressed in statutes, but are customary
Entry for Maintenance and Repairs	No statute
Entry During Tenant's Extended Absence	No statute
Entry for Showing the Property	No statute
Notice of Entry	No statute
Landlord Termination of Month-to-Month	60 days
Tenant Termination of Month-to-Month	30 days
Lease Change (Other Than Rent Amt) Notice	No statute
Retaliation Time Frame	Not specified
Tenant Exercises Legal Right	No statute
Tenant Complains to Landlord or Agency	No statute

Tenant Is Involved in Tenant Org or Union	No statute
Penalty for Evicting by Force or Intimidation	No statute
Eviction Notice for Nonpayment	Landlord can file for eviction immediately and tenant is given 7 days to pay or face eviction; if tenant has 1 previous late payment in past 12 months, an unconditional quit notice can be used immediately if landlord served notice to pay or quit every time tenant was late
Eviction Notice for Violation	Landlord can serve an unconditional quit notice

Hawaii

Rent Increase Notice	45 days
Late Fees	No statute
Returned Check Fees	$30 - Check writer is also responsible for all other costs of collection
Security Deposit Limits	1 month's rent
Security Deposit Interest	No statute
Security Deposit Bank Account	No statute
Inspection Notification	No statute
Deadline for Returning Security Deposit	14 days
Statute of Limitations for Written Contracts	6 years
Small Claims Court Limits	$3,500; no limit if security deposit case
Pet Deposits and Additional Fees	Non-refundable fees are not allowed; only the first month's rent and security deposit can be collected at the start of a tenancy
Entry for Maintenance and Repairs	Yes
Entry During Tenant's Extended Absence	Yes
Entry for Showing the Property	Yes
Notice of Entry	2 days
Landlord Termination of Month-to-Month	45 days
Tenant Termination of Month-to-Month	28 days
Lease Change (Other Than Rent Amt) Notice	45 days
Retaliation Time Frame	Not specified
Tenant Exercises Legal Right	Yes
Tenant Complains to Landlord or Agency	Yes
Tenant Is Involved in Tenant Org or Union	No

Penalty for Evicting by Force or Intimidation	2 months' rent or tenant given 2 months of free occupancy if he or she was not allowed at the property for at least 1 night; tenant has the right to stay until the end of the lease; tenant is entitled to receive attorney fees and court costs
Eviction Notice for Nonpayment	5 days to pay or quit
Eviction Notice for Violation	10 days to cure and then 20 days before landlord can file for eviction; if a nuisance issue goes beyond 24 hours, tenant has 5 days to cure and then landlord can file for eviction

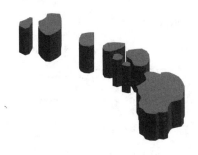

Idaho

Rent Increase Notice	15 days
Late Fees	No statute
Returned Check Fees	$20 - Check writer is also responsible for all other costs of collection
Security Deposit Limits	No statute
Security Deposit Interest	No statute
Security Deposit Bank Account	No statute
Inspection Notification	No statute
Deadline for Returning Security Deposit	21 days unless both parties agree, then up to 30 days
Statute of Limitations for Written Contracts	5 years
Small Claims Court Limits	$5,000
Pet Deposits and Additional Fees	No statute
Entry for Maintenance and Repairs	No statute
Entry During Tenant's Extended Absence	No statute
Entry for Showing the Property	No statute
Notice of Entry	No statute
Landlord Termination of Month-to-Month	1 month
Tenant Termination of Month-to-Month	1 month
Lease Change (Other Than Rent Amt) Notice	15 days
Retaliation Time Frame	No statute
Tenant Exercises Legal Right	No statute
Tenant Complains to Landlord or Agency	No statute
Tenant Is Involved in Tenant Org or Union	No statute
Penalty for Evicting by Force or Intimidation	No statute
Eviction Notice for Nonpayment	3 days to pay or quit
Eviction Notice for Violation	3 days to cure or quit

Illinois

Rent Increase Notice	30 days
Late Fees	No statute
Returned Check Fees	$25 - Check writer is also responsible for all other costs of collection
Security Deposit Limits	No statute
Security Deposit Interest	Required if owner has 25+ properties adjacent to each other or in same building; if security deposit held for longer than 6 months, must pay annually and at termination
Security Deposit Bank Account	No statute
Inspection Notification	No statute
Deadline for Returning Security Deposit	45 days if no deductions, 30 days to itemize deductions
Statute of Limitations for Written Contracts	10 years
Small Claims Court Limits	$10,000
Pet Deposits and Additional Fees	No statute
Entry for Maintenance and Repairs	No statute
Entry During Tenant's Extended Absence	No statute
Entry for Showing the Property	No statute
Notice of Entry	No statute
Landlord Termination of Month-to-Month	30 days
Tenant Termination of Month-to-Month	30 days
Lease Change (Other Than Rent Amt) Notice	30 days
Retaliation Time Frame	Not specified
Tenant Exercises Legal Right	No
Tenant Complains to Landlord or Agency	Yes
Tenant Is Involved in Tenant Org or Union	No
Penalty for Evicting by Force or Intimidation	No statute

| **Eviction Notice for Nonpayment** | 5 days to pay or quit |
| **Eviction Notice for Violation** | Landlord can serve an unconditional quit notice |

Indiana

Rent Increase Notice	30 days unless lease gives different time frame
Late Fees	No statute
Returned Check Fees	$20 - Check writer is also responsible for all other costs of collection
Security Deposit Limits	No statute
Security Deposit Interest	No statute
Security Deposit Bank Account	No statute
Inspection Notification	No statute
Deadline for Returning Security Deposit	45 days
Statute of Limitations for Written Contracts	10 years
Small Claims Court Limits	$6,000
Pet Deposits and Additional Fees	No statute
Entry for Maintenance and Repairs	Yes
Entry During Tenant's Extended Absence	No
Entry for Showing the Property	Yes
Notice of Entry	Reasonable time
Landlord Termination of Month-to-Month	1 month
Tenant Termination of Month-to-Month	1 month
Lease Change (Other Than Rent Amt) Notice	30 days unless lease gives different time frame
Retaliation Time Frame	No statute
Tenant Exercises Legal Right	No statute
Tenant Complains to Landlord or Agency	No statute
Tenant Is Involved in Tenant Org or Union	No statute
Penalty for Evicting by Force or Intimidation	No statute
Eviction Notice for Nonpayment	10 days to pay or quit
Eviction Notice for Violation	Landlord can serve an unconditional quit notice

Iowa

Rent Increase Notice	30 days
Late Fees	No statute
Returned Check Fees	$30
Security Deposit Limits	2 months' rent
Security Deposit Interest	Not required; but if paid, must pay at termination; however - any interest earned during the first 5 years is landlord's
Security Deposit Bank Account	Security deposits must be held in a separate account
Inspection Notification	No statute
Deadline for Returning Security Deposit	30 days
Statute of Limitations for Written Contracts	10 years
Small Claims Court Limits	$5,000
Pet Deposits and Additional Fees	No statute
Entry for Maintenance and Repairs	Yes
Entry During Tenant's Extended Absence	Yes
Entry for Showing the Property	Yes
Notice of Entry	24 hours
Landlord Termination of Month-to-Month	30 days
Tenant Termination of Month-to-Month	30 days
Lease Change (Other Than Rent Amt) Notice	30 days
Retaliation Time Frame	1 year
Tenant Exercises Legal Right	No
Tenant Complains to Landlord or Agency	Yes
Tenant Is Involved in Tenant Org or Union	Yes

Penalty for Evicting by Force or Intimidation	Actual damages; tenant has the right to stay until the end of the lease; tenant is entitled to receive attorney fees and court costs; if tenant terminates, landlord must return all of the security deposit
Eviction Notice for Nonpayment	3 days to pay or quit
Eviction Notice for Violation	7 days to cure or quit

Kansas

Rent Increase Notice	No statute
Late Fees	No statute
Returned Check Fees	$30
Security Deposit Limits	1 month's rent if unfurnished unit, 1½ months' rent if furnished unit
Security Deposit Interest	No statute
Security Deposit Bank Account	No statute
Inspection Notification	No statute
Deadline for Returning Security Deposit	30 days
Statute of Limitations for Written Contracts	5 years
Small Claims Court Limits	$4,000
Pet Deposits and Additional Fees	Additional pet deposit of up to ½ month's rent allowed
Entry for Maintenance and Repairs	Yes
Entry During Tenant's Extended Absence	Yes
Entry for Showing the Property	Yes
Notice of Entry	Reasonable time
Landlord Termination of Month-to-Month	30 days
Tenant Termination of Month-to-Month	30 days
Lease Change (Other Than Rent Amt) Notice	No statute
Retaliation Time Frame	Not specified
Tenant Exercises Legal Right	No
Tenant Complains to Landlord or Agency	Yes
Tenant Is Involved in Tenant Org or Union	Yes
Penalty for Evicting by Force or Intimidation	Actual damages or 1½ months' rent whichever greater; tenant has the right to stay until the end of the lease

Eviction Notice for Nonpayment	10 days to pay or quit if term of tenancy is more than 3 months, 3 days to pay or quit if term of tenancy is less than 3 months
Eviction Notice for Violation	14 days to cure and then 16 days to vacate

Kentucky

Rent Increase Notice	30 days
Late Fees	No statute
Returned Check Fees	$25
Security Deposit Limits	No statute
Security Deposit Interest	No statute
Security Deposit Bank Account	Security deposits must be held in a separate account; tenant must be told orally or in writing of the location and number of the account
Inspection Notification	No statute
Deadline for Returning Security Deposit	No statute deadline for returning; if the tenant leaves owing the last month's rent and does not request the security deposit back, the landlord may apply the security deposit to the rent owed after 30 days; if the tenant leaves owing no rent and having a refund due, the landlord must send an itemization to the tenant, but if the tenant does not respond to the landlord after 60 days, the landlord may keep the deposit
Statute of Limitations for Written Contracts	15 years
Small Claims Court Limits	$1,500
Pet Deposits and Additional Fees	No statute
Entry for Maintenance and Repairs	Yes
Entry During Tenant's Extended Absence	Yes
Entry for Showing the Property	Yes
Notice of Entry	2 days
Landlord Termination of Month-to-Month	30 days
Tenant Termination of Month-to-Month	30 days
Lease Change (Other Than Rent Amt) Notice	30 days
Retaliation Time Frame	1 year
Tenant Exercises Legal Right	No
Tenant Complains to Landlord or Agency	Yes

Tenant Is Involved in Tenant Org or Union	Yes
Penalty for Evicting by Force or Intimidation	3 months' rent; tenant has the right to stay until the end of the lease; tenant is entitled to receive attorney fees and court costs
Eviction Notice for Nonpayment	7 days to pay or quit
Eviction Notice for Violation	15 days to cure or quit

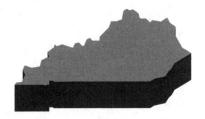

Louisiana

Rent Increase Notice	No statute
Late Fees	No statute
Returned Check Fees	$25 or 5% of the face amount of the check, whichever is greater
Security Deposit Limits	No statute
Security Deposit Interest	No statute
Security Deposit Bank Account	No statute
Inspection Notification	No statute
Deadline for Returning Security Deposit	1 month
Statute of Limitations for Written Contracts	10 years
Small Claims Court Limits	$3,000; no limit if eviction case in Justice of the Peace Courts
Pet Deposits and Additional Fees	No statute
Entry for Maintenance and Repairs	Yes
Entry During Tenant's Extended Absence	No
Entry for Showing the Property	No
Notice of Entry	No statute
Landlord Termination of Month-to-Month	10 days
Tenant Termination of Month-to-Month	10 days
Lease Change (Other Than Rent Amt) Notice	No statute
Retaliation Time Frame	No statute
Tenant Exercises Legal Right	No statute
Tenant Complains to Landlord or Agency	No statute
Tenant Is Involved in Tenant Org or Union	No statute
Penalty for Evicting by Force or Intimidation	No statute
Eviction Notice for Nonpayment	Landlord can serve an unconditional quit notice immediately
Eviction Notice for Violation	Landlord can serve an unconditional quit notice

Maine

Rent Increase Notice	45 days
Late Fees	Late fees cannot be more than 4% of the rent amount due for a 30-day period and must be indicated in writing to the tenant at the start of the tenancy; late fees can be charged when rent is 15 days late
Returned Check Fees	$25
Security Deposit Limits	2 months' rent
Security Deposit Interest	No statute
Security Deposit Bank Account	Security deposit must be held in a separate account; tenant must be told orally or in writing of the location and number of the account if the tenant requests this information
Inspection Notification	No statute
Deadline for Returning Security Deposit	21 days if tenancy at will, 30 days if written lease
Statute of Limitations for Written Contracts	6 years
Small Claims Court Limits	$4,500
Pet Deposits and Additional Fees	No statute
Entry for Maintenance and Repairs	Yes
Entry During Tenant's Extended Absence	No
Entry for Showing the Property	Yes
Notice of Entry	24 hours
Landlord Termination of Month-to-Month	30 days
Tenant Termination of Month-to-Month	30 days
Lease Change (Other Than Rent Amt) Notice	30 days
Retaliation Time Frame	6 months
Tenant Exercises Legal Right	Yes
Tenant Complains to Landlord or Agency	Yes
Tenant Is Involved in Tenant Org or Union	Yes

Penalty for Evicting by Force or Intimidation	Actual damages or $250 whichever greater; tenant is entitled to receive attorney fees and court costs
Eviction Notice for Nonpayment	7 days to pay or quit once the rent is 7 days late
Eviction Notice for Violation	Landlord can serve an unconditional quit notice

Maryland

Rent Increase Notice	1 month
Late Fees	Late fees cannot be more than 5% of the rent amount due
Returned Check Fees	$35
Security Deposit Limits	2 months' rent
Security Deposit Interest	Must pay semi-annually at a rate of 4% if deposit is greater than $50
Security Deposit Bank Account	Security deposits must be held in a separate account in a financial institution located within the state; alternatively, security deposits may be held in secured CDs or securities issued by the state or federal government
Inspection Notification	At the time the tenant pays the security deposit, the landlord must provide written notification to the tenant informing the tenant that he or she has the right to be present at the move-out inspection and what he or she needs to do to exercise that right; at least 15 days before the move-out date the tenant must send, via certified mail to the landlord, notification of the intent to move, the move-out date, and the tenant's forwarding address; upon receipt of this notice the landlord must send, via certified mail to the tenant, notification of the date and time the move-out inspection will occur; the move-out inspection must occur within 5 days before or after the move-out date given by the tenant; if the landlord does not comply with any of these procedures, the landlord forfeits the right to deduct from the security deposit for damages
Deadline for Returning Security Deposit	45 days, 10 days to itemize deductions if tenant utilizes a surety bond
Statute of Limitations for Written Contracts	3 years
Small Claims Court Limits	$5,000
Pet Deposits and Additional Fees	No statute
Entry for Maintenance and Repairs	No statute
Entry During Tenant's Extended Absence	No statute
Entry for Showing the Property	No statute

Notice of Entry	No statute
Landlord Termination of Month-to-Month	1 month; 2 months if property located in Montgomery County (except single-family residences) or in Baltimore City
Tenant Termination of Month-to-Month	1 month; 2 months if property located in Montgomery County (except single-family residences) or in Baltimore City
Lease Change (Other Than Rent Amt) Notice	1 month; 2 months if property located in Montgomery County (except single-family residences) or in Baltimore City
Retaliation Time Frame	Not specified
Tenant Exercises Legal Right	No
Tenant Complains to Landlord or Agency	Yes
Tenant Is Involved in Tenant Org or Union	Yes
Penalty for Evicting by Force or Intimidation	No statute
Eviction Notice for Nonpayment	Landlord can file for eviction immediately and tenant is given 5 days to appear in court and 4 days after ruling in landlord's favor to vacate
Eviction Notice for Violation	30 days to cure or quit; if clear and imminent danger, then 14 days to vacate

Massachusetts

Rent Increase Notice	30 days or time frame between rental payments, whichever longer
Late Fees	Late fees can be charged when rent is 30 days late
Returned Check Fees	$25
Security Deposit Limits	1 month's rent
Security Deposit Interest	Must pay annually and within 30 days of termination at a rate of 5% or the actual rate earned; no interest for last month's rent paid in advance
Security Deposit Bank Account	Security deposits must be held in a separate account in a financial institution located within the state; tenant must be told within 30 days the location and number of the account, and the amount deposited on his or her behalf
Inspection Notification	No statute
Deadline for Returning Security Deposit	30 days
Statute of Limitations for Written Contracts	6 years
Small Claims Court Limits	$2,000
Pet Deposits and Additional Fees	No statute
Entry for Maintenance and Repairs	Yes
Entry During Tenant's Extended Absence	No
Entry for Showing the Property	Yes
Notice of Entry	Not specified
Landlord Termination of Month-to-Month	30 days or time frame between rental payments, whichever longer
Tenant Termination of Month-to-Month	30 days or time frame between rental payments, whichever longer
Lease Change (Other Than Rent Amt) Notice	30 days or time frame between rental payments, whichever longer
Retaliation Time Frame	6 months
Tenant Exercises Legal Right	Yes
Tenant Complains to Landlord or Agency	Yes

Tenant Is Involved in Tenant Org or Union	Yes
Penalty for Evicting by Force or Intimidation	3 times actual damages or 3 months' rent; tenant has the right to stay until the end of the lease; tenant is entitled to receive attorney fees and court costs
Eviction Notice for Nonpayment	14 days to pay or quit; if tenant is a holdover, landlord can file for eviction immediately; lease may give different time frame; if tenant has 1 previous late payment in past 12 months, an unconditional quit notice can be used immediately if landlord served notice to pay or quit every time tenant was late
Eviction Notice for Violation	Landlord can serve an unconditional quit notice

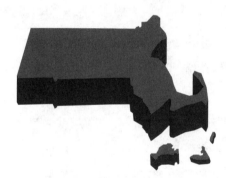

Michigan

Rent Increase Notice	No statute
Late Fees	No statute
Returned Check Fees	$25
Security Deposit Limits	1½ months' rent
Security Deposit Interest	No statute
Security Deposit Bank Account	Security deposits must be held in a separate account located at a financial institution which is regulated by the state or federal government; tenant must be told in writing within 14 days the location of the account and provided with the required disclosure in statute § 554.603 (3); landlord may use security deposits for any reason if a cash or surety bond covering all of the first $50,000 and 25% of all remaining funds is provided to the Secretary of State
Inspection Notification	No statute
Deadline for Returning Security Deposit	30 days
Statute of Limitations for Written Contracts	6 years
Small Claims Court Limits	$3,000
Pet Deposits and Additional Fees	No statute
Entry for Maintenance and Repairs	No statute
Entry During Tenant's Extended Absence	No statute
Entry for Showing the Property	No statute
Notice of Entry	No statute
Landlord Termination of Month-to-Month	Time frame between rental payments
Tenant Termination of Month-to-Month	Time frame between rental payments
Lease Change (Other Than Rent Amt) Notice	No statute
Retaliation Time Frame	90 days
Tenant Exercises Legal Right	Yes
Tenant Complains to Landlord or Agency	Yes

Tenant Is Involved in Tenant Org or Union	Yes
Penalty for Evicting by Force or Intimidation	3 times actual damages or $200 whichever greater; tenant has the right to stay until the end of the lease
Eviction Notice for Nonpayment	7 days to pay or quit
Eviction Notice for Violation	30 days to cure or quit if tenancy at will or lease allows for termination if there is a violation of terms

Minnesota

Rent Increase Notice	No statute
Late Fees	No statute
Returned Check Fees	$30 - Check writer also responsible for all other costs of collection and civil penalties may be imposed for nonpayment
Security Deposit Limits	No statute
Security Deposit Interest	No statute
Security Deposit Bank Account	No statute
Inspection Notification	No statute
Deadline for Returning Security Deposit	3 weeks, 5 days if termination due to condemnation
Statute of Limitations for Written Contracts	6 years
Small Claims Court Limits	$7,500
Pet Deposits and Additional Fees	No statute
Entry for Maintenance and Repairs	Yes
Entry During Tenant's Extended Absence	No
Entry for Showing the Property	Yes
Notice of Entry	Reasonable time
Landlord Termination of Month-to-Month	3 months or time frame between rental payments, whichever shorter
Tenant Termination of Month-to-Month	3 months or time frame between rental payments, whichever shorter
Lease Change (Other Than Rent Amt) Notice	No statute
Retaliation Time Frame	90 days
Tenant Exercises Legal Right	Yes
Tenant Complains to Landlord or Agency	Yes
Tenant Is Involved in Tenant Org or Union	No
Penalty for Evicting by Force or Intimidation	Tenant has the right to stay until the end of the lease; tenant is entitled to receive attorney fees and court costs

| **Eviction Notice for Nonpayment** | 14 days to pay or quit |
| **Eviction Notice for Violation** | Landlord can file for eviction immediately |

Mississippi

Rent Increase Notice	No statute
Late Fees	No statute
Returned Check Fees	$40
Security Deposit Limits	No statute
Security Deposit Interest	No statute
Security Deposit Bank Account	No statute
Inspection Notification	No statute
Deadline for Returning Security Deposit	45 days
Statute of Limitations for Written Contracts	3 years
Small Claims Court Limits	$2,500
Pet Deposits and Additional Fees	No statute
Entry for Maintenance and Repairs	No statute
Entry During Tenant's Extended Absence	No statute
Entry for Showing the Property	No statute
Notice of Entry	No statute
Landlord Termination of Month-to-Month	30 days
Tenant Termination of Month-to-Month	30 days
Lease Change (Other Than Rent Amt) Notice	No statute
Retaliation Time Frame	90 days
Tenant Exercises Legal Right	Not specified
Tenant Complains to Landlord or Agency	Yes
Tenant Is Involved in Tenant Org or Union	No
Penalty for Evicting by Force or Intimidation	No statute
Eviction Notice for Nonpayment	3 days to pay or quit
Eviction Notice for Violation	30 days to cure or quit

Missouri

Rent Increase Notice	No statute
Late Fees	No statute
Returned Check Fees	$25
Security Deposit Limits	2 months' rent
Security Deposit Interest	No statute
Security Deposit Bank Account	No statute
Inspection Notification	No statute
Deadline for Returning Security Deposit	30 days
Statute of Limitations for Written Contracts	10 years
Small Claims Court Limits	$3,000
Pet Deposits and Additional Fees	No statute
Entry for Maintenance and Repairs	No statute
Entry During Tenant's Extended Absence	No statute
Entry for Showing the Property	No statute
Notice of Entry	No statute
Landlord Termination of Month-to-Month	1 month
Tenant Termination of Month-to-Month	1 month
Lease Change (Other Than Rent Amt) Notice	No statute
Retaliation Time Frame	No statute
Tenant Exercises Legal Right	No statute
Tenant Complains to Landlord or Agency	No statute
Tenant Is Involved in Tenant Org or Union	No statute
Penalty for Evicting by Force or Intimidation	No statute
Eviction Notice for Nonpayment	Landlord can serve an unconditional quit notice
Eviction Notice for Violation	14 days to cure or quit; 3 days to cure or quit if unauthorized occupant or pet

Montana

Rent Increase Notice	15 days
Late Fees	No statute
Returned Check Fees	$30
Security Deposit Limits	No statute
Security Deposit Interest	No statute
Security Deposit Bank Account	No statute
Inspection Notification	No statute
Deadline for Returning Security Deposit	10 days if no deductions, 30 days if deductions
Statute of Limitations for Written Contracts	8 years
Small Claims Court Limits	$3,000
Pet Deposits and Additional Fees	Non-refundable fees are not allowed
Entry for Maintenance and Repairs	Yes
Entry During Tenant's Extended Absence	Yes
Entry for Showing the Property	Yes
Notice of Entry	24 hours
Landlord Termination of Month-to-Month	30 days
Tenant Termination of Month-to-Month	30 days
Lease Change (Other Than Rent Amt) Notice	15 days
Retaliation Time Frame	6 months
Tenant Exercises Legal Right	No
Tenant Complains to Landlord or Agency	Yes
Tenant Is Involved in Tenant Org or Union	Yes
Penalty for Evicting by Force or Intimidation	3 times actual damages or 3 months' rent whichever greater; tenant has the right to stay until the end of the lease; tenant is entitled to receive attorney fees and court costs

Eviction Notice for Nonpayment	3 days to pay or quit
Eviction Notice for Violation	14 days to cure or quit; 3 days to cure or quit if unauthorized occupant or pet

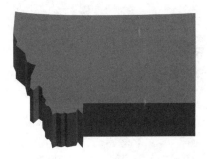

Nebraska

Rent Increase Notice	No statute
Late Fees	No statute
Returned Check Fees	$35
Security Deposit Limits	1 month's rent
Security Deposit Interest	No statute
Security Deposit Bank Account	No statute
Inspection Notification	No statute
Deadline for Returning Security Deposit	14 days
Statute of Limitations for Written Contracts	5 years
Small Claims Court Limits	$2,700
Pet Deposits and Additional Fees	Additional pet deposit of up to ¼ month's rent allowed
Entry for Maintenance and Repairs	Yes
Entry During Tenant's Extended Absence	Yes
Entry for Showing the Property	Yes
Notice of Entry	1 day
Landlord Termination of Month-to-Month	30 days
Tenant Termination of Month-to-Month	30 days
Lease Change (Other Than Rent Amt) Notice	No statute
Retaliation Time Frame	Not specified
Tenant Exercises Legal Right	No
Tenant Complains to Landlord or Agency	Yes
Tenant Is Involved in Tenant Org or Union	Yes
Penalty for Evicting by Force or Intimidation	3 months' rent; tenant has the right to stay until the end of the lease; tenant is entitled to receive attorney fees and court costs
Eviction Notice for Nonpayment	3 days to pay or quit
Eviction Notice for Violation	14 days to cure and then 16 days to vacate

Nevada

Rent Increase Notice	45 days
Late Fees	Late fees must be indicated in the lease agreement
Returned Check Fees	$25
Security Deposit Limits	3 months' rent
Security Deposit Interest	No statute
Security Deposit Bank Account	No statute
Inspection Notification	No statute
Deadline for Returning Security Deposit	30 days
Statute of Limitations for Written Contracts	6 years
Small Claims Court Limits	$5,000
Pet Deposits and Additional Fees	Non-refundable fees are allowed; the purpose of any non-refundable fee must be indicated in the lease agreement
Entry for Maintenance and Repairs	Yes
Entry During Tenant's Extended Absence	No
Entry for Showing the Property	Yes
Notice of Entry	24 hours
Landlord Termination of Month-to-Month	30 days
Tenant Termination of Month-to-Month	30 days
Lease Change (Other Than Rent Amt) Notice	30 days
Retaliation Time Frame	Not specified
Tenant Exercises Legal Right	Yes
Tenant Complains to Landlord or Agency	Yes
Tenant Is Involved in Tenant Org or Union	Yes
Penalty for Evicting by Force or Intimidation	Actual damages or $1,000 whichever greater, or tenant could be awarded both sums; tenant has the right to stay until the end of the lease; if tenant terminates, landlord must return all of the security deposit

| **Eviction Notice for Nonpayment** | 3 days to pay or quit |
| **Eviction Notice for Violation** | 3 days to cure and then 2 days to vacate |

New Hampshire

Rent Increase Notice	30 days
Late Fees	No statute
Returned Check Fees	$25
Security Deposit Limits	$100 or 1 month's rent, whichever greater; no limit if landlord and tenant share facilities
Security Deposit Interest	Only required if deposit held for a year or longer, must pay at termination; tenant can request payment every 3 years if request made within 30 days of tenancy expiration/renewal; rate must be equal to the rate paid on the bank savings account where deposited
Security Deposit Bank Account	No statute
Inspection Notification	No statute
Deadline for Returning Security Deposit	14 days
Statute of Limitations for Written Contracts	3 years
Small Claims Court Limits	$5,000
Pet Deposits and Additional Fees	No statute
Entry for Maintenance and Repairs	Yes
Entry During Tenant's Extended Absence	No
Entry for Showing the Property	Yes
Notice of Entry	Adequate notice for the circumstance
Landlord Termination of Month-to-Month	30 days; termination allowed for cause only
Tenant Termination of Month-to-Month	30 days
Lease Change (Other Than Rent Amt) Notice	30 days
Retaliation Time Frame	6 months
Tenant Exercises Legal Right	Yes
Tenant Complains to Landlord or Agency	Yes
Tenant Is Involved in Tenant Org or Union	Yes

Penalty for Evicting by Force or Intimidation	Actual damages or $1,000 whichever greater; tenant could be awarded 3 times the amount if landlord intentionally broke the law; tenant has the right to stay until the end of the lease; tenant is entitled to receive attorney fees and court costs; every day of violation is treated as a separate violation
Eviction Notice for Nonpayment	7 days to pay or quit; if tenant has 3 previous late payments in past 12 months, an unconditional quit notice can be used immediately if landlord served notice to pay or quit every time tenant was late
Eviction Notice for Violation	Landlord can serve an unconditional quit notice

New Jersey

Rent Increase Notice	1 month
Late Fees	Late fees can be charged when rent is 5 days late
Returned Check Fees	$30
Security Deposit Limits	1½ months' rent
Security Deposit Interest	Must pay annually or credit back to rent owed; landlord with less than 10 units can put deposit in any insured interest-bearing bank account; those with 10 or more must put funds in an insured money market account that matures in a year or less or in any other account that pays interest at a comparable rate to a money market account
Security Deposit Bank Account	Security deposits must be held in a separate interest-bearing account in a federally insured financial institution located within the state; tenant must be told within 30 days, and at the time of annual interest payments, of the location and type of the account, the amount deposited on his or her behalf and the interest rate
Inspection Notification	No statute
Deadline for Returning Security Deposit	30 days, 5 days if termination due to fire, flood, condemnation, evacuation; deadline does not apply if property is owner-occupied and has only 1 or 2 units if the tenant did not provide a written 30 days, notification to the landlord of the desire to invoke the law
Statute of Limitations for Written Contracts	6 years
Small Claims Court Limits	$3,000; $5,000 if security deposit case; certain suits cannot be brought in small claims court
Pet Deposits and Additional Fees	No statute
Entry for Maintenance and Repairs	No statute
Entry During Tenant's Extended Absence	No statute
Entry for Showing the Property	No statute
Notice of Entry	No statute
Landlord Termination of Month-to-Month	1 month; termination allowed for cause only

Tenant Termination of Month-to-Month	1 month
Lease Change (Other Than Rent Amt) Notice	1 month
Retaliation Time Frame	Not specified; termination not retaliation if tenant does not renew lease within 90 days of expiration
Tenant Exercises Legal Right	Yes
Tenant Complains to Landlord or Agency	Yes
Tenant Is Involved in Tenant Org or Union	Yes
Penalty for Evicting by Force or Intimidation	No statute
Eviction Notice for Nonpayment	30 days to pay or quit; if tenant has been habitually late with rent payments, an unconditional quit notice can be used immediately
Eviction Notice for Violation	3 days to cure or quit; lease must specify which violations will result in eviction

New Mexico

Rent Increase Notice	30 days before rent due date
Late Fees	Late fees cannot be more than 10% of the rent amount due per rental period; tenant must be notified of the late fee charged by the end of the next rental period
Returned Check Fees	$30
Security Deposit Limits	1 month's rent if less than 1-year lease, no limit if year or longer lease
Security Deposit Interest	Must pay annually at a rate equal to passbook rate if deposit is more than 1 month's rent and there is a year lease
Security Deposit Bank Account	No statute
Inspection Notification	No statute
Deadline for Returning Security Deposit	30 days
Statute of Limitations for Written Contracts	6 years
Small Claims Court Limits	$10,000
Pet Deposits and Additional Fees	No statute
Entry for Maintenance and Repairs	Yes
Entry During Tenant's Extended Absence	Yes
Entry for Showing the Property	Yes
Notice of Entry	24 hours
Landlord Termination of Month-to-Month	30 days
Tenant Termination of Month-to-Month	30 days
Lease Change (Other Than Rent Amt) Notice	30 days
Retaliation Time Frame	6 months
Tenant Exercises Legal Right	Yes
Tenant Complains to Landlord or Agency	Yes
Tenant Is Involved in Tenant Org or Union	Yes

Penalty for Evicting by Force or Intimidation	Actual damages and 2 months' rent and prorated portion of the rent for every day of violation; tenant has the right to stay until the end of the lease; tenant is entitled to receive attorney fees and court costs
Eviction Notice for Nonpayment	3 days to pay or quit
Eviction Notice for Violation	7 days to cure or quit

New York

Rent Increase Notice	No statute
Late Fees	No statute
Returned Check Fees	$20 - Check writer is also responsible for all other costs of collection
Security Deposit Limits	No limit unless covered by local rent control regulations
Security Deposit Interest	Must pay at prevailing rate if unit is covered under rent control or stabilization requirements or if building has 6 or more units; landlord can keep 1% admin fee a year
Security Deposit Bank Account	Security deposits are not required to be held in a financial institution unless the property has 6 or more units, in which case the financial institution must be located in the state; if security deposits are held in a financial institution, they must be held in a separate account and the tenant must be told of the location of the account and the amount deposited on his or her behalf
Inspection Notification	No statute
Deadline for Returning Security Deposit	Reasonable time
Statute of Limitations for Written Contracts	6 years
Small Claims Court Limits	$5,000; $3,000 in town and village courts
Pet Deposits and Additional Fees	No statute
Entry for Maintenance and Repairs	No statute
Entry During Tenant's Extended Absence	No statute
Entry for Showing the Property	No statute
Notice of Entry	No statute
Landlord Termination of Month-to-Month	1 month
Tenant Termination of Month-to-Month	1 month
Lease Change (Other Than Rent Amt) Notice	No statute
Retaliation Time Frame	6 months
Tenant Exercises Legal Right	Yes

Tenant Complains to Landlord or Agency	Yes
Tenant Is Involved in Tenant Org or Union	Yes
Penalty for Evicting by Force or Intimidation	3 times actual damages
Eviction Notice for Nonpayment	3 days to pay or quit
Eviction Notice for Violation	No statute for property not under rent control regulations; 10 days to cure or quit if property is under rent control unless control board sets different time frame

North Carolina

Rent Increase Notice	No statute
Late Fees	Late fees cannot be more than 5% of the rent amount due per rental period; tenant must be notified of the late fee charged by the end of the next rental period
Returned Check Fees	$25
Security Deposit Limits	1½ months' rent if month-to-month tenancy, 2 months' rent if lease term longer than 2 months
Security Deposit Interest	No statute
Security Deposit Bank Account	Security deposits must be held in a separate trust account in a federally insured financial institution located within the state; tenant must be told within 30 days the location of the account; a security bond, issued from an insurance company licensed in the state, covering all security deposits may be obtained in lieu of maintaining a separate account
Inspection Notification	No statute
Deadline for Returning Security Deposit	30 days
Statute of Limitations for Written Contracts	3 years
Small Claims Court Limits	$5,000
Pet Deposits and Additional Fees	Reasonable non-refundable pet deposit allowed
Entry for Maintenance and Repairs	No statute
Entry During Tenant's Extended Absence	No statute
Entry for Showing the Property	No statute
Notice of Entry	No statute
Landlord Termination of Month-to-Month	7 days
Tenant Termination of Month-to-Month	7 days
Lease Change (Other Than Rent Amt) Notice	No statute
Retaliation Time Frame	12 months
Tenant Exercises Legal Right	Yes

Tenant Complains to Landlord or Agency	Yes
Tenant Is Involved in Tenant Org or Union	Yes
Penalty for Evicting by Force or Intimidation	Actual damages; tenant has the right to stay until the end of the lease
Eviction Notice for Nonpayment	10 days to pay or quit
Eviction Notice for Violation	Landlord can serve an unconditional quit notice if lease allows for termination for specific violation

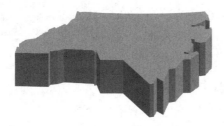

North Dakota

Rent Increase Notice	30 days
Late Fees	No statute
Returned Check Fees	$30
Security Deposit Limits	1 month's rent
Security Deposit Interest	Must pay interest if tenancy is at least 9 months; deposit must be put in an insured interest-bearing savings or checking acct
Security Deposit Bank Account	Security deposits must be held in a separate interest-bearing account in a federally insured financial institution
Inspection Notification	No statute
Deadline for Returning Security Deposit	30 days
Statute of Limitations for Written Contracts	6 years
Small Claims Court Limits	$5,000
Pet Deposits and Additional Fees	If there is a pet, the security deposit may be increased to a total of $2,500 or 2 months' rent, whichever is greater
Entry for Maintenance and Repairs	Yes
Entry During Tenant's Extended Absence	No
Entry for Showing the Property	Yes
Notice of Entry	Reasonable time
Landlord Termination of Month-to-Month	30 days
Tenant Termination of Month-to-Month	30 days; if landlord has notified tenant of a change in lease terms, then 25 days from date of notification
Lease Change (Other Than Rent Amt) Notice	30 days; tenant allowed to terminate tenancy within 25 days of notice
Retaliation Time Frame	No statute
Tenant Exercises Legal Right	No statute
Tenant Complains to Landlord or Agency	No statute
Tenant Is Involved in Tenant Org or Union	No statute

Penalty for Evicting by Force or Intimidation	3 times actual damages
Eviction Notice for Nonpayment	Landlord can serve an unconditional quit notice once rent is 3 days late
Eviction Notice for Violation	Landlord can serve an unconditional quit notice if material term of lease violated

Ohio

Rent Increase Notice	No statute
Late Fees	No statute
Returned Check Fees	$30 or 10% of the face amount of the check, whichever is greater
Security Deposit Limits	No statute
Security Deposit Interest	Must pay annually and at termination, at a rate of 5% if the tenancy is 6 months or more and the deposit is greater than $50 or 1 month's rent - whichever is greater - the interest only accrues on the excess of the $50 or 1-month rent amount
Security Deposit Bank Account	No statute
Inspection Notification	No statute
Deadline for Returning Security Deposit	30 days
Statute of Limitations for Written Contracts	15 years
Small Claims Court Limits	$3,000
Pet Deposits and Additional Fees	No statute
Entry for Maintenance and Repairs	Yes
Entry During Tenant's Extended Absence	No
Entry for Showing the Property	Yes
Notice of Entry	24 hours
Landlord Termination of Month-to-Month	30 days
Tenant Termination of Month-to-Month	30 days
Lease Change (Other Than Rent Amt) Notice	No statute
Retaliation Time Frame	Not specified
Tenant Exercises Legal Right	No
Tenant Complains to Landlord or Agency	Yes
Tenant Is Involved in Tenant Org or Union	Yes
Penalty for Evicting by Force or Intimidation	Actual damages; tenant is entitled to receive attorney fees and court costs

| **Eviction Notice for Nonpayment** | Landlord can serve an unconditional quit notice |
| **Eviction Notice for Violation** | Landlord can serve an unconditional quit notice if material term of lease violated |

Oklahoma

Rent Increase Notice	No statute
Late Fees	No statute
Returned Check Fees	$25
Security Deposit Limits	No statute
Security Deposit Interest	No statute
Security Deposit Bank Account	Security deposits must be held in a separate account
Inspection Notification	No statute
Deadline for Returning Security Deposit	30 days
Statute of Limitations for Written Contracts	5 years
Small Claims Court Limits	$6,000
Pet Deposits and Additional Fees	No statute
Entry for Maintenance and Repairs	Yes
Entry During Tenant's Extended Absence	Yes
Entry for Showing the Property	Yes
Notice of Entry	1 day
Landlord Termination of Month-to-Month	30 days
Tenant Termination of Month-to-Month	30 days
Lease Change (Other Than Rent Amt) Notice	No statute
Retaliation Time Frame	No statute
Tenant Exercises Legal Right	No statute
Tenant Complains to Landlord or Agency	No statute
Tenant Is Involved in Tenant Org or Union	No statute
Penalty for Evicting by Force or Intimidation	2 times actual damages or 2 times average monthly rent whichever greater; tenant has the right to stay until the end of the lease
Eviction Notice for Nonpayment	5 days to pay or quit
Eviction Notice for Violation	10 days to cure and then 5 days to vacate

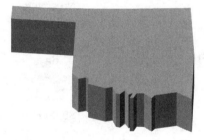

Oregon

Rent Increase Notice	No statute
Late Fees	Late fees cannot be more than a reasonable amount charged by others in the same market if a flat fee is utilized; if a daily charge is utilized, it cannot be more than 6% of the reasonable flat fee with a maximum of 5% of the rent amount due per rental period allowed; late fees can be charged when rent is 4 days late and must be indicated in the lease agreement
Returned Check Fees	$25
Security Deposit Limits	No statute
Security Deposit Interest	No statute
Security Deposit Bank Account	No statute
Inspection Notification	No statute
Deadline for Returning Security Deposit	31 days
Statute of Limitations for Written Contracts	6 years
Small Claims Court Limits	$5,000
Pet Deposits and Additional Fees	Non-refundable fees are allowed for reasonably anticipated landlord expenses (including those caused by a tenant not in compliance if indicated in the lease agreement) as long as the fees are not excessive
Entry for Maintenance and Repairs	Yes
Entry During Tenant's Extended Absence	Yes
Entry for Showing the Property	Yes
Notice of Entry	24 hours
Landlord Termination of Month-to-Month	30 days
Tenant Termination of Month-to-Month	30 days
Lease Change (Other Than Rent Amt) Notice	No statute
Retaliation Time Frame	Not specified

Tenant Exercises Legal Right	No
Tenant Complains to Landlord or Agency	Yes
Tenant Is Involved in Tenant Org or Union	Yes
Penalty for Evicting by Force or Intimidation	2 times actual damages or 2 months' rent whichever greater; tenant has the right to stay until the end of the lease
Eviction Notice for Nonpayment	72 hours to pay or quit once the rent is 8 days late or 144 hours to pay or quit once the rent is 5 days late; landlord can choose
Eviction Notice for Violation	14 days to cure and then 16 days to vacate; 10 days to cure or quit if unauthorized pet

Pennsylvania

Rent Increase Notice	No statute
Late Fees	No statute
Returned Check Fees	$30
Security Deposit Limits	2 months' rent first year of tenancy, 1 month's rent if lease term longer than 2 months
Security Deposit Interest	Must pay if tenancy longer than 2 years; interest accrues from start of 25th month of tenancy and must be paid annually after that point; landlord can deduct 1% fee
Security Deposit Bank Account	Security deposits must be held in a separate account located at a financial institution which is regulated by the state or federal government if over $100; tenant must be told the location of the account and the amount deposited on his or her behalf; a security bond, issued from a bonding company licensed in the state, covering all security deposits may be obtained in lieu of maintaining a separate account
Inspection Notification	No statute
Deadline for Returning Security Deposit	30 days
Statute of Limitations for Written Contracts	6 years
Small Claims Court Limits	$8,000; $10,000 in Philadelphia courts
Pet Deposits and Additional Fees	No statute
Entry for Maintenance and Repairs	No statute
Entry During Tenant's Extended Absence	No statute
Entry for Showing the Property	No statute
Notice of Entry	No statute
Landlord Termination of Month-to-Month	No statute
Tenant Termination of Month-to-Month	No statute
Lease Change (Other Than Rent Amt) Notice	No statute
Retaliation Time Frame	6 months
Tenant Exercises Legal Right	Yes

Tenant Complains to Landlord or Agency	No
Tenant Is Involved in Tenant Org or Union	Yes
Penalty for Evicting by Force or Intimidation	Judge determines
Eviction Notice for Nonpayment	10 days to pay or quit
Eviction Notice for Violation	Landlord can serve an unconditional quit notice

Rhode Island

Rent Increase Notice	30 days
Late Fees	No statute
Returned Check Fees	$25
Security Deposit Limits	1 month's rent
Security Deposit Interest	No statute
Security Deposit Bank Account	No statute
Inspection Notification	No statute
Deadline for Returning Security Deposit	20 days
Statute of Limitations for Written Contracts	15 years
Small Claims Court Limits	$2,500
Pet Deposits and Additional Fees	No statute
Entry for Maintenance and Repairs	Yes
Entry During Tenant's Extended Absence	Yes
Entry for Showing the Property	Yes
Notice of Entry	2 days
Landlord Termination of Month-to-Month	30 days
Tenant Termination of Month-to-Month	30 days
Lease Change (Other Than Rent Amt) Notice	30 days
Retaliation Time Frame	Not specified
Tenant Exercises Legal Right	Yes
Tenant Complains to Landlord or Agency	Yes
Tenant Is Involved in Tenant Org or Union	No
Penalty for Evicting by Force or Intimidation	3 times actual damages or 3 months' rent whichever greater; tenant has the right to stay until the end of the lease; tenant is entitled to receive attorney fees and court costs
Eviction Notice for Nonpayment	5 days to pay or quit once rent is 15 days late

Eviction Notice for Violation

20 days to cure or quit if material term of lease violated

South Carolina

Rent Increase Notice	No statute
Late Fees	No statute
Returned Check Fees	$30
Security Deposit Limits	No statute
Security Deposit Interest	No statute
Security Deposit Bank Account	No statute
Inspection Notification	No statute
Deadline for Returning Security Deposit	30 days
Statute of Limitations for Written Contracts	10 years
Small Claims Court Limits	$7,500
Pet Deposits and Additional Fees	No statute
Entry for Maintenance and Repairs	Yes
Entry During Tenant's Extended Absence	Yes
Entry for Showing the Property	Yes
Notice of Entry	24 hours
Landlord Termination of Month-to-Month	30 days
Tenant Termination of Month-to-Month	30 days
Lease Change (Other Than Rent Amt) Notice	No statute
Retaliation Time Frame	Not specified
Tenant Exercises Legal Right	No
Tenant Complains to Landlord or Agency	Yes
Tenant Is Involved in Tenant Org or Union	No
Penalty for Evicting by Force or Intimidation	2 times actual damages or 3 months' rent whichever greater; tenant has the right to stay until the end of the lease; tenant is entitled to receive attorney fees and court costs

Eviction Notice for Nonpayment	5 days to pay or quit; if lease does not conspicuously indicate that landlord may file for eviction once rent is 5 days late, landlord must give 5 days notice that eviction proceedings will be started after 5 days pay or quit notice has been given; if tenant has 1 previous late payment during their tenancy, an unconditional quit notice can be used immediately
Eviction Notice for Violation	14 days to cure or quit

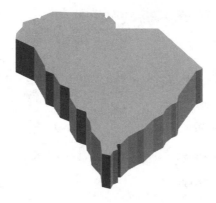

South Dakota

Rent Increase Notice	1 month
Late Fees	No statute
Returned Check Fees	$40
Security Deposit Limits	1 month's rent
Security Deposit Interest	No statute
Security Deposit Bank Account	No statute
Inspection Notification	No statute
Deadline for Returning Security Deposit	2 weeks to return deposit and/or provide explanation for any withholding; 45 days to provide an itemized accounting of all deductions made to the security deposit if the tenant requests one
Statute of Limitations for Written Contracts	6 years
Small Claims Court Limits	$8,000
Pet Deposits and Additional Fees	A security deposit exceeding the limit is allowed if special conditions pose a danger to the maintenance of the property and all parties agree
Entry for Maintenance and Repairs	No statute
Entry During Tenant's Extended Absence	No statute
Entry for Showing the Property	No statute
Notice of Entry	No statute
Landlord Termination of Month-to-Month	1 month
Tenant Termination of Month-to-Month	1 month; if landlord has notified tenant of a change in lease terms, then 15 days from date of notification
Lease Change (Other Than Rent Amt) Notice	1 month; tenant allowed to terminate tenancy within 15 days of notice
Retaliation Time Frame	180 days
Tenant Exercises Legal Right	No
Tenant Complains to Landlord or Agency	Yes

Tenant Is Involved in Tenant Org or Union	Yes
Penalty for Evicting by Force or Intimidation	2 months' rent; tenant has the right to stay until the end of the lease; if tenant terminates, landlord must return all of the security deposit
Eviction Notice for Nonpayment	3 days to pay or quit and landlord can serve an unconditional quit notice
Eviction Notice for Violation	Landlord can file for eviction immediately if lease allows for termination for specific violation

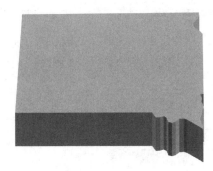

Tennessee

Rent Increase Notice	No statute
Late Fees	Late fees can be charged when rent is 5 days late and cannot be more than 10% of the late amount; however, if the fifth day is a weekend or holiday and the tenant pays the rent amount due on the following business day, a late fee cannot be charged
Returned Check Fees	$30 - Check writer is also responsible for all other costs of collection
Security Deposit Limits	No statute
Security Deposit Interest	No statute
Security Deposit Bank Account	Security deposits must be held in a separate account; tenant must be told orally or in writing the location of the account
Inspection Notification	No statute
Deadline for Returning Security Deposit	No statute, 10 days to itemize deductions
Statute of Limitations for Written Contracts	6 years
Small Claims Court Limits	$15,000; $25,000 if county population over 700,000; no limit if eviction case
Pet Deposits and Additional Fees	No statute
Entry for Maintenance and Repairs	Yes
Entry During Tenant's Extended Absence	Yes
Entry for Showing the Property	Yes
Notice of Entry	Not specified
Landlord Termination of Month-to-Month	30 days
Tenant Termination of Month-to-Month	30 days
Lease Change (Other Than Rent Amt) Notice	No statute
Retaliation Time Frame	Not specified
Tenant Exercises Legal Right	Yes
Tenant Complains to Landlord or Agency	Yes
Tenant Is Involved in Tenant Org or Union	No

Penalty for Evicting by Force or Intimidation	Actual damages and punitive damages; tenant has the right to stay until the end of the lease; tenant is entitled to receive attorney fees and court costs; if tenant terminates, landlord must return all of the security deposit
Eviction Notice for Nonpayment	14 days to pay or quit; then tenant is given 16 days to vacate
Eviction Notice for Violation	14 days to cure and then 16 days to vacate

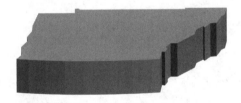

Texas

Rent Increase Notice	No statute
Late Fees	Late fees must be reasonable and close to the landlord's actual losses; late fees must be indicated in the lease agreement and can be charged when the rent is 2 days late; late fees can include an initial fee as well as a daily fee for each day the rent is late thereafter
Returned Check Fees	$30 - Other costs of collection may be charged
Security Deposit Limits	No statute
Security Deposit Interest	No statute
Security Deposit Bank Account	No statute
Inspection Notification	No statute
Deadline for Returning Security Deposit	30 days
Statute of Limitations for Written Contracts	4 years
Small Claims Court Limits	$10,000
Pet Deposits and Additional Fees	No statute
Entry for Maintenance and Repairs	No statute
Entry During Tenant's Extended Absence	No statute
Entry for Showing the Property	No statute
Notice of Entry	Not specified
Landlord Termination of Month-to-Month	1 month
Tenant Termination of Month-to-Month	1 month
Lease Change (Other Than Rent Amt) Notice	No statute
Retaliation Time Frame	6 months
Tenant Exercises Legal Right	Yes
Tenant Complains to Landlord or Agency	Yes
Tenant Is Involved in Tenant Org or Union	No

Penalty for Evicting by Force or Intimidation	Actual damages and 1 month's rent and $1,000; tenant has the right to stay until the end of the lease; tenant is entitled to receive attorney fees and court costs
Eviction Notice for Nonpayment	3 days to move; lease may give a different time frame
Eviction Notice for Violation	Landlord can serve an unconditional quit notice

Utah

Rent Increase Notice	No statute
Late Fees	No statute
Returned Check Fees	$20 - Check writer is responsible for all other costs of collection
Security Deposit Limits	No statute
Security Deposit Interest	No statute
Security Deposit Bank Account	No statute
Inspection Notification	No statute
Deadline for Returning Security Deposit	30 days or within 15 days of receipt of forwarding address from tenant, whichever is later
Statute of Limitations for Written Contracts	6 years
Small Claims Court Limits	$7,500
Pet Deposits and Additional Fees	Non-refundable fees are allowed; it is customary, though not specifically addressed in statutes, that the landlord must disclose in writing if any part of the security deposit is non-refundable when a written lease agreement is used
Entry for Maintenance and Repairs	Yes
Entry During Tenant's Extended Absence	No
Entry for Showing the Property	No
Notice of Entry	Not specified
Landlord Termination of Month-to-Month	15 days
Tenant Termination of Month-to-Month	No statute
Lease Change (Other Than Rent Amt) Notice	No statute
Retaliation Time Frame	Not specified
Tenant Exercises Legal Right	No
Tenant Complains to Landlord or Agency	Yes
Tenant Is Involved in Tenant Org or Union	No

Penalty for Evicting by Force or Intimidation	No statute
Eviction Notice for Nonpayment	3 days to move; lease may give a different time frame
Eviction Notice for Violation	3 days to cure or quit

Vermont

Rent Increase Notice	30 days
Late Fees	No statute
Returned Check Fees	$25
Security Deposit Limits	No statute
Security Deposit Interest	No statute
Security Deposit Bank Account	No statute
Inspection Notification	No statute
Deadline for Returning Security Deposit	14 days
Statute of Limitations for Written Contracts	6 years
Small Claims Court Limits	$5,000
Pet Deposits and Additional Fees	No statute
Entry for Maintenance and Repairs	Yes
Entry During Tenant's Extended Absence	No
Entry for Showing the Property	Yes
Notice of Entry	24 hours
Landlord Termination of Month-to-Month	30 days
Tenant Termination of Month-to-Month	1 rental period
Lease Change (Other Than Rent Amt) Notice	30 days
Retaliation Time Frame	Not specified
Tenant Exercises Legal Right	No
Tenant Complains to Landlord or Agency	Yes
Tenant Is Involved in Tenant Org or Union	Yes
Penalty for Evicting by Force or Intimidation	Tenant has the right to stay until the end of the lease; tenant is entitled to receive attorney fees and court costs

Eviction Notice for Nonpayment	14 days to pay or quit; if tenant has 3 previous late payments in past 12 months, an unconditional quit notice can be used immediately if landlord served notice to pay or quit every time tenant was late
Eviction Notice for Violation	Landlord can serve an unconditional quit notice

Virginia

Rent Increase Notice	No statute
Late Fees	No statute
Returned Check Fees	$35
Security Deposit Limits	2 months' rent
Security Deposit Interest	Must pay if deposit is held for more than 13 months for continued tenancy in same unit; interest accrues from start of lease and must be paid at termination; must be at rate of 1% below FED discount rate as of Jan. 1 of each year
Security Deposit Bank Account	No statute
Inspection Notification	At the time the landlord requests the tenant to vacate the property, or within 5 days of the landlord's receipt of notification from the tenant of his or her intent to vacate, the landlord must make a reasonable effort to notify the tenant of the right to be present at the move-out inspection; if the tenant wishes to be at the move-out inspection, he or she must notify the landlord in writing and the landlord must then notify the tenant of the date and time of the inspection; the move-out inspection must occur within 72 hours of the landlord's repossession of the property
Deadline for Returning Security Deposit	45 days
Statute of Limitations for Written Contracts	5 years
Small Claims Court Limits	$5,000
Pet Deposits and Additional Fees	No statute
Entry for Maintenance and Repairs	Yes
Entry During Tenant's Extended Absence	Yes
Entry for Showing the Property	Yes
Notice of Entry	24 hours
Landlord Termination of Month-to-Month	30 days if there is a written lease and tenant has resided at the property for 2 years or less, 60 days if longer; 60 days if there is no lease and tenant has resided at the property for 2 years or less, 90 days if longer

Tenant Termination of Month-to-Month	30 days
Lease Change (Other Than Rent Amt) Notice	No statute
Retaliation Time Frame	Not specified
Tenant Exercises Legal Right	Yes
Tenant Complains to Landlord or Agency	Yes
Tenant Is Involved in Tenant Org or Union	Yes
Penalty for Evicting by Force or Intimidation	Actual damages; tenant has the right to stay until the end of the lease; tenant is entitled to receive attorney fees and court costs
Eviction Notice for Nonpayment	5 days to pay or quit; if tenant has 1 previous late payment in past 12 months, an unconditional quit notice can be used immediately if landlord served notice to pay or quit every time tenant was late
Eviction Notice for Violation	21 days to cure and then 9 to vacate

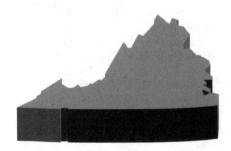

Washington

Rent Increase Notice	30 days
Late Fees	No statute
Returned Check Fees	$30 - This amount is assessed as a handling fee for returned checks; check writer is also responsible for all other costs of collection
Security Deposit Limits	No statute
Security Deposit Interest	No statute
Security Deposit Bank Account	Security deposits must be held in a separate account; tenant must be provided with a receipt for the security deposit which indicates the name and location of the financial institution where it will be held
Inspection Notification	No statute
Deadline for Returning Security Deposit	14 days
Statute of Limitations for Written Contracts	6 years
Small Claims Court Limits	$4,000
Pet Deposits and Additional Fees	Non-refundable fees are allowed; any non-refundable fees must be clearly indicated in the lease agreement as non-refundable
Entry for Maintenance and Repairs	No
Entry During Tenant's Extended Absence	No
Entry for Showing the Property	No
Notice of Entry	2 days
Landlord Termination of Month-to-Month	20 days
Tenant Termination of Month-to-Month	20 days
Lease Change (Other Than Rent Amt) Notice	30 days
Retaliation Time Frame	90 days
Tenant Exercises Legal Right	Yes
Tenant Complains to Landlord or Agency	Yes
Tenant Is Involved in Tenant Org or Union	No

Penalty for Evicting by Force or Intimidation	Actual damages and $100 for each day of no utility service if service was disconnected; tenant has the right to stay until the end of the lease; tenant is entitled to receive attorney fees and court costs
Eviction Notice for Nonpayment	3 days to pay or quit
Eviction Notice for Violation	10 days to cure or quit

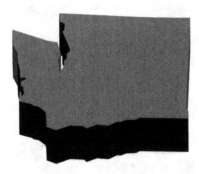

West Virginia

Rent Increase Notice	No statute
Late Fees	No statute
Returned Check Fees	$25
Security Deposit Limits	No statute
Security Deposit Interest	No statute
Security Deposit Bank Account	No statute
Inspection Notification	No statute
Deadline for Returning Security Deposit	No statute
Statute of Limitations for Written Contracts	10 years
Small Claims Court Limits	$5,000
Pet Deposits and Additional Fees	No statute
Entry for Maintenance and Repairs	No statute
Entry During Tenant's Extended Absence	No statute
Entry for Showing the Property	No statute
Notice of Entry	No statute
Landlord Termination of Month-to-Month	1 month
Tenant Termination of Month-to-Month	1 month
Lease Change (Other Than Rent Amt) Notice	No statute
Retaliation Time Frame	Not specified
Tenant Exercises Legal Right	Yes
Tenant Complains to Landlord or Agency	Yes
Tenant Is Involved in Tenant Org or Union	No
Penalty for Evicting by Force or Intimidation	No statute
Eviction Notice for Nonpayment	Landlord can file for eviction immediately
Eviction Notice for Violation	Landlord can file for eviction immediately

Wisconsin

Rent Increase Notice	No statute
Late Fees	No statute
Returned Check Fees	$20 - Check writer is also responsible for all other costs of collection
Security Deposit Limits	No statute
Security Deposit Interest	No statute
Security Deposit Bank Account	No statute
Inspection Notification	No statute
Deadline for Returning Security Deposit	21 days
Statute of Limitations for Written Contracts	6 years
Small Claims Court Limits	$5,000; no limit if eviction case
Pet Deposits and Additional Fees	No statute
Entry for Maintenance and Repairs	Yes
Entry During Tenant's Extended Absence	No
Entry for Showing the Property	Yes
Notice of Entry	Advanced notice, unless lease provides time frame
Landlord Termination of Month-to-Month	28 days
Tenant Termination of Month-to-Month	28 days
Lease Change (Other Than Rent Amt) Notice	No statute
Retaliation Time Frame	Not specified
Tenant Exercises Legal Right	Yes
Tenant Complains to Landlord or Agency	Yes
Tenant Is Involved in Tenant Org or Union	No
Penalty for Evicting by Force or Intimidation	No statute

| Eviction Notice for Nonpayment | 5 days to pay or quit if tenancy is less than 1 year or year-to-year; 5 days to pay or quit and landlord can serve an unconditional quit notice if 14 days' notice given to tenant if tenancy is month-to-month; 30 days to pay or quit if tenancy is longer than 1 year; if tenant has 1 previous late payment in past 12 months, an unconditional quit notice can be used immediately if landlord served notice to pay or quit every time tenant was late |
| Eviction Notice for Violation | Landlord can serve an unconditional quit notice |

Wyoming

Rent Increase Notice	No statute
Late Fees	No statute
Returned Check Fees	$25 - Check writer is also responsible for all other costs of collection
Security Deposit Limits	No statute
Security Deposit Interest	No statute
Security Deposit Bank Account	No statute
Inspection Notification	No statute
Deadline for Returning Security Deposit	30 days or within 15 days of receipt of forwarding address from tenant, whichever is later; 60 days if unit has damage
Statute of Limitations for Written Contracts	10 years
Small Claims Court Limits	$7,000
Pet Deposits and Additional Fees	Non-refundable fees are allowed; the landlord must disclose in writing before accepting the deposit, if any part of the security deposit is non-refundable, and the lease agreement must indicate this as well
Entry for Maintenance and Repairs	No statute
Entry During Tenant's Extended Absence	No statute
Entry for Showing the Property	No statute
Notice of Entry	No statute
Landlord Termination of Month-to-Month	No statute
Tenant Termination of Month-to-Month	No statute
Lease Change (Other Than Rent Amt) Notice	No statute
Retaliation Time Frame	No statute
Tenant Exercises Legal Right	No statute
Tenant Complains to Landlord or Agency	No statute
Tenant Is Involved in Tenant Org or Union	No statute

Penalty for Evicting by Force or Intimidation	No statute
Eviction Notice for Nonpayment	Landlord can file for eviction once rent is 3 days late and tenant is given 3 days' notice; landlord can serve an unconditional quit notice
Eviction Notice for Violation	Landlord can serve an unconditional quit notice

So, there you have it... All 50 states' most common landlord-tenant laws (plus D.C.'s). Ideally, you've found the information you sought to discover. While this *American Landlord Law* volume can't possibly address every individual legal situation, we hope it has given you the overview you need and has provided sufficient additional resources, which can steer you to the help you need...

If you ever need further advice or assistance, you can *always* **check out the official website for this entire book series** at **www.EUNTK.com** – where you'll find discussion forums, more laws and statutes, other related subjects within the series and a whole lot more... Remember, **this site is free** – and you can't beat that *for the absolute easiest way there is to learn* "Everything U Need to Know..."

For additional information about **property management** (including **tenant screening, advertising vacancies** and much more**),** please reference the *American Landlord* volume available at book retailers nationwide. If you're a tenant, then please reference the *American Tenant* volume to learn more about your rights as a renter.

We wish you the best of luck and hope **this volume has helped empower you with** *the knowledge to succeed as an* **American landlord** (or an **American tenant**).

A Radon Guide for Tenants:
U.S. Environmental Protection Agency

A Radon Guide for Tenants

"A Radon Guide for Tenants"

Environmental Law Institute (ELI) and
the U.S. Environmental Protection Agency
EPA #402-K-98-004, 1996

Contents

- Purpose Of This Guide
- What Is Radon?
- Does Your Home Have High Radon Levels?
- Can You Test For Radon Yourself?
- What Can You Do If Your Home Has High Radon Levels?
- What Can Building Owners Do About Radon Problems?
- Are Funds Available To Reduce High Radon Levels In Rental Housing?
- Renter's Radon Checklist
- Additional Resources
- Appendix: Radon Testing

Disclaimer

The Environmental Law Institute (ELI) is a not-for-profit research, training and education organization. ELI does not litigate or lobby. It works to develop and apply environmental and public health strategies that make laws more effective.

This project has been funded wholly or in part by the U.S. Environmental Protection Agency under assistance agreement to the Environmental Law Institute. It has been subjected to the Agency's review. Mention of trade names or commercial products does not constitute endorsement or recommendation for use.

Editor's Note: *This on-line version of the printed document reflects minor changes in terminology and references to EPA's Indoor Air Quality Information Clearinghouse (IAQ INFO).*

Purpose of This Guide

This guide is for people who rent their apartments or houses. The guide explains what radon is, and how to find out if there is a radon problem in your home. The guide also talks about what you can do if there are high radon levels in your home.

State radon agencies and other organizations may be able to give you additional information or assistance. Some of those offices have other materials that may help you learn more about radon. For example, the United States Environmental Protection Agency (EPA) has developed several booklets, including:

- A Citizen's Guide to Radon;
- Consumer's Guide to Radon Reduction; and
- Home Buyer's and Seller's Guide to Radon.

You can get these and other publications from EPA by calling the National Radon Hotline at 1-800-SOS-RADON [1-800-767-7236]. The Citizen's Guide to Radon is also available in Spanish [El Radón] (call 1-800-SALUD12 or your State Radon Office for a copy).

Did You Know That . . .

- Research shows that radon causes between 7,000 and 30,000 lung cancer deaths each year in the United States.
- Over one-third of all housing units in this country are rental units. Most of these are either single-family houses or apartments located below the third floor of a building.
- People living in rented houses and apartment buildings can find out whether there are high levels of radon gas in their homes. Building owners can fix radon problems by having repairs made to the building.

What is Radon?

Radon is a radioactive gas that is found in soil and rock in all parts of the United States. It is formed by the decay of uranium, which is a natural process. Radon gas is invisible, and it has no odor or taste.

What Types of Buildings Contain Radon?

- Radon may be found in all types of homes and buildings in the United States. If there is radon gas in the ground, it can seep into a building.
- Radon typically moves up from the ground into a home through drains, cracks or other holes in the foundation. Radon then can be trapped inside the home.

How Does Radon Affect Health?

- Studies show that radon is the second leading cause of lung cancer, behind cigarette smoking.
- The higher the radon level indoors, the greater the amount you breathe. Radon gas decays into radioactive particles that can get trapped in your lungs when you breathe. As they break down, these particles release small bursts of energy. This can damage lung tissue.
- Inhaling indoor air containing radon over a period of many years can increase your risk of getting lung cancer. Your chance of getting lung cancer from radon depends on how much radon is in your home and how much time you spend in your home. If you are a smoker or a former smoker, the risk of getting lung cancer from radon is even greater.

Does Your Home Have High Radon Levels?

You cannot see, smell or taste radon. Therefore, **testing** is the only way to determine the radon level in your home.

Has Your Building Been Tested Already?

- If the building you live in has been tested properly for radon, then you probably do not need to test for radon yourself. Before or after you move in to your home (whether you live in a house or apartment building), you can ask the owner if the building has been tested for radon. If the owner tells you that radon testing has been done already, you can ask for a copy of the test results. If you have questions about those results, you can call your state radon office for help, or call the National Radon Helpline at 1-800-557-2366.
- If you do not know whether your building has been tested properly for radon, you can test for radon yourself or ask the owner to test.

> **EPA Recommends Testing All Homes Below the Third Floor**
>
> Because most indoor radon comes from naturally occurring radon in the soil, high indoor levels are more likely to exist below the third floor. This is why EPA recommends testing all homes below the third floor.
>
> In some cases, high radon levels have been found at or above the third floor, due to radon movement through elevators or other air shafts in the building. If your apartment is at or above the third floor and you are concerned about this possibility, you could also decide to test for radon.

Can You Test for Radon Yourself?

- You can test for radon yourself. You can also hire a professional to test your home for radon.
- Testing for radon is easy to do, and takes very little time.
- To test for radon yourself, you must first get a radon test device. You can buy do-it-yourself radon test kits in hardware stores and other similar stores. Some laboratories provide kits through mail order. Make sure you get one from a "qualified" radon service professional or your state's requirements - the test kit will usually say so on the package.
- The price of a radon test kit starts at about ten dollars ($10.00). The price generally includes the cost of having a laboratory analyze the test. More expensive types of radon tests are also available; some of these are do-it-yourself kits, and some are used mainly by professional radon testers.
- If you cannot find a radon test kit in your community, you can order a low cost test kit from the National Radon Hotline by calling 1-800-SOS-RADON [1-800-767-7236].

Different Ways to Test For Radon

The quickest way to test for radon is with a short-term test. Short-term tests remain in your home for 2 days to 90 days, depending on the device. Long-term tests remain in your home for more than 90 days.

Because radon levels tend to vary from day to day and season to season, a long-term test is more likely to tell you your home's year-round average radon level than a short-term test.

To get more information about radon testing methods, call the National Radon Hotline at 1-800-SOS-RADON [1-800-767-7236].

How do you use a radon test kit?

It is important to follow the instructions that come with the kit. When you use any radon test, keep in mind:

- The test kit should be placed in the lowest level of your home that your family uses regularly. For example, if you live in a house and you use the basement, place the test kit there. Otherwise, use the first floor. Put the test kit in a room that is used regularly, but NOT in your kitchen or bathroom.
- Keep the test in place for as long as the instructions say, but for at least 48 hours. Then, re-seal the package and mail it to the laboratory mentioned on the package. Results should be sent to you within a few weeks.
- Keep doors and windows closed as much as possible during the test. Drafts can affect the test results.

What do radon test results mean?

- Radon levels are measured in "picocuries per liter" or "pCi/L." The higher the level, the greater the risk from long-term exposure. EPA recommends that you take action to reduce radon if the radon level in your home is 4 pCi/L or higher. (This "action level" was set at 4 pCi/L partly because it is technically possible to reduce radon to 4 pCi/L in most homes.)
- If you took a short-term test and your results were 4 pCi/L or higher, EPA recommends doing a second test to confirm the results. You can do this follow-up test yourself, or you can contact the owner about the owner doing further testing. The Appendix contains an excerpt from EPA's Citizen's Guide to Radon, which explains more about follow-up testing.
- If you have questions about what your test results mean, contact your state radon office.

What Can You Do if Your Home has High Radon Levels?

Fixing a radon problem usually involves repairs to the building. Therefore, it is generally the building owner - and not the tenant - who is authorized to have this work done. However, if your home has high radon levels, you can take steps to see that the problem is fixed.

- If your radon testing shows high radon levels, you should inform the building owner in writing. In most states, owners are required generally to keep their properties "habitable" - safe and fit for people to live in. You can give the owner a copy of your test results and discuss what steps the owner plans to take to fix the problem. The owner will probably need to do more radon testing in the building. You can ask for copies of those test results.
- If you live in an apartment building, you can share your radon information with other residents. Other residents may wish to test their own units or to discuss the matter further with the owner. (Even if your radon test showed low radon levels, there may be high levels in other parts of the building.)
- If you are concerned that a radon problem in your building is not being fixed, you may want to get more information and advice. For example, your state radon office can provide you and the building owner with more specific information about testing for and fixing radon problems. Local community organizations that work on radon or housing problems may be able to help find ways to fix the radon problem in your building. For legal advice, you can contact your local bar association for help in finding a lawyer. Or, limited income tenants can contact the nearest legal services office to find out if free legal assistance is available.

What Can Building Owners Do About Radon Problems?

As mentioned earlier, rental property owners are usually responsible for keeping their properties in a safe and fit condition. There are steps that rental property owners can take to address the problem of high radon levels.

- High radon levels can be reduced by making repairs to the building. The right system depends on the design of the building and other factors. State radon offices or the Radon Fix It Line (1-800-644-6999) can provide general information on methods for reducing radon. Also, the EPA's Consumer's Guide to Radon Reduction is a quick and easy way to learn more about the different ways to fix radon problems.
- Radon reduction costs between $500 and $2,500 for a single family home. For a larger building, the costs will depend on the size and other characteristics of the building.
- Radon reduction work generally requires a trained professional. To find out which radon reduction system is right for a building, and how much those repairs will cost, building owners should consult with a professional radon contractor.
- Many states have programs set up to train or certify radon professionals. Your state radon office can provide a list of individuals who have completed state or national programs. Or, you can call the Radon Fix It Line for free publications, referrals or how to find a "qualified" radon service professional.

Are Funds Available to Reduce High Radon Levels in Rental Housing?

- There are some federal programs that might be used to help fund radon reduction in homes that are affordable to limited income families. These programs generally give money to local agencies or groups, which then fund the work. Some examples are:

  Community Development Block Grant (CDBG) program - funds rehabilitation and repair of affordable housing. For more information, call the U.S. Department of Housing and Urban Development (HUD) at 202-708-3587.

  "203k" program - funds rehabilitation and repair of single family homes. For more information, call HUD at 202-708-2121.

  Environmental Justice Grants - funds community-based organizations and tribal governments addressing environmental concerns of people of color and low income communities. For more information, call EPA's Office of Environmental Justice at 1-800-962-6215.

- Some states, such as Maryland, have governmental programs that can provide loans for radon reduction work in limited income housing.

- Some community groups are raising funds from private companies and foundations to pay for radon reduction in limited income homes. One of these groups is the Pennsylvania Resources Council - for more information about its work, call 610-353-1555.

To find out more about federal and state programs, or about how community groups have developed local projects to fix radon problems, owners and residents can contact the government agencies and organizations listed in this guide.

Renter's Radon Checklist

- Find out whether the building you live in has been tested for radon.
- If your building has not been tested for radon, ask the building owner to test, or test your own apartment or house.
- Follow the instructions included in your radon test kit. If your short-term test shows radon levels above 4 pCi/L, EPA recommends doing a follow-up test.
- If your test shows radon levels above 4 pCi/L, notify the building owner of the test results in writing. Discuss with the owner the need for additional testing and radon reduction repairs.
- If you have high radon levels or if you need additional information and assistance about radon testing and radon repairs, contact your state radon office, the National Radon Helpline or other organizations that work on radon or housing issues.

> *If You Smoke . . .*
>
> Smoking combined with exposure to high radon levels is an even more serious health risk. If you smoke or are a former smoker, the presence of radon greatly increases your risk of lung cancer. If you stop smoking and lower your radon levels, you will reduce your lung cancer risk.

For More Information

State Radon Contacts

www.epa.gov/iaq/whereyoulive.html

If you have trouble reaching a radon office in your state, or if you would like information on tribal government radon programs, call the National Radon Helpline at 1-800-557-2366. *[You may call the **Indoor Air Quality Information Clearinghouse [IAQ INFO]** at their toll-free number **(800) 438-4318** to speak to an information specialist, **Monday through Friday, 9:00 a.m. to 5:00 p.m. eastern time.** After hours, you may leave a*

*voice message, or you may make inquiries by **fax [(703) 356-5386]** or via e-mail: iaginfo@aol.com anytime.]*

Radon Information Hotlines

The following telephone numbers are run by non-governmental, non-profit organizations.

- *To receive general information on radon:*

 National Radon Information Hotline (National Safety Council)
 1-800-SOS-RADON [1-800-767-7236]

- *To ask general questions about radon:*

 National Radon Helpline (National Safety Council)
 1-800-55-RADON [1-800-557-2366]

Non-Governmental Organizations

In addition to the radon information hotlines, you can call the following organizations for information or assistance.

- *To find out more about radon and local radon programs:*

 American Lung Association EXIT Disclaimer
 To contact your local chapter, call 1-800-LUNG-USA

 Environmental Law Institute EXIT Disclaimer
 1616 P Street, N.W., Suite 200
 Washington, D.C. 20036
 202-939-3800

 National Medical Association
 1012 10th Street, N.W.
 Washington, D.C. 20001
 202-347-1895 or 1-800-662-6563

- *To find a housing and community development organization near you that works on affordable housing issues:*

- **National Congress for Community Economic Development**
  1875 Connecticut Ave., N.W.
  Washington, D.C.
  202-234-5009

- *To find a legal services office near you that works on affordable housing issues:*

  National Legal Aid and Defender Association
  1625 K Street, N.W. Suite 800
  Washington, D.C. 20006
  (202) 452-0620

Radon Testing

The following is an excerpt from EPA's Citizen's Guide to Radon:

EPA Recommends the Following Testing Steps:

Step 1

Take a short-term test. If your result is 4 pCi/L. or higher*, take a follow-up test (Step 2) to be sure.

Step 2

Follow up with either a long-term test or a second short-term test:

- For a better understanding of your year-round average radon level, take a long-term test.
- If you need results quickly, take a second short-term test.

The higher your initial short-term test result, the more certain you can be that you should take a short-term rather than a long-term follow up test. If your first short-term test result is several times the action level - for example, about 10 pCi/L or higher - you should take a second short-term test immediately.

Step 3

- If you followed up with a long-term test: Fix your home if your long-term test result is 4pCi/L or more*.
- If you followed up with a second short-term test: The higher your short-term results, the more certain you can be that you should fix your home.

Consider fixing your home if the average of your first and second test is 4pCi/L or higher*.

* 0.02 Working Levels (WL) or higher.

Asbestos Standard for General Industry: U.S. Department of Labor

Asbestos Standard for General Industry

Asbestos Standard For General Industry

U.S. Department of Labor
Occupational Safety and Health Administration

OSHA 3095
1995 (Revised)

This informational booklet is intended to provide a generic, non-exhaustive overview of a particular standards-related topic. This publication does not itself alter or determine compliance responsibilities, which are set forth in OSHA standards themselves, and the *Occupational Safety and Health Act*. Moreover, because interpretations and enforcement policy may change over time, for additional guidance on OSHA compliance requirements, the reader should consult current administrative interpretations and decisions by the Occupational Safety and Health Review Commission and the courts.

This information will be made available to sensory impaired individuals upon request. Voice phone (202) 219-8615; Telecommunications Device for the Deaf (TDD) message referral phone: 1-800-326-2577.

Contents

Introduction
Scope and Application
Provisions of the Standard
    Permissible Exposure Limits (PELs)
        Time-Weighted Average (TWA)
        Excursion Limit (EL)
    Exposure Monitoring
    Medical Surveillance
    Recordkeeping
    Regulated Areas
Communication of Hazards
Building/Facility Owner Duties
Information and Training
Methods o f Compliance
    Control Methods
    Respiratory Protection
    Protective Clothing
    Hygiene Facilities and Practices
    Housekeeping

Other Sources of OSHA Assistance
    Safety and Health Program Management Guidelines
    State Programs
    Consultation Services
    Voluntary Protection Programs
    Training and Education

OSHA Related Publications

States with Approved Plans

OSHA Consultation Project Directory

OSHA Area Offices

Introduction

Asbestos is a widely used, mineral-based material that is resistant to heat and corrosive chemicals. Depending on the chemical composition, fibers may range in texture from coarse to silky. The properties that make asbestos fibers so valuable to industry are its high-tensile strength, flexibility, heat and chemical resistance, and good frictional properties.

Asbestos fibers enter the body by inhalation of airborne particles or by ingestion and can become embedded in the tissues of the respiratory or digestive systems. Years of exposure to asbestos can cause numerous disabling or fatal diseases. Among these diseases are asbestosis, an emphysemalike condition; lung cancer; mesothelioma, a cancerous tumor that spreads rapidly in the cells of membranes covering the lungs and body organs; and gastrointestinal cancer.

Since 1972, however, OSHA has regulated asbestos exposure in general industry thereby causing a significant decline in the use of asbestos-containing materials. The revised standard continues to protect workers, in general, who are exposed to asbestos-containing materials but now includes provisions that apply to workers performing brake and clutch repair and to those doing housekeeping in buildings and facilities where asbestos-containing materials exist.

This booklet contains ail overview of tile Occupational Safety and Health Administration's (OSHA's) worker protection requirements for exposure to asbestos in general industry and describes the steps an employer must take to reduce the levels of asbestos in the workplace. The revised rule lowers the permissible exposure limit (PEL), contains mandatory methods of control for brake and clutch repairs, and provides training provisions for maintenance and custodial workers. (OSHA has developed a separate standard and a separate pamphlet for asbestos in the construction industry. See **Related Publications** at the end of this publication for details on how to order.)

Scope and Application

OSHA's revised standards for asbestos were developed in recognition of the vastly different conditions prevailing in the workplaces for general industry (*29 Code of Federal Regulations (CFR) Part 1910.1001*), for the shipyard industry (29 *CFR Part* 1915), and for the construction industry (*29 CFR Part 1926-1101*) The information in this pamphlet applies to all occupational exposure to asbestos in general industry.

More than 685,000 workers in general industry, mostly in auto repair, are affected by the new standard. OSHA estimates, conservatively, that about 42 additional cancer deaths per year will be avoided in all industries, in addition to the lives saved of those peripherally exposed to asbestos and the lives saved by earlier OSHA standards.

Provisions of the Standard

OSHA sets out several provisions employers must follow to comply with the asbestos standard. The agency has established strict exposure limits and guidelines for exposure monitoring, medical surveillance, record keeping, regulated areas, and communication of hazards.

Permissible Exposure Limits (PELs)

Time-Weighted Average (TWA) - The employer shall ensure that no employee is exposed to an airborne concentration of asbestos in excess of 0.1 fiber per cubic centimeter of (1 f/cc) as averaged over an 8-hour TWA day.

Excursion Limit (ELT) - The employer shall ensure that no employee is exposed to an airborne concentration of asbestos in excess of 1.0 fiber per cubic centimeter of air (0.1 f/cc) as averaged over a sampling period of 30 minutes.

OSHA has adopted the term "excursion limit" to refer to the short-term permissible exposure limit to be consistent with the terminology used by the American Conference of Governmental Industrial Hygienists (ACGIH).

Exposure Monitoring

Except for brake and clutch repair where a "preferred" control method is used, each employer who has a workplace or work operation covered by this standard must assess all asbestos operations for their potential to generate airborne fibers. Where exposure may exceed the PEL, employee exposure measurements must be made from breathing zone air samples representing the 8-hour TWA and 30-minute EL for each employee.

Initial monitoring also must be performed for all employees who are, or may reasonably be expected to be, exposed to airborne concentrations of asbestos at or above the PEL and/or EL unless: (1) monitoring results conducted after March 31, 1992, meet all other standard-related requirements; and (2) the collected data demonstrate that asbestos is not capable of being released in airborne concentrations at or above the PEL and/or EL when materials are being processed, used, or handled. If initial monitoring indicates that exposures are above the PEL and/or EL, periodic monitoring must be conducted at intervals no greater than every 6 months. If either initial or periodic monitoring statistically indicates that employee exposures are below the PEL and/or EL, the employer may discontinue monitoring for those employees whose exposures are represented by such monitoring.

The employer must reinitiate monitoring whenever there has been a change in the production, process, control equipment, personnel or work practices that may result in new or additional exposures to asbestos above the PEL and/or EL, or when the employer has reason to suspect that a change may result in new or additional exposures above the PEL and/or EL.

Affected employees and their representatives must be allowed to observe monitoring and must be notified in writing, either individually or by posting results in an accessible location within 15 working days after the receipt of the results of monitoring. This written notification must contain the corrective action being taken by the employer to reduce employee exposure to asbestos on or below the PEL and/or EL wherever monitoring results indicate that the PEL and/or EL has been exceeded. If monitoring is being observed in a regulated area, the observer must be provided proper protective clothing and equipment.

Medical Surveillance

The employer must institute a medical surveillance program for all employees who are or will be exposed to airborne concentrations of asbestos at or above the PEL and/or EL. All medical examinations and procedures must be performed by or under the supervision of a licensed physician. Such exams must occur at a reasonable time and place and shall be provided at no cost to the employee. At a minimum, such examinations must include a medical and work history; a complete physical examination with emphasis on the respiratory system, the cardiovascular system, and the digestive tract; a chest X-ray; pulmonary function tests; respiratory disease standardized questionnaire as set forth in *29 CFR 1910.100I Appendix D, Part 1* of the standard; and any additional tests deemed appropriate by the examining physician. These examinations must be made available annually. Chest roentgenogram must be conducted in accordance with the following table:

Table - Frequency of Chest Roentgenogram

Years since first exposure	Age of employee		
	15 to 35	35+ to 45	45+
0 to 10	Every 5 years	Every 5 years	Every 5 years
10+	Every 5 years	Every 2 years	Every 1 year

Also, an abbreviated standardized questionnaire (see *2 9 CFR Part 1 910.1001 Appendix D Part 2* of the standard) also must be administered to the employee. Upon termination of employment, the employer must provide a termination of employment medical exam to the employee within 30 calendar days before or after the date of termination.

If adequate records exist that show the employee has been examined in accordance with the standard within the past year, no additional medical examination is required. A preemployment medical examination may not be used unless the employer pays for it.

The employer must provide the examining physician with a copy of the standard and Appendices D and E; a description of the affected employee's duties as they relate to his or her asbestos exposure; the employee's actual or anticipated exposure level; a description of any personal protective and respiratory equipment used or to be used; and information from previous medical examinations. Once the physician has completed the exam, the employer must obtain a written signed opinion from the physician. It must contain the results of the medical examination and the physician's opinion as to whether the employee has any detailed medical conditions that would place the employee at an increased risk from exposure to asbestos; any recommended limitations on the employee or upon the use of personal protective equipment such as respirators, a statement that the employee has been informed by the physician of the results of the examination, and a statement that the employee has been informed by the physician of the increased risk of lung cancer attributable to the combined effect of smoking and asbestos exposure.

The physician is not to reveal in the written opinion given to the employer specific findings or diagnoses unrelated to occupational exposure to asbestos.

The employer must provide a copy of the physician's written opinion to the affected employee within 30 days of its receipt.

Rcecordkeeping

The employer must keep an accurate record of all exposure measurements taken to monitor employee exposure to asbestos. This record must be kept for 30 years.

The employer also must maintain an accurate record for each employee subject to medical surveillance. This record must be maintained for the duration of employment plus 30 years.

In addition, the employer must maintain all employee training records for 1 year beyond the last date of employment by the employee.

All records must be made available to the OSHA Assistant Secretary, the Director of the National Institute for Occupational Safety and Health (NIOSH), affected employees, former employees, and designated representatives in accordance with *29 CFR Part 1910.20*. When the employer ceases to do business and there is no successor to receive the records for the prescribed period, the employer must notify the Director of NIOSH at least 90 days prior to the disposal of records.

Also, if handling, using, or processing any products made from or containing asbestos are exempted, the employer must establish and maintain accurate records of objective data that exempt these products. These records must be kept for the duration of products. These be kept for way duration vu of the employer's reliance upon the data.

Building and facility owners also are required to maintain records about the presence, quantity of asbestos-containing material and presumed asbestos-containing material in the building and/or facility. These records must be kept for duration of ownership and must be transferred to the successive owners.

Regulated Areas

The employer must establish and set apart a regulated area wherever airborne concentrations of asbestos and/or presumed asbestos-containing material exceed the PEL and/or EL. Only authorized personnel may enter regulated areas. All persons entering a regulated area must be supplied with and are required to an appropriate respirator.

No smoking, eating, drinking, chewing tobacco or gum, or applying cosmetics is permitted in regulated areas.

Warning signs must be provided and displayed at each regulated area and must be posted at all approaches to all regulated areas. Where necessary, signs must bear pictures or graphics, or be written in appropriate language so that all employees understand them. These signs must bear the following information:

```
Danger
Asbestos
Cancer And Lung Disease Hazard
Authorized Personnel Only
Respirators And Protective
Clothing
Are Required In This Area
```

In addition, warning labels must be affixed to all asbestos products (raw materials, mixtures, scrap) and to all containers of asbestos products, including waste containers, that may be in the workplace. The labels must comply with the requirements of 29 *CFR 1910.1200(f)* of OSHA's Hazard Communication standard and must include the following information:

```
Danger
Contains Asbestos Fibers
Avoid Creating Dust
Cancer And Lung Disease Hazard
```

Labels or Material Safety Data Sheets (MSDSs) are not required where asbestos fibers have been modified by a bonding agent, coating, binder, or other materials, if the manufacturer can demonstrate that during handling, storing, disposing, processing, or transporting no airborne concentrations of fibers of asbestos in excess of PEL and/or EL will be released or if asbestos is present in a product in a concentration of less than 1.0 percent.

Communication of Hazards

Building/Facility Owners Duties

The communication of asbestos hazards is vital. Employees engaged in housekeeping activities in public and commercial buildings with installed asbestos-containing materials may be exposed to asbestos fibers. Building owners are often the only and/or best source of information concerning that presence of previously installed asbestos-containing building materials. The standard requires building owners and employers or potentially exposed employees to institute the following

practices:

- In buildings built before 1980, treat thermal system insulation and sprayed-on and troweled-on surfacing materials as asbestos-containing materials, unless properly analyzed! and found not to contain more than 1 percent asbestos.
- Train employees who may me in contact with asbestos-containing materials to deal safely with them.
- Treat asphalt and vinyl flooring materials installed no later than 1980 as asbestos-containing, unless properly analyzed and found to contain no more than 1 percent asbestos.
- Inform employers of employees performing housekeeping activities of the presence and location of asbestos-containing materials and presumed asbestos-containing materials that may have contaminated the area.

Keep records of the presence, location, and quantity of asbestos-containing materials and presumed asbestos-containing materials present in the building for the duration of ownership and transfer these records to a successive owner.

Information and Training

Employers must develop a training program for all employees who are exposed to airborne concentrations of asbestos at or above the PEL and/or EL. Training must be provided prior to or at the thereafter. The time of initial assignment and at least yearly thereafter. The training program must inform employees about ways in which they can safeguard their health.

In addition, employers must provide an awareness training course for employees who do housekeeping operations in facilities where asbestos-containing materials or presumed asbestos-containing materials are present. The elements of the course must include the health effects of asbestos; locations, signs of damage and deterioration of asbestos-containing materials and presumed asbestos-containing materials; the proper response to fiber release episodes; and where the housekeeping requirements are found in the standard. This training must be held annually and conducted so that all employees understand it.

Also, all training materials must be available to the employees without cost and, upon request, to the Assistant 'Secretary for OSHA and the Director of NIOSH.

Methods of Compliance

Control Methods

To the extent feasible, engineering gild work practice controls must be used to reduce and maintain employee exposure at or below the PEL and/or EL. The standard, therefore, requires the employer to institute the following measures:

- Design, construct, install, and maintain local exhaust ventilation and dust collection systems according to the *American National Standard Fundamentals Governing the Design and Operation of Local Exhaust Systems*, ANSIZ9.2-1979.
- Provide a local exhaust ventilation system for all hand-operated and power-operated tools such as saws, scorers, abrasive wheels, and drills that produce or release fibers of asbestos.
- Handle, mix, apply, remove, cut, score, or work asbestos in a wet state to prevent employee exposure.
- Do not remove cement, mortar, coating, grout, plaster, or similar materials containing asbestos from bags, cartons, or other containers that are being shipped without wetting, enclosing, or ventilating them.
- Do not sand floors containing asbestos.
- Do not use compressed air to remove asbestos or materials containing asbestos unless the compressed air is used in conjunction with a ventilation system designed to capture the dust

cloud created by tile compressed air.

- Use a negative-pressure enclosure/HEPA[1] vacuum system or a low-pressure/wet cleaning method during automotive brake and clutch inspection, disassembly, repair, and assembly operations. An equivalent method also can be used if the employer demonstrates that the method being used achieves the required exposure reductions. (See *29 Part 1910.1001 Appendix F, Part C* to the standard.)
- Where no more than five pairs of brakes or five clutches are inspected, disassembled, repaired, or assembled weekly, use the control methods or work practices as set forth in *29 CFR Part 1910.1001* Appendix F to the standard.

Where engineering and work practice controls have been insufficient to reduce exposure to the required level the employer must supplement them by using respiratory protection.

Where the PEL and/or EL is exceeded the employer must establish and implement a written program to reduce employee below the engineering and work practice controls and by the use of respirators where required and permitted.

Written plans for the program must he available upon request to the Assistant Secretary for OSHA, the Director of NIOSH, and employees and their representatives. These plans must be reviewed and updated, as necessary, to reflect significant changes in the compliance program.

Employee rotation can be used as a means of compliance the PEL and/or the EL.

Respiratory Protection

Respirators must be selected, provided, and used in the following circumstances:

- While feasible engineering and work practice controls are being installed or implemented:
- During maintenance and repair activities, or other activities where engineering and work practice controls are not feasible;
- In work situations where feasible engineering and work practice controls are not yet sufficient to reduce exposure to or below the PEL and/or EL; and
- In emergencies.

Respirators must be selected from among those jointly approved by the Mine Safety and Health Administration (MSHA) and NIOSH under the provisions of *Title 30, CFR Part 11*. The employer also must provide a powered, air-purifying respirator in lieu of any negative-pressure respirator when the employee chooses it and when the respirator provides adequate protection. And, where respiratory protection is required, the employer must develop a respiratory program in accordance with *29 CFR 1910.134 (b),(d),(e), and (f)*. The respirators and the respiratory protection program must he provided to employees free of charge.

Employees who use a filter respirator must use a high-efficiency filter and must change filters whenever an increase in breathing resistance is detected. Employees who wear respirators must be allowed to wash their faces and respirator face pieces whenever necessary to prevent skin irritation associated with respirator use. An employee must not be assigned to tasks requiring the use of respirators if a physician determines that the employee is unable to function normally wearing a respirator or that the employee's safety and health or that of others would be affected by the employee's use of a respirator. In this case, the employer must assign the employee to another job or give the employee the opportunity to transfer to a different job that does not require the use of a respirator. The job must be with the same employer, in the same geographical area, and with the same seniority, status, rate of pay, if such a position is available.

The employer must ensure that a respirator issued to an employee fits properly exhibits and minimum facepiece leakage. Employers also must perform quantitative or qualitative fit tests, whichever are appropriate, at the time of initial fitting and at least every 6 months for each employee wearing negative-pressure respirators. Protocols for fit tests are set forth in *29 CFR*

1910.1001 Appendix C of the standard. Tests must be used to select facepieces that provides required protection.

Protective Clothing

For any employee exposed to airborne concentrations of asbestos that exceed the PEL and/or EL, employer must provide at no cost to the employee, and require the use of, protective clothing, such as coveralls or similar full-body clothing, head coverings, gloves, and foot coverings. In addition, wherever the possibility of eye irritation exists, face shields, vented goggles, or other appropriate protective equipment must be provided and worn. Asbestos-contaminated work clothing must be removed in change rooms and placed and stored in closed, labeled containers that prevent dispersion of the asbestos into the ambient environment. Protective clothing and equipment must be cleaned, laundered. repaired, or replaced to maintain effectiveness.

The employer must provide clean protective clothing and equipment at least weekly to each affected employee. The employer must inform any person who launders or cleans asbestos contaminated clothing or equipment of the potentially harmful effects of exposure to asbestos. In addition, the employer must be certain that the person doing the cleaning or laundering has been properly instructed on how to effectively prevent the release of airborne fibers in excess of the permissible exposure limits. For example, asbestos must never be removed from protective clothing by means of blowing or shaking.

Contaminated clothing and equipment taken out of change rooms or the workplace for cleaning, must be transported in sealed impermeable bags, or other closed impermeable containers and must be appropriately labeled.

Hygiene Facilities and Practices

Employees who are required to work in regulated areas must be provided with clean change rooms, shower facilities, and lunch rooms. Change rooms must have two separate lockers or storage facilities -- one for contaminated clothing, the other for street clothing.

They must be far enough apart to prevent accidental contamination of the employee's street clothes. Employees must shower at the end of the shift and cannot leave the workplace wearing any clothing or equipment worn during the work shift. Lunchroom facilities must have a positive-pressure filtered air supply and must be readily accessible to employees.

The employer must ensure that employees do not enter lunch room facilities with protective work clothing or equipment unless surface asbestos fibers have been removed by vacuuming or some other method that removes dust without causing the asbestos to become airborne. The employer also must ensure that employees wash their hands prior to eating, drinking, or smoking. Smoking is prohibited in regulated areas.

Housekeeping

All surfaces must be maintained as free as possible of accumulations of waste containing asbestos and/or asbestos dust. The preferred methods of cleanup are wet cleaning and/or vacuuming with HEPA filtered vacuuming equipment. Compressed air may not be used to clean surfaces contaminated by asbestos at any time. Whichever cleanup method is chosen, the equipment shall be used and a emptied in a manner that minimizes the reentry of asbestos into the workplace.

The employer also must ensure that all spills and sudden releases of asbestos-containing materials are immediately cleaned up, that sanding asbestos-containing floors is prohibited; and that low abrasion pads at speeds lower than 300 rpm and wet methods are used. If floor has sufficient finish, brushing or dry buffing is permissible. If workers are required to buff or wax asbestos containing resilient floors, building and facility owners must identify the installed material and inform employees and employers of employees doing such housekeeping work.

Asbestos waste, scrap, debris, bags, containers, equipment, and asbestos-contaminated clothing consigned for disposal must be collected and disposed of in sealed, labeled, impermeable bags or other closed, labeled impermeable containers.

Other Sources of OSHA Assistance

Safety and Health Program Management Guidelines

Effective management of worker safety and health protection is a decisive factor in reducing the extent and severity of work-related injuries and illnesses and their related costs. To assist employers and employees in developing effective safety and health programs, OSHA published recommended. *Safety and Health Program Management Guidelines (Federal Register 54 (18): 3908-3916, January 26, 1989)*. These voluntary guidelines apply to all places of employment covered by OSHA.

The guidelines identify four general elements that are critical to the development of a successful safety and health management program:

- Management commitment and employee involvement,
- Worksite analysis,
- Hazard prevention and control, and
- Safety and health training.

The guidelines recommend specific actions, under each of these general elements to achieve an effective safety and health program. A single free copy of the guidelines can be obtained from the OSHA Publications Office, U.S. Department of Labor, 200 Constitution Avenue, N.W., Room N3101, Washington, DC 20210, by sending a self-addressed mail label with your request.

State Programs

The Occupational Safety and Health Act of 1970 encourages states to develop and operate their own job safety and health plans. States with plans approved under section 18(b) of the Act must adopt standards and enforce requirements that are at least as effective as federal requirements. There are currently 25 state plan states: 23 of these states administer plans covering both private and public (state and local government) employees; the other 2 states; Connecticut and New York, cover public employees only. Plan states must adopt standards at least as effective as federal requirements within 6 months of a federal standard's promulgation. Until such time as a state standard is promulgated, federal OSHA provides interim enforcement assistance, as appropriate, in these states. A listing of approved state plans appears at the end of this publication.

Consultation Services

Consultation assistance is available on request to employers who want help in establishing and maintaining a safe and healthful workplace. Largely funded by OSHA, the service is provided at no cost to the employer. Primarily developed for smaller employers with more hazardous operations, the consultation service is delivered by state government agencies or universities employing professional safety consultants and health consultants. Comprehensive assistance includes an appraisal of all mechanical, physical work practices, and environmental hazards of the workplace and all aspects of the employer's present job safety and health program.

The program is separate from OSHA's inspection efforts. No penalties are proposed or citations issued for any safety or health problems identified by the consultant. The service is confidential.

For more information concerning consultation assistance, see the list of consultation projects at the end of this publication.

Voluntary Protection Programs (VPPs)

Voluntary Protection Programs and onsite consultation services, when coupled with an effective enforcement program, expand worker protection to help meet the goals of the OSH Act. The three VPPs -- Star, Merit, and Demonstration -- are designed to recognize outstanding achievement by companies that have successfully incorporated comprehensive safety and health programs into their total management system. They motivate others to achieve excellent safety and health results in the same outstanding way as they establish a cooperative relationship among employers, employees, and OSHA.

For additional information on VPPs and how to apply, contact the OSHA area or regional offices listed at the end of this publication.

Training and Education

OSHA area offices offer a variety of information services, such as publications, audiovisual aids, technical advice, and speakers for special engagements. OSHA Training Institute in Des Plaines, IL, provides basic and advanced courses in safety and health for federal and state compliance officers, state consultants, federal agency personnel, and private sector employers, employees, and their representatives.

OSHA also provides funds to nonprofit organizations, through grants, to conduct workplace training and education in subjects where OSHA believes there is a lack of workplace training. Grants are awarded annually. Grant recipients are expected to contribute 20 percent of the total grant cost.

For more information on grants, training and education, contact the OSHA Training institute, Office of Training and Education, 1555 Times Drive, Des Plaines, IL 60018, (708) 297-4810.

For further information on any OSHA program, contact your nearest OSHA area or regional office listed at the end of this publication.

OSHA Related Publications

A single free copy of the following materials may be obtained from the OSHA area or regional offices or contact the OSHA Publications Office, 200 Constitution Avenue, N.W., Room N3101, Washington, DC 20210, (202) 219-4667; or (202) 219-9266 (fax). Please send a self-addressed label with your written request.

All About OSHA - OSHA 2056

Asbestos Standard for Construction Industry - OSHA 3096

Asbestos Standard for Shipyards - OSHA 3145

Chemical Hazard Communication - OSHA 3084

Consultation Services for the Employer - OSHA 3047

How to Prepare for Workplace Emergencies- OSHA 3088

Job Safety and Health Protection (Poster) - OSHA 2203

OSHA: Employee Workplace Rights - OSHA 3021

OSHA Inspections - OSHA 2098

Personal Protective Equipment - OSHA 3077

Respiratory Protection - OSHA 3079

The following publications are available from the U.S. Government Printing Office, Superintendent of Documents, Washington, DC 20402, (202)512-1800. Include GPO Order No. and make checks payable to Superintendent of Documents.

Hazard Communication-A Compliance Kit - OSHA 3104
OSHA Order No. 029-010-00147-6. Cost $18.00 domestic; $22.50 foreign.

Hazard Communication Guidelines for Compliance - OSHA 3111
Order No.029-016-00127-1. Cost $1.00

Job Hazard Analysis - OSHA 3071
Order No. 029-016-00142-5. Cost: $1.00

Training Requirements in OSHA Standards and Training Guidelines - OSHA 2254
Order No. 029-016-00137-9. Cost $4.25

States with Approved Plans

Commissioner
Alaska Department of Labor
1111 West 8th Street
Room 306
Juneau AK 99801
(907) 465-2700

Director
Industrial Commission of Arizona
800 W. Washington
Phoenix, AZ 85007
(602) 542-5795

Director
California Department of Industrial Relations
455 Golden Gate Avenue
4th Floor
S. San Francisco, CA 94102
(415) 703-4590

Commissioner
Connecticut Department of Labor
200 Folly Brook Boulevard
Wethersfield, CT 06109
(203) 566-5123

Director
Hawaii Department of Labor and Industrial Relations
830 Punchbowl Street
Honolulu, HI 96813
(808) 586-8844

Commissioner
Indiana Department of Labor State Office Building

402 WestWashington Street
Room W195
Indianapolis, IN 46204
(307) 232-2378

Commissioner
Iowa Division of Labor Services
1000 E. Grand Avenue
Des Moines, IA 50319
(515) 281-3447

Secretary
Kentucky Labor Cabinet
1049 U.S. Highway, 127 South
Frankfort, KY 40601
(502) 564-3070

Commissioner
Maryland Division of Labor and industry
Department of Licensing and Regulation
501 St. Paul Place, 2nd Floor
Baltimore, MD 21202-2272
(410) 333-4179

Director
Michigan Department of Labor
Victor Office Center
201 N. Washington Square
P.O. Box 30015
Lansing, MI 48933
(517) 373-9600

Director
Michigan Department of Public Health
3423 North Logan Street
Box 30195
Lansing, MI 48909
(517) 335-8022

Commissioner
Minnesota Department of Labor and industry
443 Lafayette Road
St. Paul, MN 55155
(612) 296-2342

Director
Division of industrial Relations
400 West King Street
Carson City, NV 89710
(702) 687-3032

Secretary
New Mexico Environmental Department
Occupational Health and Safety Bureau
1190 St. Francis Drive
P.O. Box 26110
Santa Fe, NM 87502
(505) 827-7850

Commissioner
New York Department of Labor
State Office Building - Campus 12
Room 457
Albany, NY 12240
(518) 457-2741

Commissioner
North Carolina Department of Labor
319 Chapanoke Road
Raleigh, NC 27603
(919) 662-4585

Administrator
Oregon Occupational Safety and Health Division
Department of Consumer and Business Services,
Room 430
Labor and Industries Building
350 Winter Street, NE
Salem, OR 97310
(503) 378-272

Secretary
Puerto Rico Department of Labor and Human Resources
Prudencio Rivera Martinez Building
505 Munoz Rivera A-venue
Hato Rey, PR 00918
(809) 754-2119

Commissioner
South Carolina Department of Labor
3600 Forest Drive
P.O. Box 11329
Columbia, SC 29211-1329
(803) 734-9594

Commissioner
Tennessee Department of Labor
Attention: Robert Taylor
710 James Robertson Parkway
Gateway Plaza
Suite "A"- 2nd Floor
Nashville, TN 37243-0655
(615) 741-2582

Commissioner
Industrial Commission of Utah
160 East 300 South, 3rd Floor
P.O. Box 146600
Salt Lake City, UT 84114-6600
(801) 530-6880

Commissioner
Vermont Department of Labor and Industry
120 State Street
Montpelier, VT 05620
(802) 828-2788

Commissioner
Virgin Islands Department of Labor
2131 Hospital Street, Box 890
Christiansted
St. Croix, VI 00840-4666
(809) 773-1994

Commissioner
Virginia Department Department of Labor and industry
Powers-Taylor Building
13 South 13th Street
Richmond, VA 23219
(804) 786-9873

Director
Washington Department of Labor and Industries
P.O. Box 44000
Olympia, WA 98504-4000
(206) 956-4200

Administrator
Occupational Safety and Health Administration
Herschler Building,
2nd Floor East
122 West 25th Street
Cheyenne, WY 82002
(307) 777-7786

OSHA Consultation Project Directory

State	Telephone
Alabama	(205) 348 - 3033
Alaska	(907) 269 - 4939
Arizona	(602) 542 - 5795
Arkansas	(501) 682 - 4522
California	(415) 703 - 4441
Colorado	(303) 491 - 6151
Connecticut	(203) 566 - 4550
Delaware	(302) 577 - 3908
District of Columbia	(202) 576 - 6339
Florida	(904) 488 - 3044
Georgia	(404) 894 - 8274
Guam	(671) 647 - 4202
Hawaii	(808) 586 - 9116
Ida ho	(208) 385 - 3283
Illinois	(312) 814 - 2337
Indiana	(317) 232 - 2688
Iowa	(515) 281 - 5352
Kansas	(913) 296 - 4386
Kentucky	(502) 564 - 6895
Louisiana	(504) 342 - 9601
Maine	(207) 624 - 6460
Maryland	(410) 333 - 4218
Massachusetts	(617) 969 - 7177
Michigan	(517) 332 - 8250 (H)
	(517) 322 - 1809 (S)
Minnesota	(612) 297 - 2393

State	Telephone
Mississippi	(601) 987 - 3981
Missouri	(314) 751 - 3403
Montana	(406) 444 - 6418
Nebraska	(402) 471 - 4717
Nevada	(702) 486 - 5016
New Hampshire	(603) 271 - 2024
New Jersey	(609) 292 - 3923
New Mexico	(505) 827 - 2877
New York	(518) 457 - 2481
North Carolina	(919) 733 - 2360
North Dakota	(701) 221 - 5188
Ohio	(614) 644 - 2631
Oklahoma	(405) 528 - 1500
Oregon	(503) 378 - 3272
Pennsylvania	(412) 357 - 2396
Puerto Rico	(809) 754 - 2171
Rhode Island	(401) 277 - 2438
South Carolina	(803) 734 - 9599
South Dakota	(605) 688 - 4101
Tennessee	(615) 741 - 7036
Texas	(512) 440 - 3834
Utah	(801) 530 - 6868
Vermont	(802) 828 - 2765
Virginia	(804) 786 - 8707
Virgin Islands	(809) 772 - 1315
Washington	(206) 956 - 4249
West Virginia	(304) 558 - 7890
Wisconsin	(608) 266 - 8579(H)
	(414) 521 - 5188(S)
Wyoming	(307) 777 - 7786

(H)-Health
(S)- Safety

OSHA Area Offices

Area	Telephone
Albany, NY	(518) 464-6742
Albuquerque, N M	(505) 766-3411
Allentown, PA	(215) 776-0592
Anchorage, AK	(907) 271-5152
Appleton, WI	(414) 734-4521
Augusta, ME	(207) 622-8417
Austin, TX	(512) 482-5783
Avenel, NJ	(908) 750-3270
Baltimore, MD	(410) 962-2840
Baton Rouge, LA	(504) 389-0474
Bayside, NY	(718) 279-9060
Bellevue, WA	(206) 553-7520
Billings, MT	(406) 657-6649
Birmingham, AL	(205) 731-1534
Bismarck, ND	(701) 250-4521
Boise, ID	(208) 334-1867
Bowmansville, NY	(716) 684-3891
Braintree, MA	(617) 565-6924
Bridgeport, CT	(203) 579-5579
Calumet City, IT	(708) 841-3800
Carson City, NV	(702) 885-6063
Charleston, WV	(304) 347-5937

Cincinnati, OH ....(513) 841-4132
Cleveland, OH ....(216) 522-3818
Columbia, SC ....(803) 765-5904
Columbus, OH ....(614) 469-5582
Concord, NH ....(603) 225-1629
Corpus Christi, TX ....(512) 884-2694
Dallas, TX ....(214) 320-2 400
Denver, CO ....(303) 844-5285
Des Plaines IT ....(708) 803-4800
Des Moines, I A ....(515) 284-4794
Englewood, CO ....(303) 843-4500
Erie, PA ....(814) 833-5758
Fort Lauderdale, FL ....(305) 424-0242
Fort Worth, TX ....(817) 885-7025
Frankfort, KY ....(502) 227-7024
Harrisburg, PA ....(717) 782-3902
Hartford, CT ....(203) 240-3152
Hasbrouck Heights, NJ ....(201) 288-1700
Hato Rey, PR ....(809) 766-5457
Honolulu, HI ....(808) 541-2685
Houston, TX ....(713) 286-0583
Houston; TX ....(713) 591-2438
Indianapolis, IN...(317) 226-7290
Jackson, MS ....(601) 965-4606
Jacksonville, FL ....(904) 232-2895
Kansas City, MO ....(816) 426-2756
Lansing, MI ....(517) 377-1892
Little Rock, AR ....(501) 324-6291
Lubbock, TX ....(806) 743-7681
Madison, WI ....(608) 264-5388
Marlton, NJ ....(609) 757-5181
Methuen, MA ....(617) 565-8110
Milwaukee, WI ....(414) 297-3315
Minneapolis, MN ....(612) 348-1994
Mobile, AL ....(205) 441-6131
Nashville, TN ....(615) 781-5423
New York, NY ....(212) 264-9840
Norfolk, VA ....(804) 441-3820
North Aurora, IL ....(708) 896-8700
Oklahoma City, OK ....(405) 231-5351
Omaha, NE ....(402) 221-3182
Parsippany, NJ ....(201) 263-1003
Peoria, IL ....(309) 671-7033
Philadelphia, PA ....(215) 597-4955
Phoenix, AZ...(602) 640-2007
Pittsburgh, PA ....(412) 644-2903
Portland, OR ....(503) 326-2251
Providence, RI ....(401) 528-4669
Raleigh, NC ....(919) 856-4770
Salt Lake City, UT ....(801) 524-5080
San Francisco, CA ....(415) 744-7120
Savannah, GA ....(912) 652-4393
Smyrna, GA ....(404) 984-8700
Springfield, MA...(413) 785-0123
St. Louis, MO ....(314) 425-4249
Syracuse, NY ....(315) 451-0808
Tampa, FL ....(813) 626-1177
Tarrytown, NY ....(914) 682-6151

Toledo, OH ....(419) 259-7542
Tucker, GA ....(404) 493-6644
Westbury, NY ....(516) 334-3344
Wichita, KS ....(316) 269-6644
Wilkes-Barre, PA ....(717) 826-6538

U.S. Department of Labor
Occupational Safety and Health Administration
Regional Offices

Region I
(CT,* MA,ME, NH, RI,VT*)
133 Portland Street
1st Floor
Boston, MA 02114
Telephone: (617) 565-7164

Region II
(NJ, NY, * PR,* VI*)
201Varick Street
Room 670
New York, 10014
Telephone: (212) 337-2378

Region III
(DC, DE,MD,* PA, VA,* WV)
Gateway Building, Suite 2100
3535 AM Street
Philadelphia, PA 19104
Telephone:(215) 596-1201

Region IV
(AL, FL, GA, KY,*MS, NC, SC,* TN*)
1375 Peachtree Street, N.E.
Suite 587
Atlanta, GA 30367
Telephone: (404) 347-3573

Region V
(IL, IN,* MI,* OH,WI)
230 South Dearborn Street
Room 3244
Chicago, IL 60604
Telephone: (312) 353-2220

Region VI
(AR, ILA, NM,*OK, TX)
525 Griffin Street
Room 602
Dallas, TX 75202
Telephone: (214) 767-4731

Region VII
(IA,* KS, MO, NE)
City Center Square
110 Main Street, Suite 8 00
Kansas City, MO 64105
Telephone: (816)426-5861

Region VIII
(CO, MT,ND,SD,UT,* WY*)
Federal Building, Room 1576
1999 Broadway
Denver, CO 8002-5716
Telephone: (303) 391-5858

Region IX
(American Samoa, AZ,* CA,* Guam, HI,*NV,*Trust Territories of the Pacific)
71 Stevenson Street, Room 420
San Francisco, CA 94105
Atlanta, GA 30367
Telephone: (415) 744-6670

Region X
(AK, * ID, OR,* WA*)
1111 Third Avenue
Suite 715
Seattle, WA 98101-3212
Telephone: (206) 553-5930

---

[1]High-efficiency particulate air means a filter capable of trapping and retaining at least 99.97 percent of 0.3-micrometer diameter mono-disperse particles.
* These states and territories operate their own OSHA-approved job safety and health programs (Connecticut and New York plans cover public employees only). States with approved programs must have a standard that is identical to, or at least as effective, as the federal standard.

Servicemembers Civil Relief Act: Title III

Servicemembers Civil Relief Act: Title III

PUBLIC LAW 108–189—DEC. 19, 2003   117 STAT. 2845

rate limitation in subsection (a), the servicemember shall provide to the creditor written notice and a copy of the military orders calling the servicemember to military service and any orders further extending military service, not later than 180 days after the date of the servicemember's termination or release from military service.

"(2) LIMITATION EFFECTIVE AS OF DATE OF ORDER TO ACTIVE DUTY.—Upon receipt of written notice and a copy of orders calling a servicemember to military service, the creditor shall treat the debt in accordance with subsection (a), effective as of the date on which the servicemember is called to military service.

"(c) CREDITOR PROTECTION.—A court may grant a creditor relief from the limitations of this section if, in the opinion of the court, the ability of the servicemember to pay interest upon the obligation or liability at a rate in excess of 6 percent per year is not materially affected by reason of the servicemember's military service.

"(d) INTEREST.—As used in this section, the term 'interest' includes service charges, renewal charges, fees, or any other charges (except bona fide insurance) with respect to an obligation or liability.

"TITLE III—RENT, INSTALLMENT CONTRACTS, MORTGAGES, LIENS, ASSIGNMENT, LEASES

"SEC. 301. EVICTIONS AND DISTRESS.   50 USC app. 531.

"(a) COURT-ORDERED EVICTION.—

"(1) IN GENERAL.—Except by court order, a landlord (or another person with paramount title) may not—

"(A) evict a servicemember, or the dependents of a servicemember, during a period of military service of the servicemember, from premises—

"(i) that are occupied or intended to be occupied primarily as a residence; and

"(ii) for which the monthly rent does not exceed $2,400, as adjusted under paragraph (2) for years after 2003; or

"(B) subject such premises to a distress during the period of military service.

"(2) HOUSING PRICE INFLATION ADJUSTMENT.—(A) For calendar years beginning with 2004, the amount in effect under paragraph (1)(A)(ii) shall be increased by the housing price inflation adjustment for the calendar year involved.

"(B) For purposes of this paragraph—

"(i) The housing price inflation adjustment for any calendar year is the percentage change (if any) by which—

"(I) the CPI housing component for November of the preceding calendar year, exceeds

"(II) the CPI housing component for November of 1984.

"(ii) The term 'CPI housing component' means the index published by the Bureau of Labor Statistics of the Department of Labor known as the Consumer Price Index, All Urban Consumers, Rent of Primary Residence, U.S. City Average.

117 STAT. 2846   PUBLIC LAW 108–189—DEC. 19, 2003

Federal Register,
publication.

"(3) PUBLICATION OF HOUSING PRICE INFLATION ADJUST-
MENT.—The Secretary of Defense shall cause to be published
in the Federal Register each year the amount in effect under
paragraph (1)(A)(ii) for that year following the housing price
inflation adjustment for that year pursuant to paragraph (2).

Deadline.

Such publication shall be made for a year not later than 60
days after such adjustment is made for that year.
"(b) STAY OF EXECUTION.—
"(1) COURT AUTHORITY.—Upon an application for eviction
or distress with respect to premises covered by this section,
the court may on its own motion and shall, if a request is
made by or on behalf of a servicemember whose ability to
pay the agreed rent is materially affected by military service—
"(A) stay the proceedings for a period of 90 days, unless
in the opinion of the court, justice and equity require
a longer or shorter period of time; or
"(B) adjust the obligation under the lease to preserve
the interests of all parties.
"(2) RELIEF TO LANDLORD.—If a stay is granted under paragraph (1), the court may grant to the landlord (or other person
with paramount title) such relief as equity may require.
"(c) PENALTIES.—
"(1) MISDEMEANOR.—Except as provided in subsection (a),
a person who knowingly takes part in an eviction or distress
described in subsection (a), or who knowingly attempts to do
so, shall be fined as provided in title 18, United States Code,
or imprisoned for not more than one year, or both.
"(2) PRESERVATION OF OTHER REMEDIES AND RIGHTS.—The
remedies and rights provided under this section are in addition
to and do not preclude any remedy for wrongful conversion
(or wrongful eviction) otherwise available under the law to
the person claiming relief under this section, including any
award for consequential and punitive damages.
"(d) RENT ALLOTMENT FROM PAY OF SERVICEMEMBER.—To the
extent required by a court order related to property which is the
subject of a court action under this section, the Secretary concerned
shall make an allotment from the pay of a servicemember to satisfy
the terms of such order, except that any such allotment shall
be subject to regulations prescribed by the Secretary concerned
establishing the maximum amount of pay of servicemembers that
may be allotted under this subsection.
"(e) LIMITATION OF APPLICABILITY.—Section 202 is not
applicable to this section.

50 USC app. 532.

**"SEC. 302. PROTECTION UNDER INSTALLMENT CONTRACTS FOR PUR-
CHASE OR LEASE.**

"(a) PROTECTION UPON BREACH OF CONTRACT.—
"(1) PROTECTION AFTER ENTERING MILITARY SERVICE.—After
a servicemember enters military service, a contract by the
servicemember for—
"(A) the purchase of real or personal property
(including a motor vehicle); or
"(B) the lease or bailment of such property,
may not be rescinded or terminated for a breach of terms
of the contract occurring before or during that person's military
service, nor may the property be repossessed for such breach
without a court order.

PUBLIC LAW 108–189—DEC. 19, 2003   117 STAT. 2847

"(2) APPLICABILITY.—This section applies only to a contract for which a deposit or installment has been paid by the servicemember before the servicemember enters military service.

"(b) PENALTIES.—

"(1) MISDEMEANOR.—A person who knowingly resumes possession of property in violation of subsection (a), or in violation of section 107 of this Act, or who knowingly attempts to do so, shall be fined as provided in title 18, United States Code, or imprisoned for not more than one year, or both.

"(2) PRESERVATION OF OTHER REMEDIES AND RIGHTS.—The remedies and rights provided under this section are in addition to and do not preclude any remedy for wrongful conversion otherwise available under law to the person claiming relief under this section, including any award for consequential and punitive damages.

"(c) AUTHORITY OF COURT.—In a hearing based on this section, the court—

"(1) may order repayment to the servicemember of all or part of the prior installments or deposits as a condition of terminating the contract and resuming possession of the property;

"(2) may, on its own motion, and shall on application by a servicemember when the servicemember's ability to comply with the contract is materially affected by military service, stay the proceedings for a period of time as, in the opinion of the court, justice and equity require; or

"(3) may make other disposition as is equitable to preserve the interests of all parties.

"SEC. 303. MORTGAGES AND TRUST DEEDS.

50 USC app. 533.

Applicability.

"(a) MORTGAGE AS SECURITY.—This section applies only to an obligation on real or personal property owned by a servicemember that—

"(1) originated before the period of the servicemember's military service and for which the servicemember is still obligated; and

"(2) is secured by a mortgage, trust deed, or other security in the nature of a mortgage.

"(b) STAY OF PROCEEDINGS AND ADJUSTMENT OF OBLIGATION.—In an action filed during, or within 90 days after, a servicemember's period of military service to enforce an obligation described in subsection (a), the court may after a hearing and on its own motion and shall upon application by a servicemember when the servicemember's ability to comply with the obligation is materially affected by military service—

"(1) stay the proceedings for a period of time as justice and equity require, or

"(2) adjust the obligation to preserve the interests of all parties.

"(c) SALE OR FORECLOSURE.—A sale, foreclosure, or seizure of property for a breach of an obligation described in subsection (a) shall not be valid if made during, or within 90 days after, the period of the servicemember's military service except—

"(1) upon a court order granted before such sale, foreclosure, or seizure with a return made and approved by the court; or

"(2) if made pursuant to an agreement as provided in section 107.

"(d) PENALTIES.—

"(1) MISDEMEANOR.—A person who knowingly makes or causes to be made a sale, foreclosure, or seizure of property that is prohibited by subsection (c), or who knowingly attempts to do so, shall be fined as provided in title 18, United States Code, or imprisoned for not more than one year, or both.

"(2) PRESERVATION OF OTHER REMEDIES.—The remedies and rights provided under this section are in addition to and do not preclude any remedy for wrongful conversion otherwise available under law to the person claiming relief under this section, including consequential and punitive damages.

50 USC app. 534.   "SEC. 304. SETTLEMENT OF STAYED CASES RELATING TO PERSONAL PROPERTY.

"(a) APPRAISAL OF PROPERTY.—When a stay is granted pursuant to this Act in a proceeding to foreclose a mortgage on or to repossess personal property, or to rescind or terminate a contract for the purchase of personal property, the court may appoint three disinterested parties to appraise the property.

"(b) EQUITY PAYMENT.—Based on the appraisal, and if undue hardship to the servicemember's dependents will not result, the court may order that the amount of the servicemember's equity in the property be paid to the servicemember, or the servicemember's dependents, as a condition of foreclosing the mortgage, repossessing the property, or rescinding or terminating the contract.

50 USC app. 535.   "SEC. 305. TERMINATION OF RESIDENTIAL OR MOTOR VEHICLE LEASES.

"(a) TERMINATION BY LESSEE.—The lessee on a lease described in subsection (b) may, at the lessee's option, terminate the lease at any time after—

"(1) the lessee's entry into military service; or

"(2) the date of the lessee's military orders described in paragraph (1)(B) or (2)(B) of subsection (b), as the case may be.

Applicability.   "(b) COVERED LEASES.—This section applies to the following leases:

"(1) LEASES OF PREMISES.—A lease of premises occupied, or intended to be occupied, by a servicemember or a servicemember's dependents for a residential, professional, business, agricultural, or similar purpose if—

"(A) the lease is executed by or on behalf of a person who thereafter and during the term of the lease enters military service; or

"(B) the servicemember, while in military service, executes the lease and thereafter receives military orders for a permanent change of station or to deploy with a military unit for a period of not less than 90 days.

"(2) LEASES OF MOTOR VEHICLES.—A lease of a motor vehicle used, or intended to be used, by a servicemember or a servicemember's dependents for personal or business transportation if—

"(A) the lease is executed by or on behalf of a person who thereafter and during the term of the lease enters military service under a call or order specifying a period

PUBLIC LAW 108–189—DEC. 19, 2003   117 STAT. 2849

of not less than 180 days (or who enters military service under a call or order specifying a period of 180 days or less and who, without a break in service, receives orders extending the period of military service to a period of not less than 180 days); or

"(B) the servicemember, while in military service, executes the lease and thereafter receives military orders for a permanent change of station outside of the continental United States or to deploy with a military unit for a period of not less than 180 days.

"(c) MANNER OF TERMINATION.—

"(1) IN GENERAL.—Termination of a lease under subsection (a) is made—

"(A) by delivery by the lessee of written notice of such termination, and a copy of the servicemember's military orders, to the lessor (or the lessor's grantee), or to the lessor's agent (or the agent's grantee); and

"(B) in the case of a lease of a motor vehicle, by return of the motor vehicle by the lessee to the lessor (or the lessor's grantee), or to the lessor's agent (or the agent's grantee), not later than 15 days after the date of the delivery of written notice under subparagraph (A). Deadline.

"(2) DELIVERY OF NOTICE.—Delivery of notice under paragraph (1)(A) may be accomplished—

"(A) by hand delivery;

"(B) by private business carrier; or

"(C) by placing the written notice in an envelope with sufficient postage and with return receipt requested, and addressed as designated by the lessor (or the lessor's grantee) or to the lessor's agent (or the agent's grantee), and depositing the written notice in the United States mails.

"(d) EFFECTIVE DATE OF LEASE TERMINATION.—

"(1) LEASE OF PREMISES.—In the case of a lease described in subsection (b)(1) that provides for monthly payment of rent, termination of the lease under subsection (a) is effective 30 days after the first date on which the next rental payment is due and payable after the date on which the notice under subsection (c) is delivered. In the case of any other lease described in subsection (b)(1), termination of the lease under subsection (a) is effective on the last day of the month following the month in which the notice is delivered.

"(2) LEASE OF MOTOR VEHICLES.—In the case of a lease described in subsection (b)(2), termination of the lease under subsection (a) is effective on the day on which the requirements of subsection (c) are met for such termination.

"(e) ARREARAGES AND OTHER OBLIGATIONS AND LIABILITIES.— Rents or lease amounts unpaid for the period preceding the effective date of the lease termination shall be paid on a prorated basis. In the case of the lease of a motor vehicle, the lessor may not impose an early termination charge, but any taxes, summonses, and title and registration fees and any other obligation and liability of the lessee in accordance with the terms of the lease, including reasonable charges to the lessee for excess wear, use and mileage, that are due and unpaid at the time of termination of the lease shall be paid by the lessee.

PUBLIC LAW 108–189—DEC. 19, 2003   117 STAT. 2851

"(2) PRESERVATION OF OTHER REMEDIES.—The remedy and rights provided under this and do not preclude any remedy for wrongful conversion otherwise available under law to the person claiming relief under this section, including any consequential or punitive damages.

"SEC. 307. ENFORCEMENT OF STORAGE LIENS.   50 USC app. 537.

"(a) LIENS.—
"(1) LIMITATION ON FORECLOSURE OR ENFORCEMENT.—A person holding a lien on the property or effects of a servicemember may not, during any period of military service of the servicemember and for 90 days thereafter, foreclose or enforce any lien on such property or effects without a court order granted before foreclosure or enforcement.
"(2) LIEN DEFINED.—For the purposes of paragraph (1), the term 'lien' includes a lien for storage, repair, or cleaning of the property or effects of a servicemember or a lien on such property or effects for any other reason.
"(b) STAY OF PROCEEDINGS.—In a proceeding to foreclose or enforce a lien subject to this section, the court may on its own motion, and shall if requested by a servicemember whose ability to comply with the obligation resulting in the proceeding is materially affected by military service—
"(1) stay the proceeding for a period of time as justice and equity require; or
"(2) adjust the obligation to preserve the interests of all parties.
The provisions of this subsection do not affect the scope of section 303.
"(c) PENALTIES.—
"(1) MISDEMEANOR.—A person who knowingly takes an action contrary to this section, or attempts to do so, shall be fined as provided in title 18, United States Code, or imprisoned for not more than one year, or both.
"(2) PRESERVATION OF OTHER REMEDIES.—The remedy and rights provided under this section are in addition to and do not preclude any remedy for wrongful conversion otherwise available under law to the person claiming relief under this section, including any consequential or punitive damages.

"SEC. 308. EXTENSION OF PROTECTIONS TO DEPENDENTS.   50 USC app. 538.

"Upon application to a court, a dependent of a servicemember is entitled to the protections of this title if the dependent's ability to comply with a lease, contract, bailment, or other obligation is materially affected by reason of the servicemember's military service.

"TITLE IV—LIFE INSURANCE

"SEC. 401. DEFINITIONS.   50 USC app. 541.

"For the purposes of this title:
"(1) POLICY.—The term 'policy' means any individual contract for whole, endowment, universal, or term life insurance (other than group term life insurance coverage), including any benefit in the nature of such insurance arising out of membership in any fraternal or beneficial association which—
"(A) provides that the insurer may not—

Protect Your Family from Lead in Your Home: U.S. Environmental Protection Agency

Protect Your Family from Lead in Your Home

Are You Planning To Buy, Rent, or Renovate a Home Built Before 1978?

Many houses and apartments built before 1978 have paint that contains high levels of lead (called lead-based paint). Lead from paint, chips, and dust can pose serious health hazards if not taken care of properly.

OWNERS, BUYERS, and RENTERS are encouraged to check for lead (see page 6) before renting, buying or renovating pre-1978 housing.

Federal law requires that individuals receive certain information before renting, buying, or renovating pre-1978 housing:

LANDLORDS have to disclose known information on lead-based paint and lead-based paint hazards before leases take effect. Leases must include a disclosure about lead-based paint.

SELLERS have to disclose known information on lead-based paint and lead-based paint hazards before selling a house. Sales contracts must include a disclosure about lead-based paint. Buyers have up to 10 days to check for lead.

RENOVATORS disturbing more than 2 square feet of painted surfaces have to give you this pamphlet before starting work.

IMPORTANT!

Lead From Paint, Dust, and Soil Can Be Dangerous If Not Managed Properly

FACT: Lead exposure can harm young children and babies even before they are born.

FACT: Even children who seem healthy can have high levels of lead in their bodies.

FACT: People can get lead in their bodies by breathing or swallowing lead dust, or by eating soil or paint chips containing lead.

FACT: People have many options for reducing lead hazards. In most cases, lead-based paint that is in good condition is not a hazard.

FACT: Removing lead-based paint improperly can increase the danger to your family.

If you think your home might have lead hazards, read this pamphlet to learn some simple steps to protect your family.

Lead Gets in the Body in Many Ways

Childhood lead poisoning remains a major environmental health problem in the U.S.

People can get lead in their body if they:

◆ Breathe in lead dust (especially during renovations that disturb painted surfaces).

◆ Put their hands or other objects covered with lead dust in their mouths.

◆ Eat paint chips or soil that contains lead.

Lead is even more dangerous to children under the age of 6:

◆ At this age children's brains and nervous systems are more sensitive to the damaging effects of lead.

◆ Children's growing bodies absorb more lead.

◆ Babies and young children often put their hands and other objects in their mouths. These objects can have lead dust on them.

Even children who appear healthy can have dangerous levels of lead in their bodies.

Lead is also dangerous to women of childbearing age:

◆ Women with a high lead level in their system prior to pregnancy would expose a fetus to lead through the placenta during fetal development.

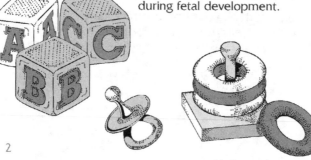

Lead's Effects

It is important to know that even exposure to low levels of lead can severely harm children.

In children, lead can cause:

◆ Nervous system and kidney damage.

◆ Learning disabilities, attention deficit disorder, and decreased intelligence.

◆ Speech, language, and behavior problems.

◆ Poor muscle coordination.

◆ Decreased muscle and bone growth.

◆ Hearing damage.

While low-lead exposure is most common, exposure to high levels of lead can have devastating effects on children, including seizures, unconsciousness, and, in some cases, death.

Although children are especially susceptible to lead exposure, lead can be dangerous for adults too.

In adults, lead can cause:

◆ Increased chance of illness during pregnancy.

◆ Harm to a fetus, including brain damage or death.

◆ Fertility problems (in men and women).

◆ High blood pressure.

◆ Digestive problems.

◆ Nerve disorders.

◆ Memory and concentration problems.

◆ Muscle and joint pain.

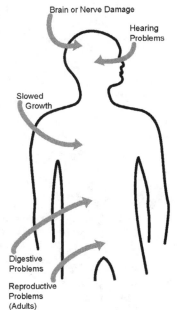

Brain or Nerve Damage

Hearing Problems

Slowed Growth

Digestive Problems

Reproductive Problems (Adults)

Lead affects the body in many ways.

3

Where Lead-Based Paint Is Found

In general, the older your home, the more likely it has lead-based paint.

Many homes built before 1978 have lead-based paint. The federal government banned lead-based paint from housing in 1978. Some states stopped its use even earlier. Lead can be found:

◆ In homes in the city, country, or suburbs.

◆ In apartments, single-family homes, and both private and public housing.

◆ Inside and outside of the house.

◆ In soil around a home. (Soil can pick up lead from exterior paint or other sources such as past use of leaded gas in cars.)

Checking Your Family for Lead

Get your children and home tested if you think your home has high levels of lead.

To reduce your child's exposure to lead, get your child checked, have your home tested (especially if your home has paint in poor condition and was built before 1978), and fix any hazards you may have. Children's blood lead levels tend to increase rapidly from 6 to 12 months of age, and tend to peak at 18 to 24 months of age.

Consult your doctor for advice on testing your children. A simple blood test can detect high levels of lead. Blood tests are usually recommended for:

◆ Children at ages 1 and 2.

◆ Children or other family members who have been exposed to high levels of lead.

◆ Children who should be tested under your state or local health screening plan.

Your doctor can explain what the test results mean and if more testing will be needed.

Identifying Lead Hazards

Lead-based paint is usually not a hazard if it is in good condition, and it is not on an impact or friction surface, like a window. It is defined by the federal government as paint with lead levels greater than or equal to 1.0 milligram per square centimeter, or more than 0.5% by weight.

Deteriorating lead-based paint (peeling, chipping, chalking, cracking or damaged) is a hazard and needs immediate attention. It may also be a hazard when found on surfaces that children can chew or that get a lot of wear-and-tear, such as:

◆ Windows and window sills.

◆ Doors and door frames.

◆ Stairs, railings, banisters, and porches.

Lead from paint chips, which you can see, and lead dust, which you can't always see, can both be serious hazards.

Lead dust can form when lead-based paint is scraped, sanded, or heated. Dust also forms when painted surfaces bump or rub together. Lead chips and dust can get on surfaces and objects that people touch. Settled lead dust can re-enter the air when people vacuum, sweep, or walk through it. The following two federal standards have been set for lead hazards in dust:

◆ 40 micrograms per square foot ($\mu g/ft^2$) and higher for floors, including carpeted floors.

◆ 250 $\mu g/ft^2$ and higher for interior window sills.

Lead in soil can be a hazard when children play in bare soil or when people bring soil into the house on their shoes. The following two federal standards have been set for lead hazards in residential soil:

◆ 400 parts per million (ppm) and higher in play areas of bare soil.

◆ 1,200 ppm (average) and higher in bare soil in the remainder of the yard.

The only way to find out if paint, dust and soil lead hazards exist is to test for them. The next page describes the most common methods used.

5

Checking Your Home for Lead

Just knowing that a home has lead-based paint may not tell you if there is a hazard.

You can get your home tested for lead in several different ways:

◆ A paint **inspection** tells you whether your home has lead-based paint and where it is located. It won't tell you whether or not your home currently has lead hazards.

◆ A **risk assessment** tells you if your home currently has any lead hazards from lead in paint, dust, or soil. It also tells you what actions to take to address any hazards.

◆ A combination risk assessment and inspection tells you if your home has any lead hazards and if your home has any lead-based paint, and where the lead-based paint is located.

Hire a trained and certified testing professional who will use a range of reliable methods when testing your home.

◆ Visual inspection of paint condition and location.

◆ A portable x-ray fluorescence (XRF) machine.

◆ Lab tests of paint, dust, and soil samples.

There are state and federal programs in place to ensure that testing is done safely, reliably, and effectively. Contact your state or local agency (see bottom of page 11) for more information, or call **1-800-424-LEAD (5323)** for a list of contacts in your area.

Home test kits for lead are available, but may not always be accurate. Consumers should not rely on these kits before doing renovations or to assure safety.

What You Can Do Now To Protect Your Family

If you suspect that your house has lead hazards, you can take some immediate steps to reduce your family's risk:

◆ **If you rent, notify your landlord of peeling or chipping paint.**

◆ **Clean up paint chips immediately.**

◆ **Clean floors, window frames, window sills, and other surfaces weekly.** Use a mop or sponge with warm water and a general all-purpose cleaner or a cleaner made specifically for lead. REMEMBER: NEVER MIX AMMONIA AND BLEACH PRODUCTS TOGETHER SINCE THEY CAN FORM A DANGEROUS GAS.

◆ **Thoroughly rinse sponges and mop heads after cleaning dirty or dusty areas.**

◆ **Wash children's hands often, especially before they eat and before nap time and bed time.**

◆ **Keep play areas clean.** Wash bottles, pacifiers, toys, and stuffed animals regularly.

◆ **Keep children from chewing window sills or other painted surfaces.**

◆ **Clean or remove shoes before entering your home to avoid tracking in lead from soil.**

◆ **Make sure children eat nutritious, low-fat meals high in iron and calcium,** such as spinach and dairy products. Children with good diets absorb less lead.

Reducing Lead Hazards In The Home

Removing lead improperly can increase the hazard to your family by spreading even more lead dust around the house.

Always use a professional who is trained to remove lead hazards safely.

In addition to day-to-day cleaning and good nutrition:

◆ You can **temporarily** reduce lead hazards by taking actions such as repairing damaged painted surfaces and planting grass to cover soil with high lead levels. These actions (called "interim controls") are not permanent solutions and will need ongoing attention.

◆ To **permanently** remove lead hazards, you should hire a certified lead "abatement" contractor. Abatement (or permanent hazard elimination) methods include removing, sealing, or enclosing lead-based paint with special materials. Just painting over the hazard with regular paint is not permanent removal.

Always hire a person with special training for correcting lead problems—someone who knows how to do this work safely and has the proper equipment to clean up thoroughly. Certified contractors will employ qualified workers and follow strict safety rules as set by their state or by the federal government.

Once the work is completed, dust cleanup activities must be repeated until testing indicates that lead dust levels are below the following:

◆ 40 micrograms per square foot ($\mu g/ft^2$) for floors, including carpeted floors;

◆ 250 $\mu g/ft^2$ for interior windows sills; and

◆ 400 $\mu g/ft^2$ for window troughs.

Call your state or local agency (see bottom of page 11) for help in locating certified professionals in your area and to see if financial assistance is available.

Remodeling or Renovating a Home With Lead-Based Paint

Take precautions before your contractor or you begin remodeling or renovating anything that disturbs painted surfaces (such as scraping off paint or tearing out walls):

◆ **Have the area tested for lead-based paint.**

◆ **Do not use a belt-sander, propane torch, high temperature heat gun, dry scraper, or dry sandpaper** to remove lead-based paint. These actions create large amounts of lead dust and fumes. Lead dust can remain in your home long after the work is done.

◆ **Temporarily move your family** (especially children and pregnant women) out of the apartment or house until the work is done and the area is properly cleaned. If you can't move your family, at least completely seal off the work area.

◆ **Follow other safety measures to reduce lead hazards.** You can find out about other safety measures by calling 1-800-424-LEAD. Ask for the brochure "Reducing Lead Hazards When Remodeling Your Home." This brochure explains what to do before, during, and after renovations.

If you have already completed renovations or remodeling that could have released lead-based paint or dust, get your young children tested and follow the steps outlined on page 7 of this brochure.

If not conducted properly, certain types of renovations can release lead from paint and dust into the air.

9

Other Sources of Lead

While paint, dust, and soil are the most common sources of lead, other lead sources also exist.

◆ **Drinking water.** Your home might have plumbing with lead or lead solder. Call your local health department or water supplier to find out about testing your water. You cannot see, smell, or taste lead, and boiling your water will not get rid of lead. If you think your plumbing might have lead in it:

- Use only cold water for drinking and cooking.

- Run water for 15 to 30 seconds before drinking it, especially if you have not used your water for a few hours.

◆ **The job.** If you work with lead, you could bring it home on your hands or clothes. Shower and change clothes before coming home. Launder your work clothes separately from the rest of your family's clothes.

◆ Old painted **toys** and **furniture.**

◆ Food and liquids stored in **lead crystal** or **lead-glazed pottery or porcelain.**

◆ **Lead smelters** or other industries that release lead into the air.

◆ **Hobbies** that use lead, such as making pottery or stained glass, or refinishing furniture.

◆ **Folk remedies** that contain lead, such as "greta" and "azarcon" used to treat an upset stomach.

For More Information

The National Lead Information Center

Call **1-800-424-LEAD (424-5323)** to learn how to protect children from lead poisoning and for other information on lead hazards. To access lead information via the web, visit **www.epa.gov/lead** and **www.hud.gov/offices/lead/.**

EPA's Safe Drinking Water Hotline

Call **1-800-426-4791** for information about lead in drinking water.

Consumer Product Safety Commission (CPSC) Hotline

To request information on lead in consumer products, or to report an unsafe consumer product or a product-related injury call **1-800-638-2772**, or visit CPSC's Web site at: **www.cpsc.gov.**

Health and Environmental Agencies

Some cities, states, and tribes have their own rules for lead-based paint activities. Check with your local agency to see which laws apply to you. Most agencies can also provide information on finding a lead abatement firm in your area, and on possible sources of financial aid for reducing lead hazards. Receive up-to-date address and phone information for your local contacts on the Internet at **www.epa.gov/lead** or contact the National Lead Information Center at **1-800-424-LEAD.**

For the hearing impaired, call the Federal Information Relay Service at **1-800-877-8339** to access any of the phone numbers in this brochure.

EPA Regional Offices

Your Regional EPA Office can provide further information regarding regulations and lead protection programs.

EPA Regional Offices

Region 1 (Connecticut, Massachusetts, Maine, New Hampshire, Rhode Island, Vermont)

Regional Lead Contact
U.S. EPA Region 1
Suite 1100 (CPT)
One Congress Street
Boston, MA 02114-2023
1 (888) 372-7341

Region 2 (New Jersey, New York, Puerto Rico, Virgin Islands)

Regional Lead Contact
U.S. EPA Region 2
2890 Woodbridge Avenue
Building 209, Mail Stop 225
Edison, NJ 08837-3679
(732) 321-6671

Region 3 (Delaware, Maryland, Pennsylvania, Virginia, Washington DC, West Virginia)

Regional Lead Contact
U.S. EPA Region 3 (3WC33)
1650 Arch Street
Philadelphia, PA 19103
(215) 814-5000

Region 4 (Alabama, Florida, Georgia, Kentucky, Mississippi, North Carolina, South Carolina, Tennessee)

Regional Lead Contact
U.S. EPA Region 4
61 Forsyth Street, SW
Atlanta, GA 30303
(404) 562-8998

Region 5 (Illinois, Indiana, Michigan, Minnesota, Ohio, Wisconsin)

Regional Lead Contact
U.S. EPA Region 5 (DT-8J)
77 West Jackson Boulevard
Chicago, IL 60604-3666
(312) 886-6003

Region 6 (Arkansas, Louisiana, New Mexico, Oklahoma, Texas)

Regional Lead Contact
U.S. EPA Region 6
1445 Ross Avenue, 12th Floor
Dallas, TX 75202-2733
(214) 665-7577

Region 7 (Iowa, Kansas, Missouri, Nebraska)

Regional Lead Contact
U.S. EPA Region 7
(ARTD-RALI)
901 N. 5th Street
Kansas City, KS 66101
(913) 551-7020

Region 8 (Colorado, Montana, North Dakota, South Dakota, Utah, Wyoming)

Regional Lead Contact
U.S. EPA Region 8
999 18th Street, Suite 500
Denver, CO 80202-2466
(303) 312-6021

Region 9 (Arizona, California, Hawaii, Nevada)

Regional Lead Contact
U.S. Region 9
75 Hawthorne Street
San Francisco, CA 94105
(415) 947-4164

Region 10 (Alaska, Idaho, Oregon, Washington)

Regional Lead Contact
U.S. EPA Region 10
Toxics Section WCM-128
1200 Sixth Avenue
Seattle, WA 98101-1128
(206) 553-1985

CPSC Regional Offices

Your Regional CPSC Office can provide further information regarding regulations and consumer product safety.

Eastern Regional Center
Consumer Product Safety Commission
201 Varick Street, Room 903
New York, NY 10014
(212) 620-4120

Western Regional Center
Consumer Product Safety Commission
1301 Clay Street, Suite 610-N
Oakland, CA 94612
(510) 637-4050

Central Regional Center
Consumer Product Safety Commission
230 South Dearborn Street, Room 2944
Chicago, IL 60604
(312) 353-8260

HUD Lead Office

Please contact HUD's Office of Healthy Homes and Lead Hazard Control for information on lead regulations, outreach efforts, and lead hazard control and research grant programs.

U.S. Department of Housing and Urban Development
Office of Healthy Homes and Lead Hazard Control
451 Seventh Street, SW, P-3206
Washington, DC 20410
(202) 755-1785

U.S. EPA Washington DC 20460   EPA747-K-99-001
U.S. CPSC Washington DC 20207   June 2003
U.S. HUD Washington DC 20410

Carbon Monoxide Fact Sheet:
U.S. Environmental Protection Agency

Carbon Monoxide Fact Feet

United States
Environmental Protection
Agency

Indoor Environments Division (6609J)
Office of Air and Radiation

EPA-402-F-96-005
October 1996

 EPA | ## Protect Your Family and Yourself from Carbon Monoxide Poisoning

Carbon Monoxide Can Be Deadly

You can't see or smell carbon monoxide, but at high levels it can kill a person in minutes. Carbon monoxide (CO) is produced whenever any fuel such as gas, oil, kerosene, wood, or charcoal is burned. If appliances that burn fuel are maintained and used properly, the amount of CO produced is usually not hazardous. However, if appliances are not working properly or are used incorrectly, dangerous levels of CO can result. Hundreds of people die accidentally every year from CO poisoning caused by malfunctioning or improperly used fuel-burning appliances. Even more die from CO produced by idling cars. Fetuses, infants, elderly people, and people with anemia or with a history of heart or respiratory disease can be especially susceptible. Be safe. Practice the DO's and DON'Ts of carbon monoxide.

CO Poisoning Symptoms

Know the symptoms of CO poisoning. At moderate levels, you or your family can get severe headaches, become dizzy, mentally confused, nauseated, or faint. You can even die if these levels persist for a long time. Low levels can cause shortness of breath, mild nausea, and mild headaches, and may have longer-term effects on your health. Since many of these symptoms are similar to those of the flu, food poisoning, or other illnesses, you may not think that CO poisoning could be the cause.

Play it Safe

If you experience symptoms that you think could be from CO poisoning:

✓ DO *GET FRESH AIR IMMEDIATELY.* Open doors and windows, turn off combustion appliances and *leave the house*.

✓ DO *GO TO AN EMERGENCY ROOM and tell the physician you suspect CO poisoning.* If CO poisoning has occurred, it can often be diagnosed by a blood test done soon after exposure.

✓ DO Be prepared to answer the following questions for the doctor:

- Do your symptoms occur only in the house? Do they disappear or decrease when you leave home and reappear when you return?
- Is anyone else in your household complaining of similar symptoms? Did everyone's symptoms appear about the same time?
- Are you using any fuel-burning appliances in the home?
- Has anyone inspected your appliances lately? Are you certain they are working properly?

Prevention **is the Key to Avoiding Carbon Monoxide Poisoning**

✓ DO have your fuel-burning appliances -- including oil and gas furnaces, gas water heaters, gas ranges and ovens, gas dryers, gas or kerosene space heaters, fireplaces, and wood stoves -- inspected by a trained professional at the beginning of every heating

season. Make certain that the flues and chimneys are connected, in good condition, and not blocked.

✓ **DO** choose appliances that vent their fumes to the outside whenever possible, have them properly installed, and maintain them according to manufacturers' instructions.

✓ **DO** read and follow all of the instructions that accompany any fuel-burning device. If you cannot avoid using an unvented gas or kerosene space heater, *carefully follow the cautions* that come with the device. Use the proper fuel and keep doors to the rest of the house open. Crack a window to ensure enough air for ventilation and proper fuel-burning.

✓ **DO** call EPA's IAQ INFO Clearinghouse (**1-800-438-4318**) or the Consumer Product Safety Commission (**1-800-638-2772**) for more information on how to reduce your risks from CO and other combustion gases and particles.

✗ **DON'T** idle the car in a garage -- even if the garage door to the outside is open. Fumes can build up very quickly in the garage and living area of your home.

✗ **DON'T** use a gas oven to heat your home, even for a short time.

✗ **DON'T** *ever* use a charcoal grill indoors -- even in a fireplace.

✗ **DON'T** sleep in any room with an unvented gas or kerosene space heater.

✗ **DON'T** use any gasoline-powered engines (mowers, weed trimmers, snow blowers, chain saws, small engines or generators) in enclosed spaces.

✗ **DON'T** ignore symptoms, particularly if more than one person is feeling them. You could lose consciousness and die if you do nothing.

A Few Words About CO Detectors

Carbon Monoxide Detectors are widely available in stores and you may want to consider buying one as a back up -- *BUT NOT AS A REPLACEMENT* for proper use and maintenance of your fuel-burning appliances. However, it is important for you to know that the technology of CO detectors is still developing, that there are several types on the market, and that they are not generally considered to be as reliable as the smoke detectors found in homes today. Some CO detectors have been laboratory-tested, and their performance varied. Some performed well, others failed to alarm even at very high CO levels, and still others alarmed even at very low levels that don't pose any immediate health risk. And unlike a smoke detector, where you can easily confirm the cause of the alarm, CO is invisible and odorless, so it's harder to tell if an alarm is false or a real emergency.

So What's a Consumer to Do?

First, don't let buying a CO detector lull you into a false sense of security. Preventing CO from becoming a problem in your home is better than relying on an alarm. Follow the checklist of DOs and DON'Ts above.

Second, if you shop for a CO detector, do some research on features and don't select solely on the basis of cost. Non-governmental organizations such as Consumers Union (publisher of *Consumer Reports*), the American Gas Association, and Underwriters Laboratories (UL) can help you make an informed decision. Look for UL certification on any detector you purchase.

Carefully follow manufacturers' instructions for its placement, use, and maintenance.

If the CO detector alarm goes off:

- Make sure it is your CO detector and not your smoke detector.
- Check to see if any member of the household is experiencing symptoms of poisoning.
- If they are, get them out of the house immediately and seek medical attention. Tell the doctor that you suspect CO poisoning.
- If no one is feeling symptoms, ventilate the home with fresh air, turn off all potential sources of CO -- your oil or gas furnace, gas water heater, gas range and oven, gas dryer, gas or kerosene space heater and any vehicle or small engine.
- Have a qualified technician inspect your fuel-burning appliances and chimneys to make sure they are operating correctly and that there is nothing blocking the fumes from being vented out of the house.

A Brief Guide to Mold, Moisture, and Your Home:
U.S. Environmental Protection Agency

A Brief Guide to Mold, Moisture, and Your Home

EPA 402-K-02-003

This Guide provides information and guidance for homeowners and renters on how to clean up residential mold problems and how to prevent mold growth.

U.S. Environmental Protection Agency
Office of Air and Radiation
Indoor Environments Division
1200 Pennsylvania Avenue
Mailcode: 6609J
Washington, DC 20460
www.epa.gov/iaq

A BRIEF GUIDE TO MOLD, MOISTURE, AND YOUR HOME

Contents

	Page
Mold Basics	
Why is mold growing in my home?	2
Can mold cause health problems?	2
How do I get rid of mold?	3
Mold Cleanup	
Who should do the cleanup?	4
Mold Cleanup Guidelines	6
What to Wear When Cleaning Moldy Areas	8
How Do I Know When the Remediation or Cleanup is Finished?	9
Moisture and Mold Prevention and Control Tips	10
Actions that will help to reduce humidity	11
Actions that will help prevent condensation	12
Testing or sampling for mold	13
Hidden Mold	14
Cleanup and Biocides	15
Additional Resources	16

MOLD **BASICS**

- **The key to mold control is moisture control.**

- **If mold is a problem in your home, you should clean up the mold promptly *and* fix the water problem.**

- **It is important to dry water-damaged areas and items within 24-48 hours to prevent mold growth.**

Why is mold growing in my home? Molds are part of the natural environment. Outdoors, molds play a part in nature by breaking down dead organic matter such as fallen leaves and dead trees, but indoors, mold growth should be avoided. Molds reproduce by means of tiny spores; the spores are invisible to the naked eye and float through outdoor and indoor air. Mold may begin growing indoors when mold spores land on surfaces that are wet. There are many types of mold, and none of them will grow without water or moisture.

Mold growing outdoors on firewood. Molds come in many colors; both white and black molds are shown here.

Can mold cause health problems? Molds are usually not a problem indoors, unless mold spores land on a wet or damp spot and begin growing. Molds have the potential to cause health problems. Molds produce allergens (substances that can cause allergic reactions), irritants, and in some cases, potentially toxic substances (mycotoxins).

Inhaling or touching mold or mold spores may cause allergic reactions in sensitive individuals. Allergic responses include hay fever-type symptoms, such as sneezing, runny nose, red eyes, and skin rash (dermatitis). Allergic reactions to mold are common. They can be immediate or delayed. Molds can also cause asthma attacks in people with asthma who are allergic to mold. In addition, mold exposure can irritate the eyes, skin, nose, throat, and lungs of both mold-allergic and non-allergic people. Symptoms other than the allergic and irritant types are not commonly reported as a result of inhaling mold.

Research on mold and health effects is ongoing. This brochure provides a brief overview; it does not describe all potential health effects related to mold exposure. For more detailed information consult a health professional. You may also wish to consult your state or local health department.

How do I get rid of mold? It is impossible to get rid of all mold and mold spores indoors; some mold spores will be found floating through the air and in house dust. The mold spores will not grow if moisture is not present. Indoor mold growth can and should be prevented or controlled by controlling moisture indoors. If there is mold growth in your home, you must clean up the mold **and** fix the water problem. If you clean up the mold, but don't fix the water problem, then, most likely, the mold problem will come back.

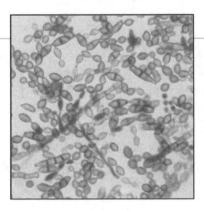

Magnified mold spores.

Molds can gradually destroy the things they grow on. You can prevent damage to your home and furnishings, save money, and avoid potential health problems by controlling moisture and eliminating mold growth.

Leaky window — mold is beginning to rot the wooden frame and windowsill.

If you already have a mold problem –
ACT QUICKLY.
Mold damages what it grows on. The longer it grows, the more damage it can cause.

Who should do the cleanup? Who should do the cleanup depends on a number of factors. One consideration is the size of the mold problem. If the moldy area is less than about 10 square feet (less than roughly a 3 ft. by 3 ft. patch), in most cases, you can handle the job yourself, following the guidelines below. However:

■ If there has been a lot of water damage, and/or mold growth covers more than 10 square feet, consult the U.S. Environmental Protection Agency (EPA) guide: *Mold Remediation in Schools and Commercial Buildings.* Although focused on schools and commercial buildings, this document is applicable to other building types. It is available free by calling the EPA Indoor Air Quality Information Clearinghouse at (800) 438-4318, or on the Internet at: www.epa.gov/mold.

- If you choose to hire a contractor (or other professional service provider) to do the cleanup, make sure the contractor has experience cleaning up mold. Check references and ask the contractor to follow the recommendations in EPA's *Mold Remediation in Schools and Commercial Buildings*, the guidelines of the American Conference of Governmental Industrial Hygenists (ACGIH), or other guidelines from professional or government organizations.

- If you suspect that the heating/ventilation/air conditioning (HVAC) system may be contaminated with mold (it is part of an identified moisture problem, for instance, or there is mold near the intake to the system), consult EPA's guide *Should You Have the Air Ducts in Your Home Cleaned?* before taking further action. Do not run the HVAC system if you know or suspect that it is contaminated with mold - it could spread mold throughout the building. Visit www.epa.gov/iaq/pubs/ airduct.html, or call (800) 438-4318 for a free copy.

- If the water and/or mold damage was caused by sewage or other contaminated water, then call in a professional who has experience cleaning and fixing buildings damaged by contaminated water.

- If you have health concerns, consult a health professional before starting cleanup.

MOLD **CLEANUP** GUIDELINES

BATHROOM TIP
Places that are often or always damp can be hard to maintain completely free of mold. If there's some mold in the shower or elsewhere in the bathroom that seems to reappear, increasing the ventilation (running a fan or opening a window) and cleaning more frequently will usually prevent mold from recurring, or at least keep the mold to a minimum.

Tips and techniques The tips and techniques presented in this section will help you clean up your mold problem. Professional cleaners or remediators may use methods not covered in this publication. Please note that mold may cause staining and cosmetic damage. It may not be possible to clean an item so that its original appearance is restored.

■ Fix plumbing leaks and other water problems as soon as possible. Dry all items completely.

■ Scrub mold off hard surfaces with detergent and water, and dry completely.

Mold growing on the underside of a plastic lawnchair in an area where rainwater drips through and deposits organic material.

Mold growing on a piece of ceiling tile.

- Absorbent or porous materials, such as ceiling tiles and carpet, may have to be thrown away if they become moldy. Mold can grow on or fill in the empty spaces and crevices of porous materials, so the mold may be difficult or impossible to remove completely.

- Avoid exposing yourself or others to mold (see discussions: **What to Wear When Cleaning Moldy Areas** and **Hidden Mold**.)

- Do not paint or caulk moldy surfaces. Clean up the mold and dry the surfaces before painting. Paint applied over moldy surfaces is likely to peel.

- If you are unsure about how to clean an item, or if the item is expensive or of sentimental value, you may wish to consult a specialist. Specialists in furniture repair, restoration, painting, art restoration and conservation, carpet and rug cleaning, water damage, and fire or water restoration are commonly listed in phone books. Be sure to ask for and check references. Look for specialists who are affiliated with professional organizations.

Mold growing on a suitcase stored in a humid basement.

It is important to take precautions to **LIMIT YOUR EXPOSURE** to mold and mold spores.

■ **Avoid breathing in mold or mold spores**. In order to limit your exposure to airborne mold, you may want to wear an N-95 respirator, available at many hardware stores and from companies that advertise on the Internet. (They cost about $12 to $25.) Some N-95 respirators resemble a paper dust mask with a nozzle on the front, others are made primarily of plastic or rubber and have removable cartridges that trap most of the mold spores from entering. In order to be effective, the respirator or mask must fit properly, so carefully follow the instructions supplied with the respirator. Please note that the Occupational Safety and Health Administration (OSHA) requires that respirators fit properly (fit testing) when used in an occupational setting; consult OSHA for more information (800-321-OSHA or osha.gov/).

8

- **Wear gloves**. Long gloves that extend to the middle of the forearm are recommended. When working with water and a mild detergent, ordinary household rubber gloves may be used. If you are using a disinfectant, a biocide such as chlorine bleach, or a strong cleaning solution, you should select gloves made from natural rubber, neoprene, nitrile, polyurethane, or PVC (see **Cleanup and Biocides**). Avoid touching mold or moldy items with your bare hands.

- **Wear goggles**. Goggles that do not have ventilation holes are recommended. Avoid getting mold or mold spores in your eyes.

Cleaning while wearing N-95 respirator, gloves, and goggles.

How do I know when the remediation or cleanup is finished? You must have completely fixed the water or moisture problem before the cleanup or remediation can be considered finished.

- You should have completed mold removal. Visible mold and moldy odors should not be present. Please note that mold may cause staining and cosmetic damage.

- You should have revisited the site(s) shortly after cleanup and it should show no signs of water damage or mold growth.

- People should have been able to occupy or re-occupy the area without health complaints or physical symptoms.

- Ultimately, this is a judgment call; there is no easy answer. If you have concerns or questions call the EPA Indoor Air Quality Information Clearinghouse at (800) 438-4318.

MOISTURE AND MOLD
PREVENTION AND
CONTROL TIPS

MOISTURE
Control is the Key to
Mold Control

Mold growing on the surface of a unit ventilator.

■ When water leaks or spills occur indoors - **ACT QUICKLY**.
If wet or damp materials or areas are dried 24-48 hours after a leak or spill happens, in most cases mold will not grow.

■ Clean and repair roof gutters regularly.

■ Make sure the ground slopes away from the building foundation, so that water does not enter or collect around the foundation.

■ Keep air conditioning drip pans clean and the drain lines unobstructed and flowing properly.

Condensation on the inside of a windowpane.

- Keep indoor humidity low. If possible, keep indoor humidity below 60 percent (ideally between 30 and 50 percent) relative humidity. Relative humidity can be measured with a moisture or humidity meter, a small, inexpensive ($10-$50) instrument available at many hardware stores.

- If you see condensation or moisture collecting on windows, walls or pipes - ACT QUICKLY to dry the wet surface and reduce the moisture/water source. Condensation can be a sign of high humidity.

Actions that will help to reduce humidity:

- Vent appliances that produce moisture, such as clothes dryers, stoves, and kerosene heaters to the outside where possible. (Combustion appliances such as stoves and kerosene heaters produce water vapor and will increase the humidity unless vented to the outside.)

- Use air conditioners and/or de-humidifiers when needed.

- Run the bathroom fan or open the window when showering. Use exhaust fans or open windows whenever cooking, running the dishwasher or dishwashing, etc.

Actions that will help prevent condensation:

- Reduce the humidity (see preceeding page).

- Increase ventilation or air movement by opening doors and/or windows, when practical. Use fans as needed.

- Cover cold surfaces, such as cold water pipes, with insulation.

- Increase air temperature.

Mold growing on a wooden headboard in a room with high humidity.

Renters: Report all plumbing leaks and moisture problems immediately to your building owner, manager, or superintendent. In cases where persistent water problems are not addressed, you may want to contact local, state, or federal health or housing authorities.

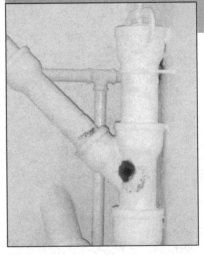

Rust is an indicator that condensation occurs on this drainpipe. The pipe should be insulated to prevent condensation.

Testing or sampling for mold Is sampling for mold needed? **In most cases, if visible mold growth is present, sampling is unnecessary.** Since no EPA or other federal limits have been set for mold or mold spores, sampling cannot be used to check a building's compliance with federal mold standards. Surface sampling may be useful to determine if an area has been adequately cleaned or remediated. Sampling for mold should be conducted by professionals who have specific experience in designing mold sampling protocols, sampling methods, and interpreting results. Sample analysis should follow analytical methods recommended by the American Industrial Hygiene Association (AIHA), the American Conference of Governmental Industrial Hygienists (ACGIH), or other professional organizations.

HIDDEN **MOLD**

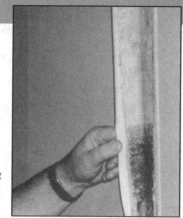

Mold growing on the back side of wallpaper.

Suspicion of hidden mold You may suspect hidden mold if a building smells moldy, but you cannot see the source, or if you know there has been water damage and residents are reporting health problems. Mold may be hidden in places such as the back side of dry wall, wallpaper, or paneling, the top side of ceiling tiles, the underside of carpets and pads, etc. Other possible locations of hidden mold include areas inside walls around pipes (with leaking or condensing pipes), the surface of walls behind furniture (where condensation forms), inside ductwork, and in roof materials above ceiling tiles (due to roof leaks or insufficient insulation).

Investigating hidden mold problems Investigating hidden mold problems may be difficult and will require caution when the investigation involves disturbing potential sites of mold growth. For example, removal of wallpaper can lead to a massive release of spores if there is mold growing on the underside of the paper. If you believe that you may have a hidden mold problem, consider hiring an experienced professional.

14

Cleanup and Biocides Biocides are substances that can destroy living organisms. The use of a chemical or biocide that kills organisms such as mold (chlorine bleach, for example) is not recommended as a routine practice during mold cleanup. There may be instances, however, when professional judgment may indicate its use (for example, when immune-compromised individuals are present). In most cases, it is not possible or desirable to sterilize an area; a background level of mold spores will remain - these spores will not grow if the moisture problem has been resolved. If you choose to use disinfectants or biocides, always ventilate the area and exhaust the air to the outdoors. Never mix chlorine bleach solution with other cleaning solutions or detergents that contain ammonia because toxic fumes could be produced.

Please note: Dead mold may still cause allergic reactions in some people, so it is not enough to simply kill the mold, it must also be removed.

Water stain on a basement wall — locate and fix the source of the water promptly.

ADDITIONAL **RESOURCES**

For more information on mold related issues including mold cleanup and moisture control/condensation/humidity issues, you can call the EPA Indoor Air Quality Information Clearinghouse at

(800) 438-4318.

Or visit:

www.epa.gov/mold

Mold growing on fallen leaves.

This document is available on the Environmental Protection Agency, Indoor Environments Division website at: www.epa.gov/mold

NOTES

Acknowledgements

EPA would like to thank Paul Ellringer, PE, CIH, for providing the photo on page 14.

Please note that this document presents recommendations. EPA does not regulate mold or mold spores in indoor air.

Fair Housing Poster:
U.S. Department of Housing
and Urban Development

Fair Housing Poster

U. S. Department of Housing and Urban Development

EQUAL HOUSING OPPORTUNITY

We Do Business in Accordance With the Federal Fair Housing Law

(The Fair Housing Amendments Act of 1988)

It is illegal to Discriminate Against Any Person Because of Race, Color, Religion, Sex, Handicap, Familial Status, or National Origin

---

- In the sale or rental of housing or residential lots
- In advertising the sale or rental of housing
- In the financing of housing

- In the provision of real estate brokerage services
- In the appraisal of housing
- Blockbusting is also illegal

Anyone who feels he or she has been discriminated against may file a complaint of housing discrimination:

    1-800-669-9777 (Toll Free)
    1-800-927-9275 (TTY)

U.S. Department of Housing and Urban Development
Assistant Secretary for Fair Housing and Equal Opportunity
Washington, D.C. 20410

Previous editions are obsolete   form HUD-928.1 (2/2003)

Fair Housing Act:
Federal Housing Administration

Fair Housing Act

FAIR HOUSING ACT

Sec. 800. [42 U.S.C. 3601 note] Short Title

This title may be cited as the "Fair Housing Act".

Sec. 801. [42 U.S.C. 3601] Declaration of Policy

It is the policy of the United States to provide, within constitutional limitations, for fair housing throughout the United States.

Sec. 802. [42 U.S.C. 3602] Definitions

As used in this subchapter--

(a) "Secretary" means the Secretary of Housing and Urban Development.

(b) "Dwelling" means any building, structure, or portion thereof which is occupied as, or designed or intended for occupancy as, a residence by one or more families, and any vacant land which is offered for sale or lease for the construction or location thereon of any such building, structure, or portion thereof.

(c) "Family" includes a single individual.

(d) "Person" includes one or more individuals, corporations, partnerships, associations, labor organizations, legal representatives, mutual companies, joint-stock companies, trusts, unincorporated organizations, trustees, trustees in cases under title 11 [of the United States Code], receivers, and fiduciaries.

(e) "To rent" includes to lease, to sublease, to let and otherwise to grant for a consideration the right to occupy premises not owned by the occupant.

(f) "Discriminatory housing practice" means an act that is unlawful under section 804, 805, 806, or 818 of this title.

(g) "State" means any of the several States, the District of Columbia, the Commonwealth of Puerto Rico, or any of the territories and possessions of the United States.

(h) "Handicap" means, with respect to a person--

   (1) a physical or mental impairment which substantially limits one or more of such person's major life activities,

   (2) a record of having such an impairment, or

   (3) being regarded as having such an impairment, but such term does not include current, illegal use of or addiction to a controlled substance (as defined in section 102 of the Controlled Substances Act (21 U.S.C. 802)).

(i) "Aggrieved person" includes any person who--

(1) claims to have been injured by a discriminatory housing practice; or

(2) believes that such person will be injured by a discriminatory housing practice that is about to occur.

(j) "Complainant" means the person (including the Secretary) who files a complaint under section 810.

(k) "Familial status" means one or more individuals (who have not attained the age of 18 years) being domiciled with--

(1) a parent or another person having legal custody of such individual or individuals; or

(2) the designee of such parent or other person having such custody, with the written permission of such parent or other person.

The protections afforded against discrimination on the basis of familial status shall apply to any person who is pregnant or is in the process of securing legal custody of any individual who has not attained the age of 18 years.

(l) "Conciliation" means the attempted resolution of issues raised by a complaint, or by the investigation of such complaint, through informal negotiations involving the aggrieved person, the respondent, and the Secretary.

(m) "Conciliation agreement" means a written agreement setting forth the resolution of the issues in conciliation.

(n) "Respondent" means--

(1) the person or other entity accused in a complaint of an unfair housing practice; and

(2) any other person or entity identified in the course of investigation and notified as required with respect to respondents so identified under section 810(a).

(o) "Prevailing party" has the same meaning as such term has in section 722 of the Revised Statutes of the United States (42 U.S.C. 1988).

[42 U.S.C. 3602 note] Neither the term "individual with handicaps" nor the term "handicap" shall apply to an individual solely because that individual is a transvestite.

Sec. 803. [42 U.S.C. 3603] Effective dates of certain prohibitions

(a) Subject to the provisions of subsection (b) of this section and section 807 of this title, the prohibitions against discrimination in the sale or rental of housing set forth in section 804 of this title shall apply:

(1) Upon enactment of this subchapter, to--

(A) dwellings owned or operated by the Federal Government;

(B) dwellings provided in whole or in part with the aid of loans, advances, grants, or contributions made by the Federal Government, under agreements entered into after November 20, 1962, unless payment due thereon has been made in full prior to April 11, 1968;

(C) dwellings provided in whole or in part by loans insured, guaranteed, or otherwise secured by the credit of the Federal Government, under agreements entered into after November 20, 1962, unless payment thereon has been made in full prior to April 11, 1968: **Provided**, That nothing contained in subparagraphs (B) and (C) of this subsection shall be applicable to dwellings solely by virtue of the fact that they are subject to mortgages held by an FDIC or FSLIC institution; and

(D) dwellings provided by the development or the redevelopment of real property purchased, rented, or otherwise obtained from a State or local public agency receiving Federal financial assistance for slum clearance or urban renewal with respect to such real property under loan or grant contracts entered into after November 20, 1962.

(2) After December 31, 1968, to all dwellings covered by paragraph (1) and to all other dwellings except as exempted by subsection (b) of this section.

(b)Nothing in section 804 of this title (other than subsection (c)) shall apply to--

(1) any single-family house sold or rented by an owner: **Provided**, That such private individual owner does not own more than three such single-family houses at any one time: **Provided further**, That in the case of the sale of any such single-family house by a private individual owner not residing in such house at the time of such sale or who was not the most recent resident of such house prior to such sale, the exemption granted by this subsection shall apply only with respect to one such sale within any twenty-four month period: **Provided further**, That such bona fide private individual owner does not own any interest in, nor is there owned or reserved on his behalf, under any express or voluntary agreement, title to or any right to all or a portion of the proceeds from the sale or rental of, more than three such single-family houses at any one time: **Provided further**, That after December 31, 1969, the sale or rental of any such single-family house shall be excepted from the application of this subchapter only if such house is sold or rented (A) without the use in any manner of the sales or rental facilities or the sales or rental services of any real estate broker, agent, or salesman, or of such facilities or services of any person in the business of selling or renting dwellings, or of any employee or agent of any such broker, agent, salesman, or person and (B) without the publication, posting or mailing, after notice, of any advertisement or written notice in violation of section 804(c) of this title; but nothing in this proviso shall prohibit the use of attorneys, escrow agents, abstractors, title companies, and other such professional assistance as necessary to perfect or transfer the title, or

(2)rooms or units in dwellings containing living quarters occupied or intended to be occupied by no more than four families living independently of each other, if the owner actually maintains and occupies one of such living quarters as his residence.

(c)For the purposes of subsection (b) of this section, a person shall be deemed to be in the business of selling or renting dwellings if--

(1) he has, within the preceding twelve months, participated as principal in three or more transactions involving the sale or rental of any dwelling or any interest therein, or

(2) he has, within the preceding twelve months, participated as agent, other than in the sale of his own personal residence in providing sales or rental facilities or sales or rental services in two or more transactions involving the sale or rental of any dwelling or any interest therein, or

(3) he is the owner of any dwelling designed or intended for occupancy by, or occupied by, five or more families.

Sec. 804. [42 U.S.C. 3604] Discrimination in sale or rental of housing and other prohibited practices

As made applicable by section 803 of this title and except as exempted by sections 803(b) and 807 of this title, it shall be unlawful--

(a) To refuse to sell or rent after the making of a bona fide offer, or to refuse to negotiate for the sale or rental of, or otherwise make unavailable or deny, a dwelling to any person because of race, color, religion, sex, familial status, or national origin.

(b) To discriminate against any person in the terms, conditions, or privileges of sale or rental of a dwelling, or in the provision of services or facilities in connection therewith, because of race, color, religion, sex, familial status, or national origin.

(c) To make, print, or publish, or cause to be made, printed, or published any notice, statement, or advertisement, with respect to the sale or rental of a dwelling that indicates any preference, limitation, or discrimination based on race, color, religion, sex, handicap, familial status, or national origin, or an intention to make any such preference, limitation, or discrimination.

(d) To represent to any person because of race, color, religion, sex, handicap, familial status, or national origin that any dwelling is not available for inspection, sale, or rental when such dwelling is in fact so available.

(e) For profit, to induce or attempt to induce any person to sell or rent any dwelling by representations regarding the entry or prospective entry into the neighborhood of a person or persons of a particular race, color, religion, sex, handicap, familial status, or national origin.

(f)

(1) To discriminate in the sale or rental, or to otherwise make unavailable or deny, a dwelling to any buyer or renter because of a handicap of--

(A) that buyer or renter,

(B) a person residing in or intending to reside in that dwelling after it is so sold, rented, or made available; or

(C) any person associated with that buyer or renter.

(2) To discriminate against any person in the terms, conditions, or privileges of sale or

rental of a dwelling, or in the provision of services or facilities in connection with such dwelling, because of a handicap of--

(A) that person; or

(B) a person residing in or intending to reside in that dwelling after it is so sold, rented, or made available; or

(C) any person associated with that person.

(3) For purposes of this subsection, discrimination includes--

(A) a refusal to permit, at the expense of the handicapped person, reasonable modifications of existing premises occupied or to be occupied by such person if such modifications may be necessary to afford such person full enjoyment of the premises, except that, in the case of a rental, the landlord may where it is reasonable to do so condition permission for a modification on the renter agreeing to restore the interior of the premises to the condition that existed before the modification, reasonable wear and tear excepted.

(B) a refusal to make reasonable accommodations in rules, policies, practices, or services, when such accommodations may be necessary to afford such person equal opportunity to use and enjoy a dwelling; or

(C) in connection with the design and construction of covered multifamily dwellings for first occupancy after the date that is 30 months after the date of enactment of the Fair Housing Amendments Act of 1988, a failure to design and construct those dwelling in such a manner that--

(i) the public use and common use portions of such dwellings are readily accessible to and usable by handicapped persons;

(ii) all the doors designed to allow passage into and within all premises within such dwellings are sufficiently wide to allow passage by handicapped persons in wheelchairs; and

(iii) all premises within such dwellings contain the following features of adaptive design:

(I) an accessible route into and through the dwelling;

(II) light switches, electrical outlets, thermostats, and other environmental controls in accessible locations;

(III) reinforcements in bathroom walls to allow later installation of grab bars; and

(IV) usable kitchens and bathrooms such that an individual in a wheelchair can maneuver about the space.

(4) Compliance with the appropriate requirements of the American National Standard for buildings and facilities providing accessibility and usability for physically handicapped people (commonly cited as "ANSI A117.1") suffices to satisfy the requirements of paragraph (3)(C)(iii).

(5)

(A) If a State or unit of general local government has incorporated into its laws the requirements set forth in paragraph (3)(C), compliance with such laws shall be deemed to satisfy the requirements of that paragraph.

(B) A State or unit of general local government may review and approve newly constructed covered multifamily dwellings for the purpose of making determinations as to whether the design and construction requirements of paragraph (3)(C) are met.

(C) The Secretary shall encourage, but may not require, States and units of local government to include in their existing procedures for the review and approval of newly constructed covered multifamily dwellings, determinations as to whether the design and construction of such dwellings are consistent with paragraph (3)(C), and shall provide technical assistance to States and units of local government and other persons to implement the requirements of paragraph (3)(C).

(D) Nothing in this title shall be construed to require the Secretary to review or approve the plans, designs or construction of all covered multifamily dwellings, to determine whether the design and construction of such dwellings are consistent with the requirements of paragraph 3(C).

(6)

(A) Nothing in paragraph (5) shall be construed to affect the authority and responsibility of the Secretary or a State or local public agency certified pursuant to section 810(f)(3) of this Act to receive and process complaints or otherwise engage in enforcement activities under this title.

(B) Determinations by a State or a unit of general local government under paragraphs (5)(A) and (B) shall not be conclusive in enforcement proceedings under this title.

(7) As used in this subsection, the term "covered multifamily dwellings" means--

(A) buildings consisting of 4 or more units if such buildings have one or more elevators; and

(B) ground floor units in other buildings consisting of 4 or more units.

(8) Nothing in this title shall be construed to invalidate or limit any law of a State or political subdivision of a State, or other jurisdiction in which this title shall be effective, that requires dwellings to be designed and constructed in a manner that affords handicapped persons greater access than is required by this title.

(9) Nothing in this subsection requires that a dwelling be made available to an individual

whose tenancy would constitute a direct threat to the health or safety of other individuals or whose tenancy would result in substantial physical damage to the property of others.

Sec. 805. [42 U.S.C. 3605] Discrimination in Residential Real Estate-Related Transactions

(a) In General.--It shall be unlawful for any person or other entity whose business includes engaging in residential real estate-related transactions to discriminate against any person in making available such a transaction, or in the terms or conditions of such a transaction, because of race, color, religion, sex, handicap, familial status, or national origin.

(b) Definition.--As used in this section, the term "residential real estate-related transaction" means any of the following:

(1) The making or purchasing of loans or providing other financial assistance--

(A) for purchasing, constructing, improving, repairing, or maintaining a dwelling; or

(B) secured by residential real estate.

(2) The selling, brokering, or appraising of residential real property.

(c) Appraisal Exemption.--Nothing in this title prohibits a person engaged in the business of furnishing appraisals of real property to take into consideration factors other than race, color, religion, national origin, sex, handicap, or familial status.

Sec. 806. [42 U.S.C. 3606] Discrimination in provision of brokerage services

After December 31, 1968, it shall be unlawful to deny any person access to or membership or participation in any multiple-listing service, real estate brokers' organization or other service, organization, or facility relating to the business of selling or renting dwellings, or to discriminate against him in the terms or conditions of such access, membership, or participation, on account of race, color, religion, sex, handicap, familial status, or national origin.

Sec. 807. [42 U.S.C. 3607] Religious organization or private club exemption

(a) Nothing in this subchapter shall prohibit a religious organization, association, or society, or any nonprofit institution or organization operated, supervised or controlled by or in conjunction with a religious organization, association, or society, from limiting the sale, rental or occupancy of dwellings which it owns or operates for other than a commercial purpose to persons of the same religion, or from giving preference to such persons, unless membership in such religion is restricted on account of race, color, or national origin. Nor shall anything in this subchapter prohibit a private club not in fact open to the public, which as an incident to its primary purpose or purposes provides lodgings which it owns or operates for other than a commercial purpose, from limiting the rental or occupancy of such lodgings to its members or from giving preference to its members.

(b)

(1) Nothing in this title limits the applicability of any reasonable local, State, or Federal restrictions regarding the maximum number of occupants permitted to occupy a dwelling. Nor does any provision in this title regarding familial status apply with respect to housing

for older persons.

(2) As used in this section "housing for older persons" means housing --

(A) provided under any State or Federal program that the Secretary determines is specifically designed and operated to assist elderly persons (as defined in the State or Federal program); or

(B) intended for, and solely occupied by, persons 62 years of age or older; or

(C) intended and operated for occupancy by persons 55 years of age or older, and--

(i) at least 80 percent of the occupied units are occupied by at least one person who is 55 years of age or older;

(ii) the housing facility or community publishes and adheres to policies and procedures that demonstrate the intent required under this subparagraph; and

(iii) the housing facility or community complies with rules issued by the Secretary for verification of occupancy, which shall--

(I) provide for verification by reliable surveys and affidavits; and

(II) include examples of the types of policies and procedures relevant to a determination of compliance with the requirement of clause (ii). Such surveys and affidavits shall be admissible in administrative and judicial proceedings for the purposes of such verification.

(3) Housing shall not fail to meet the requirements for housing for older persons by reason of:

(A) persons residing in such housing as of the date of enactment of this Act who do not meet the age requirements of subsections (2)(B) or (C): **Provided**, That new occupants of such housing meet the age requirements of sections (2)(B) or (C); or

(B) unoccupied units: **Provided**, That such units are reserved for occupancy by persons who meet the age requirements of subsections (2)(B) or (C).

(4) Nothing in this title prohibits conduct against a person because such person has been convicted by any court of competent jurisdiction of the illegal manufacture or distribution of a controlled substance as defined in section 102 of the Controlled Substances Act (21 U.S.C. 802).

(5)

(A) A person shall not be held personally liable for monetary damages for a violation of this title if such person reasonably relied, in good faith, on the application of the exemption under this subsection relating to housing for older persons.

(B) For the purposes of this paragraph, a person may only show good faith reliance on the application of the exemption by showing that--

(i) such person has no actual knowledge that the facility or community is not, or will not be, eligible for such exemption; and

(ii) the facility or community has stated formally, in writing, that the facility or community complies with the requirements for such exemption.

Sec. 808. [42 U.S.C. 3608] Administration

(a) Authority and responsibility

The authority and responsibility for administering this Act shall be in the Secretary of Housing and Urban Development.

(b) Assistant Secretary

The Department of Housing and Urban Development shall be provided an additional Assistant Secretary.

(c) Delegation of authority; appointment of administrative law judges; location of conciliation meetings; administrative review

The Secretary may delegate any of his functions, duties and power to employees of the Department of Housing and Urban Development or to boards of such employees, including functions, duties, and powers with respect to investigating, conciliating, hearing, determining, ordering, certifying, reporting, or otherwise acting as to any work, business, or matter under this subchapter. The person to whom such delegations are made with respect to hearing functions, duties, and powers shall be appointed and shall serve in the Department of Housing and Urban Development in compliance with sections 3105, 3344, 5372, and 7521 of title 5 [of the United States Code]. Insofar as possible, conciliation meetings shall be held in the cities or other localities where the discriminatory housing practices allegedly occurred. The Secretary shall by rule prescribe such rights of appeal from the decisions of his administrative law judges to other administrative law judges or to other officers in the Department, to boards of officers or to himself, as shall be appropriate and in accordance with law.

(d) Cooperation of Secretary and executive departments and agencies in administration of housing and urban development programs and activities to further fair housing purposes

All executive departments and agencies shall administer their programs and activities relating to housing and urban development (including any Federal agency having regulatory or supervisory authority over financial institutions) in a manner affirmatively to further the purposes of this subchapter and shall cooperate with the Secretary to further such purposes.

(e) Functions of Secretary

The Secretary of Housing and Urban Development shall--

(1) make studies with respect to the nature and extent of discriminatory housing practices in representative communities, urban, suburban, and rural, throughout the United States;

(2) publish and disseminate reports, recommendations, and information derived from such

studies, including an annual report to the Congress--

(A) specifying the nature and extent of progress made nationally in eliminating discriminatory housing practices and furthering the purposes of this title, obstacles remaining to achieving equal housing opportunity, and recommendations for further legislative or executive action; and

(B) containing tabulations of the number of instances (and the reasons therefor) in the preceding year in which--

(i) investigations are not completed as required by section 810(a)(1)(B);

(ii) determinations are not made within the time specified in section 810(g); and

(iii) hearings are not commenced or findings and conclusions are not made as required by section 812(g);

(3) cooperate with and render technical assistance to Federal, State, local, and other public or private agencies, organizations, and institutions which are formulating or carrying on programs to prevent or eliminate discriminatory housing practices;

(4) cooperate with and render such technical and other assistance to the Community Relations Service as may be appropriate to further its activities in preventing or eliminating discriminatory housing practices;

(5) administer the programs and activities relating to housing and urban development in a manner affirmatively to further the policies of this subchapter; and

(6) annually report to the Congress, and make available to the public, data on the race, color, religion, sex, national origin, age, handicap, and family characteristics of persons and households who are applicants for, participants in, or beneficiaries or potential beneficiaries of, programs administered by the Department to the extent such characteristics are within the coverage of the provisions of law and Executive orders referred to in subsection (f) which apply to such programs (and in order to develop the data to be included and made available to the public under this subsection, the Secretary shall, without regard to any other provision of law, collect such information relating to those characteristics as the Secretary determines to be necessary or appropriate).

(f) The provisions of law and Executive orders to which subsection (e)(6) applies are--

(1) title VI of the Civil Rights Act of 1964;

(2) title VIII of the Civil Rights Act of 1968;

(3) section 504 of the Rehabilitation Act of 1973;

(4) the Age Discrimination Act of 1975;

(5) the Equal Credit Opportunity Act;

(6) section 1978 of the Revised Statutes (42 U.S.C. 1982);

(7) section 8(a) of the Small Business Act;

(8) section 527 of the National Housing Act;

(9) section 109 of the Housing and Community Development Act of 1974;

(10) section 3 of the Housing and Urban Development Act of 1968;

(11) Executive Orders 11063, 11246, 11625, 12250, 12259, and 12432; and

(12) any other provision of law which the Secretary specifies by publication in the Federal Register for the purpose of this subsection.

Sec. 808a. [42 U.S.C. 3608a] Collection of certain data

(a) In general

To assess the extent of compliance with Federal fair housing requirements (including the requirements established under title VI of Public Law 88-352 [42 U.S.C.A. {2000d et seq.] and title VIII of Public Law 90-284 [42 U.S.C.A. {3601 et seq.]), the Secretary of Housing and Urban Development and the Secretary of Agriculture shall each collect, not less than annually, data on the racial and ethnic characteristics of persons eligible for, assisted, or otherwise benefiting under each community development, housing assistance, and mortgage and loan insurance and guarantee program administered by such Secretary. Such data shall be collected on a building by building basis if the Secretary involved determines such collection to be appropriate.

(b) Reports to Congress

The Secretary of Housing and Urban Development and the Secretary of Agriculture shall each include in the annual report of such Secretary to the Congress a summary and evaluation of the data collected by such Secretary under subsection (a) of this section during the preceding year.

Sec. 809. [42 U.S.C. 3609] Education and conciliation; conferences and consultations; reports

Immediately after April 11, 1968, the Secretary shall commence such educational and conciliatory activities as in his judgment will further the purposes of this subchapter. He shall call conferences of persons in the housing industry and other interested parties to acquaint them with the provisions of this subchapter and his suggested means of implementing it, and shall endeavor with their advice to work out programs of voluntary compliance and of enforcement. He may pay per diem, travel, and transportation expenses for persons attending such conferences as provided in section 5703 of Title 5. He shall consult with State and local officials and other interested parties to learn the extent, if any, to which housing discrimination exists in their State or locality, and whether and how State or local enforcement programs might be utilized to combat such discrimination in connection with or in place of, the Secretary's enforcement of this subchapter. The Secretary shall issue reports on such conferences and consultations as he deems appropriate.

Sec. 810. [42 U.S.C. 3610] Administrative Enforcement; Preliminary Matters

(a) Complaints and Answers. --

   (1)

      (A)

         (i) An aggrieved person may, not later than one year after an alleged discriminatory housing practice has occurred or terminated, file a complaint with the Secretary alleging such discriminatory housing practice. The Secretary, on the Secretary's own initiative, may also file such a complaint.

         (ii) Such complaints shall be in writing and shall contain such information and be in such form as the Secretary requires.

         (iii) The Secretary may also investigate housing practices to determine whether a complaint should be brought under this section.

      (B) Upon the filing of such a complaint--

         (i) the Secretary shall serve notice upon the aggrieved person acknowledging such filing and advising the aggrieved person of the time limits and choice of forums provided under this title;

         (ii) the Secretary shall, not later than 10 days after such filing or the identification of an additional respondent under paragraph (2), serve on the respondent a notice identifying the alleged discriminatory housing practice and advising such respondent of the procedural rights and obligations of respondents under this title, together with a copy of the original complaint;

         (iii) each respondent may file, not later than 10 days after receipt of notice from the Secretary, an answer to such complaint; and

         (iv) the Secretary shall make an investigation of the alleged discriminatory housing practice and complete such investigation within 100 days after the filing of the complaint (or, when the Secretary takes further action under subsection (f)(2) with respect to a complaint, within 100 days after the commencement of such further action), unless it is impracticable to do so.

      (C) If the Secretary is unable to complete the investigation within 100 days after the filing of the complaint (or, when the Secretary takes further action under subsection (f)(2) with respect to a complaint, within 100 days after the commencement of such further action), the Secretary shall notify the complainant and respondent in writing of the reasons for not doing so.

      (D) Complaints and answers shall be under oath or affirmation, and may be reasonably and fairly amended at any time.

   (2)

      (A) A person who is not named as a respondent in a complaint, but who is identified as a respondent in the course of investigation, may be joined as an additional or substitute respondent upon written notice, under paragraph (1), to such person, from the Secretary.

(B) Such notice, in addition to meeting the requirements of paragraph (1), shall explain the basis for the Secretary's belief that the person to whom the notice is addressed is properly joined as a respondent.

(b) Investigative Report and Conciliation. --

(1) During the period beginning with the filing of such complaint and ending with the filing of a charge or a dismissal by the Secretary, the Secretary shall, to the extent feasible, engage in conciliation with respect to such complaint.

(2) A conciliation agreement arising out of such conciliation shall be an agreement between the respondent and the complainant, and shall be subject to approval by the Secretary.

(3) A conciliation agreement may provide for binding arbitration of the dispute arising from the complaint. Any such arbitration that results from a conciliation agreement may award appropriate relief, including monetary relief.

(4) Each conciliation agreement shall be made public unless the complainant and respondent otherwise agree and the Secretary determines that disclosure is not required to further the purposes of this title.

(5)

(A) At the end of each investigation under this section, the Secretary shall prepare a final investigative report containing--

(i) the names and dates of contacts with witnesses;

(ii) a summary and the dates of correspondence and other contacts with the aggrieved person and the respondent;

(iii) a summary description of other pertinent records;

(iv) a summary of witness statements; and

(v) answers to interrogatories.

(B) A final report under this paragraph may be amended if additional evidence is later discovered.

(c) Failure to Comply With Conciliation Agreement. -- Whenever the Secretary has reasonable cause to believe that a respondent has breached a conciliation agreement, the Secretary shall refer the matter to the Attorney General with a recommendation that a civil action be filed under section 814 for the enforcement of such agreement.

(d) Prohibitions and Requirements With Respect to Disclosure of Information. --

(1) Nothing said or done in the course of conciliation under this title may be made public or used as evidence in a subsequent proceeding under this title without the written consent of the persons concerned.

(2) Notwithstanding paragraph (1), the Secretary shall make available to the aggrieved person and the respondent, at any time, upon request following completion of the

Secretary's investigation, information derived from an investigation and any final investigative report relating to that investigation.

(e) Prompt Judicial Action. --

(1) If the Secretary concludes at any time following the filing of a complaint that prompt judicial action is necessary to carry out the purposes of this title, the Secretary may authorize a civil action for appropriate temporary or preliminary relief pending final disposition of the complaint under this section. Upon receipt of such authorization, the Attorney General shall promptly commence and maintain such an action. Any temporary restraining order or other order granting preliminary or temporary relief shall be issued in accordance with the Federal Rules of Civil Procedure. The commencement of a civil action under this subsection does not affect the initiation or continuation of administrative proceedings under this section and section 812 of this title.

(2) Whenever the Secretary has reason to believe that a basis may exist for the commencement of proceedings against any respondent under section 814(a) and 814(c) or for proceedings by any governmental licensing or supervisory authorities, the Secretary shall transmit the information upon which such belief is based to the Attorney General, or to such authorities, as the case may be.

(f) Referral for State or Local Proceedings. --

(1) Whenever a complaint alleges a discriminatory housing practice--

(A) within the jurisdiction of a State or local public agency; and

(B) as to which such agency has been certified by the Secretary under this subsection; the Secretary shall refer such complaint to that certified agency before taking any action with respect to such complaint.

(2) Except with the consent of such certified agency, the Secretary, after that referral is made, shall take no further action with respect to such complaint unless--

(A) the certified agency has failed to commence proceedings with respect to the complaint before the end of the 30th day after the date of such referral;

(B) the certified agency, having so commenced such proceedings, fails to carry forward such proceedings with reasonable promptness; or

(C) the Secretary determines that the certified agency no longer qualifies for certification under this subsection with respect to the relevant jurisdiction.

(3)

(A) The Secretary may certify an agency under this subsection only if the Secretary determines that--

(i) the substantive rights protected by such agency in the jurisdiction with respect to which certification is to be made;

(ii) the procedures followed by such agency;

(iii) the remedies available to such agency; and

(iv) the availability of judicial review of such agency's action;

are substantially equivalent to those created by and under this title.

(B) Before making such certification, the Secretary shall take into account the current practices and past performance, if any, of such agency.

(4) During the period which begins on the date of the enactment of the Fair Housing Amendments Act of 1988 and ends 40 months after such date, each agency certified (including an agency certified for interim referrals pursuant to 24 CFR 115.11, unless such agency is subsequently denied recognition under 24 CFR 115.7) for the purposes of this title on the day before such date shall for the purposes of this subsection be considered certified under this subsection with respect to those matters for which such agency was certified on that date. If the Secretary determines in an individual case that an agency has not been able to meet the certification requirements within this 40-month period due to exceptional circumstances, such as the infrequency of legislative sessions in that jurisdiction, the Secretary may extend such period by not more than 8 months.

(5) Not less frequently than every 5 years, the Secretary shall determine whether each agency certified under this subsection continues to qualify for certification. The Secretary shall take appropriate action with respect to any agency not so qualifying.

(g) Reasonable Cause Determination and Effect. --

(1) The Secretary shall, within 100 days after the filing of the complaint (or, when the Secretary takes further action under subsection (f)(2) with respect to a complaint, within 100 days after the commencement of such further action), determine based on the facts whether reasonable cause exists to believe that a discriminatory housing practice has occurred or is about to occur, unless it is impracticable to do so, or unless the Secretary has approved a conciliation agreement with respect to the complaint. If the Secretary is unable to make the determination within 100 days after the filing of the complaint (or, when the Secretary takes further action under subsection (f)(2) with respect to a complaint, within 100 days after the commencement of such further action), the Secretary shall notify the complainant and respondent in writing of the reasons for not doing so.

(2)

(A) If the Secretary determines that reasonable cause exists to believe that a discriminatory housing practice has occurred or is about to occur, the Secretary shall, except as provided in subparagraph (C), immediately issue a charge on behalf of the aggrieved person, for further proceedings under section 812.

(B) Such charge--

(i) shall consist of a short and plain statement of the facts upon which the Secretary has found reasonable cause to believe that a discriminatory housing practice has occurred or is about to occur;

(ii) shall be based on the final investigative report; and

(iii) need not be limited to the facts or grounds alleged in the complaint filed under section 810(a).

(C) If the Secretary determines that the matter involves the legality of any State or local zoning or other land use law or ordinance, the Secretary shall immediately refer the matter to the Attorney General for appropriate action under section 814, instead of issuing such charge.

(3) If the Secretary determines that no reasonable cause exists to believe that a discriminatory housing practice has occurred or is about to occur, the Secretary shall promptly dismiss the complaint. The Secretary shall make public disclosure of each such dismissal.

(4) The Secretary may not issue a charge under this section regarding an alleged discriminatory housing practice after the beginning of the trial of a civil action commenced by the aggrieved party under an Act of Congress or a State law, seeking relief with respect to that discriminatory housing practice.

(h) Service of Copies of Charge. -- After the Secretary issues a charge under this section, the Secretary shall cause a copy thereof, together with information as to how to make an election under section 812(a) and the effect of such an election, to be served--

(1) on each respondent named in such charge, together with a notice of opportunity for a hearing at a time and place specified in the notice, unless that election is made; and

(2) on each aggrieved person on whose behalf the complaint was filed.

Sec. 811. [42 U.S.C. 3611] Subpoenas; Giving of Evidence

(a) In General. -- The Secretary may, in accordance with this subsection, issue subpoenas and order discovery in aid of investigations and hearings under this title. Such subpoenas and discovery may be ordered to the same extent and subject to the same limitations as would apply if the subpoenas or discovery were ordered or served in aid of a civil action in the United States district court for the district in which the investigation is taking place.

(b) Witness Fees. -- Witnesses summoned by a subpoena under this title shall be entitled to same witness and mileage fees as witnesses in proceedings in United States district courts. Fees payable to a witness summoned by a subpoena issued at the request of a party shall be paid by that party or, where a party is unable to pay the fees, by the Secretary.

(c) Criminal Penalties. --

(1) Any person who willfully fails or neglects to attend and testify or to answer any lawful inquiry or to produce records, documents, or other evidence, if it is in such person's power to do so, in obedience to the subpoena or other lawful order under subsection (a), shall be fined not more than $100,000 or imprisoned not more than one year, or both.

(2) Any person who, with intent thereby to mislead another person in any proceeding under

this title--

> (A) makes or causes to be made any false entry or statement of fact in any report, account, record, or other document produced pursuant to subpoena or other lawful order under subsection (a);

> (B) willfully neglects or fails to make or to cause to be made full, true, and correct entries in such reports, accounts, records, or other documents; or

> (C) willfully mutilates, alters, or by any other means falsifies any documentary evidence;

> shall be fined not more than $100,000 or imprisoned not more than one year, or both.

Sec. 812. [42 U.S.C. 3612] Enforcement by Secretary

(a) Election of Judicial Determination. -- When a charge is filed under section 810, a complainant, a respondent, or an aggrieved person on whose behalf the complaint was filed, may elect to have the claims asserted in that charge decided in a civil action under subsection (o) in lieu of a hearing under subsection (b). The election must be made not later than 20 days after the receipt by the electing person of service under section 810(h) or, in the case of the Secretary, not later than 20 days after such service. The person making such election shall give notice of doing so to the Secretary and to all other complainants and respondents to whom the charge relates.

(b) Administrative Law Judge Hearing in Absence of Election. -- If an election is not made under subsection (a) with respect to a charge filed under section 810, the Secretary shall provide an opportunity for a hearing on the record with respect to a charge issued under section 810. The Secretary shall delegate the conduct of a hearing under this section to an administrative law judge appointed under section 3105 of title 5, United States Code. The administrative law judge shall conduct the hearing at a place in the vicinity in which the discriminatory housing practice is alleged to have occurred or to be about to occur.

(c) Rights of Parties. -- At a hearing under this section, each party may appear in person, be represented by counsel, present evidence, cross-examine witnesses, and obtain the issuance of subpoenas under section 811. Any aggrieved person may intervene as a party in the proceeding. The Federal Rules of Evidence apply to the presentation of evidence in such hearing as they would in a civil action in a United States district court.

(d) Expedited Discovery and Hearing. --

> (1) Discovery in administrative proceedings under this section shall be conducted as expeditiously and inexpensively as possible, consistent with the need of all parties to obtain relevant evidence.

> (2) A hearing under this section shall be conducted as expeditiously and inexpensively as possible, consistent with the needs and rights of the parties to obtain a fair hearing and a complete record.

> (3) The Secretary shall, not later than 180 days after the date of enactment of this

subsection, issue rules to implement this subsection.

(e) Resolution of Charge. -- Any resolution of a charge before a final order under this section shall require the consent of the aggrieved person on whose behalf the charge is issued.

(f) Effect of Trial of Civil Action on Administrative Proceedings. -- An administrative law judge may not continue administrative proceedings under this section regarding any alleged discriminatory housing practice after the beginning of the trial of a civil action commenced by the aggrieved party under an Act of Congress or a State law, seeking relief with respect to that discriminatory housing practice.

(g) Hearings, Findings and Conclusions, and Order. -- (

(1) The administrative law judge shall commence the hearing under this section no later than 120 days following the issuance of the charge, unless it is impracticable to do so. If the administrative law judge is unable to commence the hearing within 120 days after the issuance of the charge, the administrative law judge shall notify the Secretary, the aggrieved person on whose behalf the charge was filed, and the respondent, in writing of the reasons for not doing so.

(2) The administrative law judge shall make findings of fact and conclusions of law within 60 days after the end of the hearing under this section, unless it is impracticable to do so. If the administrative law judge is unable to make findings of fact and conclusions of law within such period, or any succeeding 60-day period thereafter, the administrative law judge shall notify the Secretary, the aggrieved person on whose behalf the charge was filed, and the respondent, in writing of the reasons for not doing so.

(3) If the administrative law judge finds that a respondent has engaged or is about to engage in a discriminatory housing practice, such administrative law judge shall promptly issue an order for such relief as may be appropriate, which may include actual damages suffered by the aggrieved person and injunctive or other equitable relief. Such order may, to vindicate the public interest, assess a civil penalty against the respondent--

(A) in an amount not exceeding $11,000 if the respondent has not been adjudged to have committed any prior discriminatory housing practice;

(B) in an amount not exceeding $27,500 if the respondent has been adjudged to have committed one other discriminatory housing practice during the 5-year period ending on the date of the filing of this charge; and

(C) in an amount not exceeding $55,000 if the respondent has been adjudged to have committed 2 or more discriminatory housing practices during the 7-year period ending on the date of the filing of this charge;

except that if the acts constituting the discriminatory housing practice that is the object of the charge are committed by the same natural person who has been previously adjudged to have committed acts constituting a discriminatory housing practice, then the civil penalties set forth in subparagraphs (B) and (C) may be imposed without regard to the period of time within which any subsequent discriminatory housing practice occurred.

(4) No such order shall affect any contract, sale, encumbrance, or lease consummated before the issuance of such order and involving a bona fide purchaser, encumbrancer, or tenant without actual notice of the charge filed under this title.

(5) In the case of an order with respect to a discriminatory housing practice that occurred in the course of a business subject to a licensing or regulation by a governmental agency, the Secretary shall, not later than 30 days after the date of the issuance of such order (or, if such order is judicially reviewed, 30 days after such order is in substance affirmed upon such review)--

    (A) send copies of the findings of fact, conclusions of law, and the order, to that governmental agency; and

    (B) recommend to that governmental agency appropriate disciplinary action (including, where appropriate, the suspension or revocation of the license of the respondent).

(6) In the case of an order against a respondent against whom another order was issued within the preceding 5 years under this section, the Secretary shall send a copy of each such order to the Attorney General.

(7) If the administrative law judge finds that the respondent has not engaged or is not about to engage in a discriminatory housing practice, as the case may be, such administrative law judge shall enter an order dismissing the charge. The Secretary shall make public disclosure of each such dismissal.

(h) Review by Secretary; Service of Final Order. --

    (1) The Secretary may review any finding, conclusion, or order issued under subsection (g). Such review shall be completed not later than 30 days after the finding, conclusion, or order is so issued; otherwise the finding, conclusion, or order becomes final.

    (2) The Secretary shall cause the findings of fact and conclusions of law made with respect to any final order for relief under this section, together with a copy of such order, to be served on each aggrieved person and each respondent in the proceeding.

(i) Judicial Review. --

    (1) Any party aggrieved by a final order for relief under this section granting or denying in whole or in part the relief sought may obtain a review of such order under chapter 158 of title 28, United States Code.

    (2) Notwithstanding such chapter, venue of the proceeding shall be in the judicial circuit in which the discriminatory housing practice is alleged to have occurred, and filing of the petition for review shall be not later than 30 days after the order is entered.

(j) Court Enforcement of Administrative Order Upon Petition by Secretary. --

    (1) The Secretary may petition any United States court of appeals for the circuit in which the discriminatory housing practice is alleged to have occurred or in which any respondent

resides or transacts business for the enforcement of the order of the administrative law judge and for appropriate temporary relief or restraining order, by filing in such court a written petition praying that such order be enforced and for appropriate temporary relief or restraining order.

(2) The Secretary shall file in court with the petition the record in the proceeding. A copy of such petition shall be forthwith transmitted by the clerk of the court to the parties to the proceeding before the administrative law judge.

(k) Relief Which May Be Granted. --

(1) Upon the filing of a petition under subsection (i) or (j), the court may--

(A) grant to the petitioner, or any other party, such temporary relief, restraining order, or other order as the court deems just and proper;

(B) affirm, modify, or set aside, in whole or in part, the order, or remand the order for further proceedings; and

(C) enforce such order to the extent that such order is affirmed or modified.

(2) Any party to the proceeding before the administrative law judge may intervene in the court of appeals.

(3) No objection not made before the administrative law judge shall be considered by the court, unless the failure or neglect to urge such objection is excused because of extraordinary circumstances.

(l) Enforcement Decree in Absence of Petition for Review. -- If no petition for review is filed under subsection (i) before the expiration of 45 days after the date the administrative law judge's order is entered, the administrative law judge's findings of fact and order shall be conclusive in connection with any petition for enforcement--

(1) which is filed by the Secretary under subsection (j) after the end of such day; or

(2) under subsection (m).

(m) Court Enforcement of Administrative Order Upon Petition of Any Person Entitled to Relief. -- If before the expiration of 60 days after the date the administrative law judge's order is entered, no petition for review has been filed under subsection (i), and the Secretary has not sought enforcement of the order under subsection (j), any person entitled to relief under the order may petition for a decree enforcing the order in the United States court of appeals for the circuit in which the discriminatory housing practice is alleged to have occurred.

(n) Entry of Decree. -- The clerk of the court of appeals in which a petition for enforcement is filed under subsection (1) or (m) shall forthwith enter a decree enforcing the order and shall transmit a copy of such decree to the Secretary, the respondent named in the petition, and to any other parties to the proceeding before the administrative law judge.

(o) Civil Action for Enforcement When Election Is Made for Such Civil Action. --

(1) If an election is made under subsection (a), the Secretary shall authorize, and not later than 30 days after the election is made the Attorney General shall commence and maintain, a civil action on behalf of the aggrieved person in a United States district court seeking relief under this subsection. Venue for such civil action shall be determined under chapter 87 of title 28, United States Code.

(2) Any aggrieved person with respect to the issues to be determined in a civil action under this subsection may intervene as of right in that civil action.

(3) In a civil action under this subsection, if the court finds that a discriminatory housing practice has occurred or is about to occur, the court may grant as relief any relief which a court could grant with respect to such discriminatory housing practice in a civil action under section 813. Any relief so granted that would accrue to an aggrieved person in a civil action commenced by that aggrieved person under section 813 shall also accrue to that aggrieved person in a civil action under this subsection. If monetary relief is sought for the benefit of an aggrieved person who does not intervene in the civil action, the court shall not award such relief if that aggrieved person has not complied with discovery orders entered by the court.

(p) Attorney's Fees. -- In any administrative proceeding brought under this section, or any court proceeding arising therefrom, or any civil action under section 812, the administrative law judge or the court, as the case may be, in its discretion, may allow the prevailing party, other than the United States, a reasonable attorney's fee and costs. The United States shall be liable for such fees and costs to the extent provided by section 504 of title 5, United States Code, or by section 2412 of title 28, United States Code.

Sec. 813. [42 U.S.C. 3613] Enforcement by Private Persons

(a) Civil Action. --

(1)

(A) An aggrieved person may commence a civil action in an appropriate United States district court or State court not later than 2 years after the occurrence or the termination of an alleged discriminatory housing practice, or the breach of a conciliation agreement entered into under this title, whichever occurs last, to obtain appropriate relief with respect to such discriminatory housing practice or breach.

(B) The computation of such 2-year period shall not include any time during which an administrative proceeding under this title was pending with respect to a complaint or charge under this title based upon such discriminatory housing practice. This subparagraph does not apply to actions arising from a breach of a conciliation agreement.

(2) An aggrieved person may commence a civil action under this subsection whether or not a complaint has been filed under section 810(a) and without regard to the status of any such complaint, but if the Secretary or a State or local agency has obtained a conciliation agreement with the consent of an aggrieved person, no action may be filed under this subsection by such aggrieved person with respect to the alleged discriminatory housing practice which forms the basis for such complaint except for the purpose of enforcing the

terms of such an agreement.

(3) An aggrieved person may not commence a civil action under this subsection with respect to an alleged discriminatory housing practice which forms the basis of a charge issued by the Secretary if an administrative law judge has commenced a hearing on the record under this title with respect to such charge.

(b) Appointment of Attorney by Court. -- Upon application by a person alleging a discriminatory housing practice or a person against whom such a practice is alleged, the court may--

(1) appoint an attorney for such person; or

(2) authorize the commencement or continuation of a civil action under subsection (a) without the payment of fees, costs, or security, if in the opinion of the court such person is financially unable to bear the costs of such action.

(c) Relief Which May Be Granted. --

(1) In a civil action under subsection (a), if the court finds that a discriminatory housing practice has occurred or is about to occur, the court may award to the plaintiff actual and punitive damages, and subject to subsection (d), may grant as relief, as the court deems appropriate, any permanent or temporary injunction, temporary restraining order, or other order (including an order enjoining the defendant from engaging in such practice or ordering such affirmative action as may be appropriate).

(2) In a civil action under subsection (a), the court, in its discretion, may allow the prevailing party, other than the United States, a reasonable attorney's fee and costs. The United States shall be liable for such fees and costs to the same extent as a private person.

(d) Effect on Certain Sales, Encumbrances, and Rentals. -- Relief granted under this section shall not affect any contract, sale, encumbrance, or lease consummated before the granting of such relief and involving a bona fide purchaser, encumbrancer, or tenant, without actual notice of the filing of a complaint with the Secretary or civil action under this title.

(e) Intervention by Attorney General. -- Upon timely application, the Attorney General may intervene in such civil action, if the Attorney General certifies that the case is of general public importance. Upon such intervention the Attorney General may obtain such relief as would be available to the Attorney General under section 814(e) in a civil action to which such section applies.

Sec. 814. [42 U.S.C. 3614] Enforcement by the Attorney General

(a) Pattern or Practice Cases. -- Whenever the Attorney General has reasonable cause to believe that any person or group of persons is engaged in a pattern or practice of resistance to the full enjoyment of any of the rights granted by this title, or that any group of persons has been denied any of the rights granted by this title and such denial raises an issue of general public importance, the Attorney General may commence a civil action in any appropriate United States district court.

(b) On Referral of Discriminatory Housing Practice or Conciliation Agreement for Enforcement. --

(1)

    (A) The Attorney General may commence a civil action in any appropriate United States district court for appropriate relief with respect to a discriminatory housing practice referred to the Attorney General by the Secretary under section 810(g).

    (B) A civil action under this paragraph may be commenced not later than the expiration of 18 months after the date of the occurrence or the termination of the alleged discriminatory housing practice.

(2)

    (A) The Attorney General may commence a civil action in any appropriate United States district court for appropriate relief with respect to breach of a conciliation agreement referred to the Attorney General by the Secretary under section 810(c).

    (B) A civil action may be commenced under this paragraph not later than the expiration of 90 days after the referral of the alleged breach under section 810(c).

(c) Enforcement of Subpoenas. -- The Attorney General, on behalf of the Secretary, or other party at whose request a subpoena is issued, under this title, may enforce such subpoena in appropriate proceedings in the United States district court for the district in which the person to whom the subpoena was addressed resides, was served, or transacts business.

(d) Relief Which May Be Granted in Civil Actions Under Subsections (a) and (b). --

    (1) In a civil action under subsection (a) or (b), the court--

        (A) may award such preventive relief, including a permanent or temporary injunction, restraining order, or other order against the person responsible for a violation of this title as is necessary to assure the full enjoyment of the rights granted by this title;

        (B) may award such other relief as the court deems appropriate, including monetary damages to persons aggrieved; and

        (C) may, to vindicate the public interest, assess a civil penalty against the respondent--

            (i) in an amount not exceeding $55,000, for a first violation; and

            (ii) in an amount not exceeding $110,000, for any subsequent violation.

    (2) In a civil action under this section, the court, in its discretion, may allow the prevailing party, other than the United States, a reasonable attorney's fee and costs. The United States shall be liable for such fees and costs to the extent provided by section 2412 of title 28, United States Code.

(e) Intervention in Civil Actions. -- Upon timely application, any person may intervene in a civil action commenced by the Attorney General under subsection (a) or (b) which involves an alleged discriminatory housing practice with respect to which such person is an aggrieved person or a

conciliation agreement to which such person is a party. The court may grant such appropriate relief to any such intervening party as is authorized to be granted to a plaintiff in a civil action under section 813.

Sec. 814a. Incentives for Self-Testing and Self-Correction

(a) Privileged Information. --

(1) Conditions For Privilege. -- A report or result of a self-test (as that term is defined by regulation of the Secretary) shall be considered to be privileged under paragraph (2) if any person-

(A) conducts, or authorizes an independent third party to conduct, a self- test of any aspect of a residential real estate related lending transaction of that person, or any part of that transaction, in order to determine the level or effectiveness of compliance with this title by that person; and

(B) has identified any possible violation of this title by that person and has taken, or is taking, appropriate corrective action to address any such possible violation.

(2) Privileged Self-Test. -- If a person meets the conditions specified in subparagraphs (A) and (B) of paragraph (1) with respect to a self-test described in that paragraph, any report or results of that self-test-

(A) shall be privileged; and

(B) may not be obtained or used by any applicant, department, or agency in any --

(i) proceeding or civil action in which one or more violations of this title are alleged; or

(ii) examination or investigation relating to compliance with this title.

(b) Results of Self-Testing. --

(1) In General. -- No provision of this section may be construed to prevent an aggrieved person, complainant, department, or agency from obtaining or using a report or results of any self-test in any proceeding or civil action in which a violation of this title is alleged, or in any examination or investigation of compliance with this title if --

(A) the person to whom the self-test relates or any person with lawful access to the report or the results --

(i) voluntarily releases or discloses all, or any part of, the report or results to the aggrieved person, complainant, department, or agency, or to the general public; or

(ii) refers to or describes the report or results as a defense to charges of violations of this title against the person to whom the self-test relates; or

(B) the report or results are sought in conjunction with an adjudication or admission of a violation of this title for the sole purpose of determining an appropriate penalty or remedy.

(2) Disclosure for Determination of Penalty or Remedy. -- Any report or results of a self-test that are disclosed for the purpose specified in paragraph (1)(B) --

(A) shall be used only for the particular proceeding in which the adjudication or admission referred to in paragraph (1)(B) is made; and

(B) may not be used in any other action or proceeding.

(c) Adjudication. -- An aggrieved person, complainant, department, or agency that challenges a privilege asserted under this section may seek a determination of the existence and application of that privilege in --

(1) a court of competent jurisdiction; or

(2) an administrative law proceeding with appropriate jurisdiction.

(2) Regulations. --

(A) In General. -- Not later than 6 months after the date of enactment of this Act, in consultation with the Board and after providing notice and an opportunity for public comment, the Secretary of Housing and Urban Development shall prescribe final regulations to implement section 814A of the Fair Housing Act, as added by this section.

(B) Self-Test. --

(i) Definition. -- The regulations prescribed by the Secretary under subparagraph (A) shall include a definition of the term "self-test" for purposes of section 814A of the Fair Housing Act, as added by this section.

(ii) Requirement for Self-Test. -- The regulations prescribed by the Secretary under subparagraph (A) shall specify that a self-test shall be sufficiently extensive to constitute a determination of the level and effectiveness of the compliance by a person engaged in residential real estate related lending activities with the Fair Housing Act.

(iii) Substantial Similarity to Certain Equal Credit Opportunity Act Regulations. -- The regulations prescribed under subparagraph (A) shall be substantially similar to the regulations prescribed by the Board to carry out section 704A of the Equal Credit Opportunity Act, as added by this section.

(C) Applicability. --

(1) In General. -- Except as provided in paragraph (2), the privilege provided for in section 704a of the Equal Credit Opportunity Act or section 814a of the Fair Housing Act (as those sections are added by this section) shall apply to a

self-test (as that term is defined pursuant to the regulations prescribed under subsection (a)(2) or (b)(2) of this section, as appropriate) conducted before, on, or after the effective date of the regulations prescribed under subsection (a)(2) or (b)(2), as appropriate.

(2) Exception. -- The privilege referred to in paragraph (1) does not apply to such a self-test conducted before the effective date of the regulations prescribed under subsection (a) or (b), as appropriate, if --

(A) before that effective date, a complaint against the creditor or person engaged in residential real estate related lending activities (as the case may be) was --

(i) formally filed in any court of competent jurisdiction; or

(ii) the subject of an ongoing administrative law proceeding;

(B) in the case of section 704a of the Equal Credit Opportunity Act, the creditor has waived the privilege pursuant to subsection (b)(1)(A)(i) of that section; or

(C) in the case of section 814a of the Fair Housing Act, the person engaged in residential real estate related lending activities has waived the privilege pursuant to subsection (b)(1)(A)(i) of that section.

Sec. 815. [42 U.S.C. 3614a] Rules to Implement Title

The Secretary may make rules (including rules for the collection, maintenance, and analysis of appropriate data) to carry out this title. The Secretary shall give public notice and opportunity for comment with respect to all rules made under this section.

Sec. 816. [42 U.S.C. 3615] Effect on State laws

Nothing in this subchapter shall be constructed to invalidate or limit any law of a State or political subdivision of a State, or of any other jurisdiction in which this subchapter shall be effective, that grants, guarantees, or protects the same rights as are granted by this subchapter; but any law of a State, a political subdivision, or other such jurisdiction that purports to require or permit any action that would be a discriminatory housing practice under this subchapter shall to that extent be invalid.

Sec. 817. [42 U.S.C. 3616] Cooperation with State and local agencies administering fair housing laws; utilization of services and personnel; reimbursement; written agreements; publication in

Federal Register

The Secretary may cooperate with State and local agencies charged with the administration of State and local fair housing laws and, with the consent of such agencies, utilize the services of such agencies and their employees and, notwithstanding any other provision of law, may reimburse such agencies and their employees for services rendered to assist him in carrying out this subchapter. In furtherance of such cooperative efforts, the Secretary may enter into written agreements with such State or local agencies. All agreements and terminations thereof shall be published in the Federal Register.

Sec. 818. [42 U.S.C. 3617] Interference, coercion, or intimidation; enforcement by civil action

It shall be unlawful to coerce, intimidate, threaten, or interfere with any person in the exercise or enjoyment of, or on account of his having exercised or enjoyed, or on account of his having aided or encouraged any other person in the exercise or enjoyment of, any right granted or protected by section 803, 804, 805, or 806 of this title.

Sec. 819. [42 U.S.C. 3618] Authorization of appropriations

There are hereby authorized to be appropriated such sums as are necessary to carry out the purposes of this subchapter.

Sec. 820. [42 U.S.C. 3619] Separability of provisions

If any provision of this subchapter or the application thereof to any person or circumstances is held invalid, the remainder of the subchapter and the application of the provision to other persons not similarly situated or to other circumstances shall not be affected thereby.

(Sec. 12 of 1988 Act). [42 U.S.C. 3601 note] Disclaimer of Preemptive Effect on Other Acts

Nothing in the Fair Housing Act as amended by this Act limits any right, procedure, or remedy available under the Constitution or any other Act of the Congress not so amended.

(Sec. 13 of 1988 Act). [42 U.S.C. 3601 note] Effective Date and Initial Rulemaking

(a) Effective Date. -- This Act and the amendments made by this Act shall take effect on the 180th day beginning after the date of the enactment of this Act.

(b) Initial Rulemaking. -- In consultation with other appropriate Federal agencies, the Secretary shall, not later than the 180th day after the date of the enactment of this Act, issue rules to implement title VIII as amended by this Act. The Secretary shall give public notice and opportunity for comment with respect to such rules.

(Sec. 14 of 1988 Act). [42 U.S.C. 3601 note] Separability of Provisions

If any provision of this Act or the application thereof to any person or circumstances is held invalid, the remainder of the Act and the application of the provision to other persons not similarly situated or to other circumstances shall not be affected thereby.

Section 901. (Title IX As Amended) [42 U.S.C. 3631] Violations; bodily injury; death; penalties

Whoever, whether or not acting under color of law, by force or threat of force willfully injures, intimidates or interferes with, or attempts to injure, intimidate or interfere with--

(a) any person because of his race, color, religion, sex, handicap (as such term is defined in section 802 of this Act), familial status (as such term is defined in section 802 of this Act), or national origin and because he is or has been selling, purchasing, renting, financing occupying, or contracting or negotiating for the sale, purchase, rental, financing or occupation of any dwelling, or applying for or participating in any service, organization, or facility relating to the business of selling or renting dwellings; or

Bonus CD-ROM:
The American Landlord Law Resource Center

System Requirements:

★ **Windows 2000, XP or Vista (with CD-ROM Drive)**
★ **Adobe Reader (Version 7 or Higher - Available as a Free Download)**
★ **Internet Connection (Recommended)**

The enclosed CD-ROM is outfitted with rental forms, agreements and publications, among many other invaluable resources *[some forms and agreements may need to be modified (or amended) to accommodate new or existing laws in your state]*. Each form comes equipped with fields that can be highlighted and then hovered with your mouse for pop-up instructions. You can even personalize each form and agreement with your contact information and logo *[see the illustrations on the following pages]*.

Installation Instructions

Insert the CD into your CD-ROM drive and follow the onscreen instructions. If the installation process does not automatically begin, click the **START** button, then click **RUN** and type in the following: **D:\americanlandlordlaw.exe** and click **OK** to begin following the onscreen instructions. *(If the location of your CD-ROM begins with a letter other than **D**, you must replace it with the proper drive letter.)*

Terms of Use

All copyrighted forms are provided for your personal use only and may not be redistributed or sold.
Note: The contents of this CD-ROM are not intended as a substitute for the advice of an attorney.

How to Personalize a Rental Form

Instructions:
1. Insert your IMAGE
2. Enter 'PROPE
3. REPLACE ALL of this te
4. Click on 'PRINT FORM' whe

Highlight instructions to delete or replace with your contact information

Everything U Need to Know...

Click here to insert image/logo

Insert a logo or image from your computer to display on the top right of your form

...l Application

Applicant Information

Property address applying for: **1002 Nor_**

Name:

Date of birth: | SSN:

Current address:

City: | ZIP Code:

Own | Ren | How long?

Previous

City: | ZIP Code:

Owned | How long?

Forms with landlord required fields can be completed onscreen before printing

Employment

Current employer:

Employer address: | How long?

City: | State | ZIP Code:

Phone:

Position:

Emergency Conta

Name of a person not residi

Address:

City: | State | ode: | Phone:

Your personalized information cannot be saved - so be sure to print multiple copies for future use

Relationship:

References

Name: | Address: | Phone:

The End Result

JOHN Z. DOE RENTAL PROPERTY LLC
2008 Western Avenue
Anytown, USA 12345
PH (555) 555-1212
FX (555) 555-1313

JZD
Rental Property LLC

Residential Rental Application

Applicant Information

Property address applying for: 1002 North Canyon Rd , Unit #3, Anytown, USA 12345

Name:		
Date of birth:	SSN:	Phone:
Current address:		
City:	State:	ZIP Code:
Own Rent (Please circle) Monthly payment or rent:		How long?
Previous address:		
City:	State:	ZIP Code:
Owned Rented (Please circle) Monthly payment or rent:		How long?

Employment Information

Current employer:		
Employer address:		How long?
City:	State:	ZIP Code:
Phone:	E-mail:	Fax:
Position:	Hourly Salary (Please circle)	Annual income:

Emergency Contact

Name of a person not residing with you:			
Address:			
City:	State:	ZIP Code:	Phone:
Relationship:			

References

Name:	Address:	Phone:

Have you ever been convicted of a crime? (yes / no) If so, please explain all offenses including where, when and why:

Have you ever been evicted? (yes / no) If so, please explain where, when and why:

I acknowledge that falsification or omission of any information on this rental application may result in the immediate dismissal or retraction of an offer of tenancy. I hereby voluntarily consent to and authorize the AmerUSA Corporation ("AmerUSA"), acting as the landlord's designated screening organization for the above referenced rental property, to obtain my consumer report and render a credit decision. I further authorize all persons and organizations that may have information relevant to this research to disclose such information to the landlord's authorized agent, AmerUSA. I hereby release the landlord and its authorized agent, AmerUSA, from all claims and liabilities of any nature in connection with this research, results and decision. A photocopy of this authorization will be considered valid. I understand that I have specific prescribed rights as a consumer under the federal Fair Credit Reporting Act ('FCRA') and have received a copy of those rights titled "FCRA Summary of Rights."

Signature of applicant:	Date:

This form provided by USLandlord.com

Index

A...

abandonment of property, 165, 167
Alabama, 170-171
Alaska, 172-173
AmericanLandlord.com, 67, 167
application fees, *see* fees
Arizona, 174-175
Arkansas, 176-177
asbestos, 97-98
asset protection, 91
assignees, *see* occupants
attorney
  fees, 166
  finding, 165-166
  hiring for eviction, 151, 160, 164
  insurance paying for, 90-91
  protecting your assets, 91
  when necessary, 164-165

B...

bounced checks, 5, 12-15, 104

C...

California, 98, 118, 165, 178-179
carbon monoxide, 99

carpeting, 47-48
case law, 18, 167
CDC, *see* Centers for Disease Control and Prevention
Centers for Disease Control and Prevention, 99
cleaning fees, *see* fees
Colorado, 180-181
common areas, 65
compensatory damages, 90
complaints, tenant, 9, 65-67, 132, 141
condition of property, 35, 43, 47, 89-90
Connecticut, 182-183
co-tenants, *see* occupants
court summons, 159
crime, 119
cure or quit notice, 152

D...

damage to property, 43, 121, 124, 125, 165
Delaware, 184-185
discrimination, 9, 28, 58, 90-91, 161, 164
District of Columbia, 186-187

E...

emergencies, 66, 77
entry to property, 74-85
environmental hazards, 93-101
Environmental Protection Agency, 94-96, 99, 100-101
EPA, *see* Environmental Protection Agency
EUNTK.com, 67, 167
eviction
  assignees and, 124
  attorney, hiring for, 151, 160, 164, 165-166
  cause, 144
  complaint, 159
  damage to the property and, 165
  documenting problems leading to, 141, 160
  illegal, 145-146, 149
  losing suit, 161
  military personnel and, 161
  non-payment of rent, 152
  notice to cure or quit, 152, 156-158
  notice to pay or quit, 152, 153-155
  notice to quit, 144
  penalties if by force, 147-149
  removing tenant from property, 149, 161
  retaliation and, 132, 141
  security deposit and, 48, 160
  steps of, 144
  subtenants and, 124
  summons, 159

eviction (continued)
  trial, 159-160
  types of, 144
  unconditional quit, 145, 152
  winning suit, 160-161
extended absence of tenant, 77-79

F...

fees
  allowable, 59-61
  application, 56
  bounced check, 12-15
  cleaning, 56-57
  late, 9-12
  pet, 28, 57-61
financial protection, 90-91
fixtures, 46-47
Florida, 65, 100, 118, 165, 188-189
form of payment, rent, 5

G...

garnishment of wages, 160, 165
Georgia, 190-191

H...

Hawaii, 4, 192-193

I...

Idaho, 194-195
Illinois, 196-197

increasing rent, 6-9, 104-107, 114-115
Indiana, 98, 198-199
injuries on property, 87-91, 93-101
inspection, *see also* condition of
    property, move-out, security deposit
  cleaning after, 38-39
  contact information for, 32
  co-tenants and, 49, 121
  itemizing damage, 43
  move-out, 32, 35-38, 49, 121
  occupants present at, 35, 121
  repairs after, 38-39, 48
  secret, 74
  wear and tear, 32, 42, 47-48
insurance, 90-91
interest, security deposit and, 21-24,
    43-46
Iowa, 200-201

K...

Kansas, 202-203
Kentucky, 204-205

L...

landlord responsibilities, 64-67, 87-91,
    94-101, 124
last month's rent, 57
late fees, *see* fees
laws, *see* statutes
lead, 94-96
lease agreement
  asbestos disclosure in, 98

lease agreement (continued)
  assignment to new owner, 29
  assignment to new tenant, 118, 124-125,
      128-130
  cleaning requirements and, 32
  extended absences and, 77
  fixtures and, 46
  modifying, 103-115, 118, 125
  occupants and, 28, 118, 119, 124-130
  prohibiting items, 99
  providing for changes, 104
  radon disclosure in, 100
  rent payments and, 4-5, 6
  statute of limitations for lawsuits, 50-51
lease termination, *see also* eviction
  agreement, 122-123
  assignment of lease and, 118
  co-tenants and, 49, 120-123
  move-out letter, 32-34
  notification required, 107-111
  subtenants and, 118
  unpaid rent and, 48
liability
  landlord, 87-91, 98-99, 124
  tenant, 98, 99, 119
limited liability company, 91
Louisiana, 80, 206-207

M...

mailbox, getting a, 5
Maine, 208-209
maintenance, *see* repairs
management office, 4

Maryland, 98, 210-211
Massachusetts, 212-213
mediation, 119
Michigan, 141, 214-215
military duty, 130, 161
Minnesota, 216-217
Mississippi, 218-219
Missouri, 220-221
mold, 98-99
Montana, 98, 222-223
move-out, *see also* inspection, lease
    termination, security deposit
  cleaning, 38-39, 56-57
  co-tenants and, 49, 120-121
  fixtures, 46-47
  inspection, 32, 35-38, 49, 121
  letter, 32-34
  notice of, 48
  repairs, 38-39
  unpaid rent at, 48

N...

National Lead Information Center, 96
National Safety Council, 101
Nebraska, 224-225
negligence, 88-89
Nevada, 226-227
New Hampshire, 228-229
New Jersey, 98, 230-231
New Mexico, 232-233
New York, 98, 234-235
non-refundable fees, *see* fees
North Carolina, 236-237

North Dakota, 238-239
notice to cure or quit, 152
notice to pay or quit, 152
notice to quit, 144
notification time requirements
  entry to property, 83-85
  eviction for lease violation, 156-158
  eviction for nonpayment of rent,
      153-155
  final inspection, 35-38
  increasing rent, 6-9, 57, 104, 114-115
  landlord termination, 108-109
  lease modification, 112-113
  tenant termination, 110-111
NSC, *see* National Safety Council

O...

occupants
  abandoning property, 165, 167
  assignees, 118, 124-125, 128-130
  changing, 104
  co-tenants, 49, 118, 119-122, 125
  complaints from, 9, 65-67, 132, 141
  extended absence of, 77-79
  lease agreement and, 28, 118, 119,
      124-130
  persistently troubling, 145
  present at inspection, 35, 121
  privacy of, 80, 90-91
  security deposit and, 28, 120-121, 124
  subtenants, 118, 124, 125-127, 130

Occupational Safety and Health
Administration, 97-98
Ohio, 240-241
Oklahoma, 242-243
Oregon, 64, 244-245
OSHA, *see* Occupational Safety and
Health Administration

P...

painting, 47
partial payment, rent, 5-6
pay or quit notice, 152
penalties, illegal eviction, 147-149
Pennsylvania, 246-247
personal injury lawsuits, 90
pets, 28, 57-61, 104
policies, 141
privacy of tenants, 80, 90-91
punitive damages, 90

R...

radon gas, 100-101
relationship with tenant, 28, 32, 77, 120
rent
assignees and, 124-125, 128, 130
bounced, 5, 12-15, 104
co-tenants and, 119, 121-122
control, 9
form of payment, 5
garnishing wages for, 160
increasing, 6-9, 57, 104, 114-115, 125
last month's, 57

rent (continued)
late, 9-12
lease agreement and, 4-5, 6
mailbox for, 5
partial payments, 5-6
repair and deduct, 66-67, 70-71
retaliation and, 132, 141
subtenants and, 124
unpaid, 48
when due, 4
where due, 4
withholding, 66-67, 68-69, 161
repair and deduct, 66-67, 70-71
repairs
asbestos exposure and, 97-98
consequences for not making, 66-67,
87-90
entry for, 74-76
landlord's duty to make, 64-67, 87-90
liability and, 87-90, 98-99
maintenance schedule, 65-66
scheduling time for, 74
security deposit deductions for, 48, 57
statutes regarding, 68-71
tenant's responsibilities for, 66, 120-121
time frame for, 88-90
retaliation, 9, 28, 131-141
Rhode Island, 248-249

S...

sample forms
assignment of lease, 129
lead-based paint disclosure, 95

sample forms (continued)
  modification of lease, 106
  move-out letter, 34
  subletting agreement, 126-127
  termination of lease, 123
security deposit, *see also* fees
  carpet and, 47-48
  co-tenants and, 49, 120-121, 125
  deductions, 38-39, 43, 48, 56-57
  disputes over, 46-48
  eviction and, 48, 160
  fixtures and, 46-47
  increasing, 28, 57, 125
  interest on, 21-24, 43-46
  last month's rent and, 57
  limits, 18-20, 58
  painting and, 47
  pets and, 28, 57-61
  returning, 32, 39-42, 43, 49
  subtenants and, 124, 130
  time limits for return, 39-42
  transferring to new owner, 29
  unpaid rent and, 48
  wear and tear and, 32, 42, 47-48
  where kept, 24-27
self-help eviction, 145-146, 149
selling rental property, 29, 80-82
service animals, 58
Servicemembers Civil Relief Act, 161
showing property, 80-82
small claims court, *see also* statute of
    limitations
  amount limits for suits, 52-53
  eviction and, 159-160

small claims court (continued)
  finding yourself in, 42, 49
South Carolina, 250-251
South Dakota, 252-253
statute of limitations, lease lawsuits,
    50-51
statutes, 67, 68-71, 167
subtenants, *see* occupants

T...

tenants, *see* occupants
Tennessee, 254-255
termination of lease, *see* lease
    termination
Texas, 98, 256-257
time frame for retaliation, 132-134, 141
trial, eviction, 160

U...

unconditional quit, 145, 152
Utah, 80, 258-259

V...

Vermont, 65, 260-261
violence, 119
Virginia, 262-263

W...

Washington, 264-265
waterbeds, 28

wear and tear, 32, 42, 47-48
West Virginia, 266-267
Wisconsin, 56, 268-269
withholding, 66-67, 68-69, 161
Wyoming, 270-271

Notes

Notes

Notes

Notes

Also available:

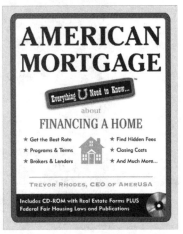

We would like to hear from you!

Please email us your comments or suggestions about *American Landlord Law* or any other volume from the Everything U Need to Know... series. Whether it's an idea for a new volume or a comment about an existing one, it's always a distinct pleasure to hear what *you* have to say...

feedback@euntk.com